Written in the Stars
Unlocking the Secrets of your Birth Chart to Create the Life of Your Dreams

Written in the Stars

Unlocking the Secrets of your Birth Chart to Create the Life of Your Dreams

Jenna Weston

AN OFFICIAL PUBLICATION OF MANIFESTATIONMINDS LLC

Written in the Stars
Unlocking the Secrets of Your Birth Chart to Create the Life of Your
Dreams

Written by
Jenna Weston, B.S., M.P.A.

Self-published by ManifestationMinds LLC

Website: ManifestationMinds.com
Email: Jenna@ManifestationMinds.com

ISBN: 979-8-9925989-0-2

Disclaimer:
This book is for informational purposes only. The content is not intended
to provide medical, financial, or legal advice. Readers are encouraged to
seek professional guidance specific to their individual circumstances.

Artwork and Design:
All cover design, drawings, and artwork featured in this book were created
solely by the author, Jenna Weston. Unauthorized use or reproduction of
this artwork is strictly prohibited.

All quotes and links used in this book are either public domain or used with
permission from the original copyright holder. For specific inquiries,
contact Jenna@ManifestationMinds.com

Printed in the United States of America
2025

To those who, like me, are on a journey to uncover their truth,

I once heard the quote, *"Live your truth, and it will set you free,"* and this quote has been my anchor through every step of this journey. It reminded me to look inward, to uncover what truly mattered to me, and to follow my passions with courage and trust. This book is the result of that belief—a reminder that when you honor your truth, life has a way of unfolding exactly as it should.

To my readers and supporters—none of this would have been possible without you. Thank you for your trust, your encouragement, and for being a part of this journey with me.

And thank you to the Universe for bringing the signs, synchronicities, and people I needed to step into this version of myself.

With all my love and gratitude,
Jenna

"Astrology is a science in itself and contains an illuminating body of knowledge. It taught me many things, and I am greatly indebted to it."
- Albert Einstein

Contents

Contents

Contents

Contents

1. Preface

Astrology has been a guiding light in my life, helping me understand myself, my connections with other people, and the world around me in ways I never thought possible. For as long as I can remember, I've been fascinated by astrology, but I really began to study it in-depth in 2019. As soon as I turned 18, I ran to the tattoo shop and got my first tattoo of the Scorpio symbol on the back of my neck. It was a physical expression of my love for astrology and my own Scorpio energy.

Like many of you, I was once a beginner, looking at a birth chart and feeling completely overwhelmed. But over time, I learned that astrology isn't just a set of generic meanings that vaguely apply to everyone, but that our birth charts are deeply personal, reflecting the unique energy and patterns that shape who we are.

Whether you are just beginning your journey or have been studying astrology for years, this book is designed to guide you step by step through the process of reading your birth chart. I know it may seem daunting at first, but I'll be here to teach you everything you need to know. By the time you finish this book, you'll not only be able to interpret your birth chart but also grasp the intricacies that make astrology such a powerful tool.

Don't be discouraged if you don't grasp something the first time. With practice and repetition, you will come to understand this multifaceted topic. It took me years to reach this level of knowledge, and I truly believe you are more than capable of achieving the same. Be patient and trust the process—the ability to read and understand your chart will pay off in more ways than you can imagine.

This book offers insights and guidance to help you deepen your understanding of astrology. While many astrology books focus solely on signs, houses, and planets, this book goes far beyond that. Here, you'll learn about objects, angles, ruling planets and their influence based on where they are located in the chart, degrees, aspects, orbs of influence, elements, modality, and so much more. I also include an in-depth look at Lana Del Rey's birth chart where I break down her chart completely using everything covered in the book.

One of the ways this book takes a different approach is by focusing on the individual meanings of signs, planets, and houses before combining them. For example, instead of jumping straight into what it means to have your Sun in Scorpio, I first explain the traits of Scorpio as a sign and then discuss the role of the Sun in astrology. This way, you can understand both the sign and the planet on their own before exploring how they work together. This method allows for a deeper understanding of how each part of your birth chart contributes to the bigger picture and also allows you to read anyone's birth chart with ease and understanding.

This book uses the Placidus system, one of the most widely used house systems in astrology. In the Placidus system, the houses are not divided equally by degrees (like the whole house system), but rather based on the time it takes for a zodiac sign to rise over the horizon at your place of birth. This system reflects the natural movement of the Earth and results in varying house sizes, which can affect how certain signs and planets fall into different houses. Using this system allows for a more personalized interpretation of the birth chart, giving deeper insights into how planetary placements influence various areas of your life.

By the end of the book, you'll have the opportunity to apply everything you've learned in a DIY birth chart section, where you can fill in your own chart and reflect on how the planets, signs, and houses connect to influence your life.

While my future books will explore favorable placements and aspects for love, money, career, etc., it's essential to first build a strong understanding of the basics. Only then can you truly unlock the deeper potential of astrology.

Astrology is more than just a tool for self-awareness. It is a tool for empowerment, giving you the knowledge to create the life of your dreams.

Let's unlock the stars together,

Jenna

2.
The Basics of Astrology and the Tools You Need

When criticized by a skeptic about astrology, he reportedly responded, "I have studied the matter. You, sir, have not."
- Isaac Newton

A Brief Introduction to Astrology

Astrology is an ancient practice rooted in the observation of celestial movements and their impact on life on Earth. For thousands of years, astrologers have studied the positions of the stars, planets, and other cosmic bodies to understand how these heavenly cycles influence human behavior, events, and natural phenomena. Through this practice, astrology has developed into a system that connects the patterns in the sky with the patterns in our everyday lives.

At the core of astrology is the birth chart, also known as a natal chart. This chart is a personalized map of the sky, showing the exact positions of the Sun, Moon, planets, and other key points at the moment and location of your birth. It serves as a unique cosmic blueprint, offering insights into your personality, life path, and the different energies that influence your experiences in various areas of life.

What Is a Birth Chart?

A birth chart is a circular diagram that divides the sky into 12 sections, called houses, each representing a different area of your life. The positions of the Sun, Moon, planets, objects, and points are plotted along this chart within the 12 zodiac signs, and their placements at the time of your birth offer insights into your life path.

In a birth chart, there are several key components:
- **The Houses**: These 12 sections represent different areas of life, such as career, relationships, and health. Each house governs a specific domain and helps determine how various facets of your life will be influenced by the planets.
- **The Zodiac Signs**: Each planet and celestial point is placed in one of the 12 zodiac signs (Aries, Taurus, Gemini, etc.). These signs influence how the energy of that planet is expressed. For example, having Mars in Leo would give your actions a bold, confident flavor, while Mars in Virgo would express itself in a more detail-oriented, practical way.
- **The Planets and Celestial Points**: The Sun, Moon, planets, objects, and other key points, such as the Ascendant (Rising Sign)

5

and Midheaven, are plotted around the chart based on their positions at the exact time of your birth. These celestial bodies represent different aspects of your personality and life path, such as how you express emotions (Moon), communicate (Mercury), or pursue goals (Mars).

Your birth chart is unique to you, just as your fingerprint is. Even if someone shares the same birthday, slight differences in the time and location of birth can create a completely different chart.

How to Calculate Your Birth Chart

To create your birth chart, you need three key pieces of information:

- **Date of Birth**: The exact day, month, and year you were born.
- **Time of Birth**: The precise time of day you were born, down to the minute if possible. This is crucial because even a slight variation can change key elements of your chart, such as your Ascendant and the placement of the planets in the houses.
- **Place of Birth**: The city or town where you were born, as this determines your geographic location, which is essential for calculating the positions of the planets and points like the Ascendant and Midheaven.

Once you have this information, you can use an online birth chart calculator or astrology software to generate your chart. Many websites offer free chart generation tools, or you can consult an astrologer to create a more personalized interpretation.

Tools You'll Need

While there are many resources available for calculating and interpreting your birth chart, here are the essential tools you'll need to get started:

-**Birth Information**: As mentioned, you'll need your date, time, and place of birth.
- **Astrology Software or Online Chart Calculators**: These tools allow you to enter your birth information and instantly generate your natal chart. They display the layout of the planets, houses, and zodiac signs at the time of your birth.
- **House System**: When generating your chart, you'll likely come

across different house systems. The most commonly used is the Placidus system (which this book follows), but others, like the Whole Sign or Equal House systems, also exist. Each system calculates house divisions differently, which can slightly change the placements of planets and house cusps in a birth chart, but the core interpretations remain similar.

Why Accurate Birth Data Matters

The accuracy of your birth chart depends on the precision of the information you provide, especially your birth time. The exact time of birth is crucial because it determines your rising sign and house placements, which can shift throughout the day. Without this detail, important elements of your chart—like your Ascendant and house positions—might not fully capture your unique astrological profile. If you're unsure of your birth time, it's worth checking your birth certificate or reaching out to the hospital where you were born.

3. The Zodiac Signs

"I don't believe in astrology; I'm a Sagittarius and we're skeptical."
- Arthur C. Clarke

The Role of Zodiac Signs in Astrology

In astrology, the zodiac signs form the foundation of a birth chart, each representing unique qualities, traits, and modes of expression. The 12 signs of the zodiac act as the lens through which the different areas of life are experienced. When looking at a birth chart, these signs indicate how various energies manifest in different aspects of a person's life. Each sign has its own distinct characteristics, influencing personality, behavior, and the way one interacts with the world. This section will explore the qualities of each zodiac sign and how they bring their own flavor to the planets, houses, and other elements in the chart.

Positive and "Negative" Expressions of Zodiac Signs

People can either embody the positive or "negative" aspects of their signs, and this can influence how the sign is expressed through them. For example, a Leo might express the positive traits of confidence and generosity or the shadow side of arrogance and stubbornness. Similarly, a Virgo could showcase diligence and helpfulness or, on the flip side, become overly critical and anxious. Understanding how both the light and shadow aspects of a sign manifest provides a more holistic view of a person's behavior and tendencies. I like to use the term "un-evolved" to describe individuals who primarily exude the "negative" expressions of their sign. However, everyone has the potential to embody their sign's highest qualities—it's simply a matter of self-awareness and growth. By recognizing where you may be expressing the lower vibrations of your sign, you can consciously shift toward its more evolved traits. This variability in expression makes it important to reflect on how you are channeling the energies of your zodiac sign and where there may be room for growth or balance.

The Importance of Cusps

A cusp marks the transition between two signs, and a planet positioned at this boundary can influence how its energy is expressed. Individuals with a planet on the cusp may embody qualities of both signs, creating a unique blend that adds depth to their personality. If you have a placement on the cusp, exploring both signs can help you better understand how these combined energies manifest in your life.

This concept applies to any planet, point, or object in your chart that falls at the boundary between two signs. Whether it's a planet like Mars, a point like the Ascendant, or an object like Chiron, a cusp placement carries influence from both signs, making its interpretation more nuanced. Examining both signs involved will provide deeper insight into how this energy expresses itself in your birth chart.

Ruling Planets and Their Influence

Each zodiac sign in astrology is associated with a ruling planet, which significantly influences the sign's characteristics and the way its energy is expressed in a birth chart. A ruling planet acts as the celestial guide for its respective sign, imparting its qualities and style. For example, Mars, the planet of action and drive, rules Aries, endowing it with courage and assertiveness. Similarly, Venus, the planet of love and beauty, rules both Taurus and Libra, shaping their love for harmony, beauty, and connection.

Understanding a sign's ruling planet offers deeper insight into how that sign functions and what drives its core motivations. The influence of the ruling planet can be seen in how each sign approaches life, from the fiery enthusiasm of Leo, ruled by the Sun, to the structured discipline of Capricorn, ruled by Saturn. This connection between the signs and their ruling planets enriches the interpretation of a birth chart, highlighting how planetary energy uniquely colors each sign's influence on the houses, aspects, and overall chart dynamics.

Elements and Modality

In addition to ruling planets, each sign is associated with an element—Fire, Earth, Air, or Water—and a modality—Cardinal, Fixed, or Mutable—which further shapes the sign's characteristics and expression. I touch on these concepts briefly here, but we will explore them in greater depth later in the book. Understanding the element and modality of a sign adds more layers to the interpretation, helping you grasp how each sign's energy flows and interacts with other dynamics in the chart.

Aries (March 21 - April 19)

Symbol: ♈

Aries is the first sign of the zodiac, represented by the symbol of the Ram, and it represents the beginning of the astrological year. Ruled by Mars, the planet of action, aggression, and drive, Aries embodies raw, unbridled energy. This sign is connected with the element of Fire, which further enhances its qualities of passion, warmth, and dynamism. Individuals born under this sign are known for their forward-thinking mentality, assertiveness, and a relentless desire to create new paths.

Symbol: The Ram

The symbol of Aries is the Ram, an animal known for its boldness, strength, and directness, perfectly representing the dynamic and assertive nature of those born under this sign. Rams are fearless creatures that charge forward without hesitation, a reflection of Aries' impulsive, pioneering spirit. This symbolism captures Aries' desire to lead, initiate, and take bold action. Just as the Ram uses its horns to break through obstacles, Aries is known for their determination and willingness to confront challenges head-on. The Ram also signifies vitality and drive, traits that fuel Aries' pursuit of new adventures and uncharted territories. As the first sign of the zodiac, Aries embodies the energy of new beginnings, leadership, and the courage to take the first step, much like the Ram who paves the way in the wild. This symbolism emphasizes Aries' role as the zodiac's trailblazer, always ready to forge ahead with confidence and enthusiasm.

Ruling Planet: Mars

Mars, the ruler of Aries, is the planet of war, action, and vitality. It bestows upon Aries a natural inclination towards confrontation and competitiveness. This influence drives them to be fearless and direct, often giving them the courage to pursue their goals with single-minded determination. The Martian energy infuses

Aries with a boldness that allows them to dive into challenges headfirst, often without hesitation.

Key Traits:
- **Bold and Ambitious:** Aries possesses an unyielding drive to succeed and often sets ambitious goals. Their fiery determination ensures they don't just wait for opportunities—they create them. They view life as a series of challenges to be conquered, and they're seldom satisfied unless they are pushing the limits of what's possible. This ambition also makes them natural leaders who are adept at inspiring others to take action.
- **Energetic and Enthusiastic:** Mars' influence provides Aries with an almost inexhaustible supply of energy. They are constantly on the move, chasing new experiences and eagerly diving into projects. This fervor for life can be infectious, as their enthusiasm often inspires those around them to get involved and pursue their own passions.
- **Confident and Assertive:** Aries is marked by an innate confidence and self-assuredness. They often exude a magnetic presence that commands attention and respect. When an Aries has an opinion, they're not shy about voicing it. Their assertiveness enables them to step into leadership roles easily, as they are not afraid to make swift, sometimes difficult, decisions.
- **Impulsive and Impatient:** One of Aries' more challenging traits is their impulsivity. The need for quick action and results can lead to decisions made without careful consideration. They often prefer to jump headfirst into situations, trusting their instincts rather than dwelling on the finer details. While this approach can lead to exciting discoveries, it can also result in missteps or unintended consequences. Their impatience can make them quick to frustration, particularly when they feel that progress is being hindered.
- **Independent and Adventurous:** Aries places a high value on personal freedom and autonomy. They despise feeling confined or restricted and are always in search of their next adventure. This sign embodies the spirit of exploration, often displaying an

eagerness to try new things and break new ground. While this independence is a great strength, it can also result in a tendency to disregard others' input or advice, particularly if they feel it interferes with their personal objectives.

Strengths:

- **Courageous:** Aries is naturally fearless and will often take on challenges that others shy away from. Their courage isn't just physical but also mental and emotional, as they are willing to confront difficult situations or have uncomfortable conversations to get to the truth.
- **Independent:** Self-reliance is at the core of the Aries personality. They prefer to carve their own path, rarely leaning on others for support or direction. This self-motivation enables them to be highly productive and goal-oriented.
- **Dynamic:** With their boundless energy, Aries can juggle multiple tasks simultaneously. They thrive in environments where they are constantly stimulated and given the freedom to express their dynamic nature.
- **Direct:** Honesty is a hallmark of the Aries communication style. They prefer to be straightforward and clear, which can be refreshing to those around them. However, this bluntness can sometimes come off as harsh or tactless, especially when discussing sensitive subjects.
- **Innovative:** Aries' pioneering spirit makes them natural innovators. They are always looking for new, more efficient ways to solve problems. Their willingness to take risks often leads them to be at the forefront of technological, artistic, or social advancements.

Challenges:

- **Impulsive:** Aries is prone to act before thinking things through, often diving into situations with little regard for potential risks. This can lead to hasty decisions or taking actions they might later regret.
- **Impatient:** Waiting is not in Aries' nature. They have a desire for

instant gratification and can become easily frustrated when things don't move at their desired pace. This impatience can sometimes result in conflicts, especially when working within a group that operates at a slower speed.

- **Short-Tempered:** The fiery temperament of Aries makes them quick to anger, especially when they feel their independence is being threatened or when they encounter obstacles. However, they usually cool down just as fast, rarely holding onto grudges for long.

- **Reckless:** In their desire to explore and experience life fully, Aries can be prone to taking unnecessary risks. Their adventurous nature sometimes leads them to disregard caution, resulting in situations that could have been avoided with a more careful approach.

- **Self-Centered:** Aries' focus on their personal goals can sometimes make them seem self-centered. They can become so absorbed in their pursuits that they overlook the needs and feelings of others, leading to potential conflicts in relationships.

Element: Fire

Aries is ruled by the element of Fire, which symbolizes energy, inspiration, and action. Fire signs are known for their dynamic, enthusiastic, and progressive spirits, and Aries, as the first sign of the zodiac, exemplifies these qualities. The Fire element fuels Aries' boldness, independence, and relentless drive to take the lead and venture into new possibilities. This intense inner flame gives Aries the courage to innovate and motivate others, making them pioneers in their endeavors. Fire also represents passion and spontaneity, both of which manifest in Aries' energetic approach to life. However, just as fire can be both creative and destructive, Aries' impulsive nature and quick temper can sometimes lead to challenges. Learning to harness and direct this fiery energy constructively is a key part of Aries' personal growth.

Modality: Cardinal

Aries belongs to the Cardinal modality, which is associated with action, initiation, and leadership. As a Cardinal sign, Aries is driven to start new projects and push forward into unknown territory. Cardinal signs are the initiators of the zodiac, and Aries, as the first sign, represents the spark of energy that begins new cycles. This modality enhances Aries' natural tendency to take charge, paving the way for others to follow. The Cardinal energy makes Aries proactive and eager to lead, often jumping into action with little hesitation. However, while Aries excels at starting things, they may sometimes struggle with seeing tasks through to completion, as their focus can quickly shift to the next exciting challenge. Balancing this drive to begin with the patience to follow through is key to Aries' growth.

Aries' Lesson:

For Aries, the challenge is to harness their powerful energy and direct it in a constructive way. Learning patience, tempering impulsiveness, and understanding the value of collaboration can help Aries achieve their full potential without burning bridges along the way.

Taurus (April 20 - May 20)

Symbol: ♉

Taurus, the second sign of the zodiac, is symbolized by the Bull, a creature known for its strength, determination, and steadfastness. This sign is ruled by Venus, the planet of love, beauty, and material pleasure, which endows Taurus with an affinity for comfort, luxury, and all things pleasurable. As an Earth sign, Taurus is grounded, practical, and focused on the physical realm. Taureans are known for their patience, reliability, and a deep-rooted need for stability and security in all aspects of life.

Symbol: The Bull

The symbol of Taurus is the Bull, an animal that represents strength, stability, and a steadfast nature, all key traits of this grounded Earth sign. Bulls are known for their calm, patient demeanor but also for their immense power and determination when provoked. This symbolism reflects Taurus' steady and reliable nature, as well as their persistence in achieving their goals. Just as a bull remains unmoved until it chooses to act, Taurus is known for their patience and deliberate approach to life, preferring to take their time and carefully plan their actions. However, like the Bull, once Taurus sets their mind on something, they are nearly unstoppable, displaying immense willpower and resilience. The Bull also symbolizes Taurus' connection to the material world, comfort, and sensual pleasures, as Taurus is deeply attuned to beauty, nature, and physical enjoyment. This symbolism highlights Taurus' strong need for security, both emotionally and materially, as well as their deep appreciation for the finer things in life.

Ruling Planet: Venus

Venus, the goddess of love and beauty, governs Taurus, imparting qualities of sensuality, harmony, and a love for the finer things in life. This planetary influence makes Taurus individuals deeply appreciative of aesthetics, art, and the pleasures of the senses.

Venus's presence in this sign also fosters a loving and loyal nature, as well as a strong desire for comfort and security. Taurus, under Venus's guidance, seeks to create a life of beauty, whether through relationships, surroundings, or personal style.

Key Traits:
- **Patient and Reliable:** Taurus is known for its patience and reliability. They have a calm demeanor and prefer to take their time when making decisions, ensuring that they make the right choice rather than a hasty one. This patience makes them dependable friends and partners who are always there when needed. Once Taurus commits to something, they see it through to the end, often outlasting others with their steady, persistent energy.
- **Loyal and Devoted:** Loyalty is a hallmark of Taurus. Whether in friendships, romantic relationships, or professional commitments, Taurus individuals are unwavering in their support and dedication. They take their relationships seriously and are deeply committed to the people they care about. This loyalty is not easily earned, but once it is, a Taurus will stand by their loved ones through thick and thin.
- **Practical and Grounded:** As an Earth sign, Taurus is inherently practical and grounded. They approach life with a realistic mindset, preferring facts and concrete evidence over abstract ideas. This practicality extends to all areas of their life, from their career choices to their daily routines. They value hard work and are willing to put in the effort to achieve their goals, often displaying a strong sense of responsibility and duty.
- **Sensual and Pleasure-Seeking:** Ruled by Venus, Taurus has a natural affinity for beauty, luxury, and sensual pleasures. They are attuned to their physical senses and often seek comfort through touch, taste, sound, and sight. Whether it's indulging in a delicious meal, enjoying a piece of art, or lounging in a cozy environment, Taurus knows how to appreciate life's pleasures. This sensuality also extends to their romantic relationships, where they are affectionate and attentive partners.
- **Stubborn and Resistant to Change:** One of Taurus's most

defining traits is its stubbornness. Once they set their mind on something, it's nearly impossible to sway them. This tenacity can be both a strength and a challenge, as it makes them incredibly determined but also resistant to change. Taurus prefers stability and consistency, often feeling uncomfortable when faced with sudden shifts or disruptions. They need time to adjust to new situations, and their reluctance to adapt quickly can sometimes lead to conflicts, especially in fast-paced environments.

Strengths:
- **Dependable:** Taurus is a rock of stability in both their personal and professional lives. They are the friend you can always count on, the employee who consistently delivers, and the partner who remains faithful.
- **Patient:** Taurus's patience allows them to handle challenges with a calm and steady approach. They are not easily flustered and can navigate difficulties without losing their composure.
- **Practical:** With their feet firmly planted on the ground, Taurus is adept at managing practical matters. They are resourceful and skilled at turning ideas into reality, often excelling in careers that require careful planning and execution.
- **Sensuous:** Taurus has a deep appreciation for the finer things in life. Their love of beauty and pleasure enhances their experiences, allowing them to create a life filled with comfort and joy.
- **Persistent:** Once a Taurus sets their sights on a goal, they pursue it with relentless determination. Their persistence often leads them to success, as they are not easily deterred by obstacles.

Challenges:
- **Stubborn:** The Bull's obstinate nature can make Taurus unwilling to budge, even when it's in their best interest to do so. They can become fixated on their viewpoint, leading to conflicts in relationships or at work.
- **Materialistic:** Taurus's desire for comfort and security can sometimes translate into materialism. They may place a high value on possessions and financial stability, which can lead to an

overemphasis on wealth or status.

- Possessive: In relationships, Taurus can be quite possessive and sometimes jealous. Their need for security makes them wary of anything that might threaten their sense of stability, which can lead to controlling behaviors.

- Resistant to Change: Taurus's preference for routine and familiarity can make them resistant to change. They may struggle with adapting to new circumstances or ideas, often preferring to stick with what they know.

- Self-Indulgent: With their love for luxury and pleasure, Taurus can sometimes become overly self-indulgent. They may have difficulty exercising moderation, leading to habits of excess in eating, spending, or other areas of life.

Element: Earth

Taurus belongs to the Earth element, which reflects its connection to the physical world and its practical, grounded nature. Earth signs are known for their stability, reliability, and focus on tangible results, making them the builders and sustainers of the zodiac. Taurus, in particular, embodies these qualities through its deep-rooted need for security, comfort, and material well-being. As an Earth sign, Taurus values consistency and is adept at creating a solid foundation in both personal and professional aspects of life. The Earth element also highlights Taurus' appreciation for the senses—whether through nature, art, or physical pleasures—allowing them to savor the beauty and richness of life. This grounding influence is what makes Taurus dependable and devoted, but it also contributes to their resistance to change, as they prefer the familiar and stable over the unpredictable.

Modality: Fixed

Taurus is a Fixed sign, representing stability, endurance, and determination. Fixed signs are known for their ability to maintain and sustain what has been started, making them the pillars of the zodiac. For Taurus, this manifests as a deep commitment to their goals, relationships, and routines. They are steady, reliable, and rarely swayed once their mind is made up, which makes them incredibly persistent and hardworking. However, this Fixed energy can also contribute to Taurus' resistance to change, as they tend to cling to the familiar and comfortable. While their Fixed modality helps Taurus remain dedicated and grounded, learning to embrace flexibility and adaptability is crucial for their personal growth.

Taurus's Lesson:

For Taurus, the challenge is to learn flexibility and embrace change. While their stability is one of their greatest strengths, it can also hold them back from experiencing growth and new opportunities. By learning to let go of their stubbornness and becoming more open to change, Taurus can find a balance between comfort and progress, enhancing their life with both security and new experiences.

Gemini (May 21 - June 20)

Symbol: ♊

Gemini, the third sign of the zodiac, is symbolized by the Twins, representing the duality and multifaceted nature of those born under this sign. Ruled by Mercury, the planet of communication, intellect, and curiosity, Gemini individuals are known for their versatility, adaptability, and sharp wit. As an Air sign, Gemini is concerned with the realm of ideas, social interactions, and mental stimulation. They are characterized by their desire to learn, explore, and engage with the world through conversation and the exchange of information.

Symbol: The Twins

The symbol of Gemini is the Twins, representing duality, communication, and the versatile and dynamic qualities associated with this Air sign. The Twins reflect Gemini's ability to see and understand multiple perspectives, as well as their adaptable, curious personality. This symbolism captures Gemini's versatility and their natural talent for juggling different ideas, roles, or projects at once. The Twins also signify the intellectual and social nature of Gemini, who is always eager to engage in conversation, share knowledge, and learn from others. Just as the Twins suggest a dual aspect, Gemini is known for their quick-thinking and ability to effortlessly switch between contrasting viewpoints or experiences, embodying both sides of a situation with ease. The symbol also points to Gemini's restlessness and desire for constant mental stimulation, as they seek variety and thrive on new ideas and interactions. This duality reflects Gemini's natural ability to connect with others, adapt to change, and explore the world through an ever-curious, inquisitive mind.

Ruling Planet: Mercury

Mercury, the messenger of the gods, is the planet of communication, intellect, and travel. Its influence on Gemini is evident in their quick-thinking, articulate speech, and thirst for knowledge. Gemini's unpredictable nature makes them fast learners who can easily switch between topics or activities. This planet also grants them a playful, curious demeanor, constantly urging them to seek out new experiences and connect with others. However, Mercury's fast-paced energy can also make Gemini restless and prone to scattering their focus.

Key Traits:
  - **Adaptable and Versatile:** Geminis are natural chameleons, capable of adapting to new situations and environments with ease. Their versatility allows them to thrive in a variety of roles and social settings, as they can quickly adjust their behavior and attitudes to suit the circumstances. This trait also makes them open-minded and willing to explore new perspectives, often leading them to be the ones who bridge gaps between differing viewpoints.
  - **Intelligent and Curious:** The influence of Mercury endows Gemini with a sharp intellect and insatiable curiosity. They are avid learners who are constantly seeking out new information, whether through reading, conversation, or hands-on experience. Their minds are always buzzing with ideas, and they enjoy discussing and debating various topics. This love of knowledge makes them natural storytellers, as they can absorb information from a multitude of sources and weave it into engaging narratives.
  - **Communicative and Witty:** Gemini is known for its gift of gab. They are highly expressive and articulate, communicating their thoughts clearly and effectively. Their conversational skills are exceptional, as they can effortlessly navigate through various topics, keeping others engaged with their wit and charm. Geminis have a playful sense of humor and often use clever wordplay to entertain and lighten the mood. They thrive in social environments where they can exchange ideas and connect with different types of people.
  - **Energetic and Restless:** With their minds constantly racing, Geminis are full of energy and enthusiasm. They are always on the go, exploring new places, meeting new people, and diving into new projects. This boundless energy can make them seem scattered, as

they often juggle multiple interests or tasks at once. While this restlessness can lead to exciting adventures and discoveries, it can also result in a lack of focus and follow-through on long-term commitments.

- **Dual Nature and Changeable:** The symbol of the Twins reflects the duality inherent in Gemini's nature. They can exhibit different personalities, sometimes seeming contradictory. One moment they may be lively and sociable, and the next, quiet and introspective. This changeability makes them unpredictable, and it can be challenging for others to fully understand their true nature. However, this duality also gives Gemini the ability to see multiple sides of a situation, making them excellent mediators and negotiators.

Strengths:

- **Adaptable:** Gemini's flexibility allows them to navigate change with ease. They can quickly acclimate to new environments, roles, or perspectives, making them excellent at problem-solving and innovation.

- **Intellectual:** Their love for learning and mental stimulation means that Geminis are well-informed and knowledgeable on a wide range of topics. They are often seen as the "know-it-alls" of the zodiac, though their curiosity is driven by genuine interest rather than ego.

- **Communicative:** Geminis are natural communicators. They can express complex ideas in an accessible manner, often becoming the life of social gatherings. Their expressiveness and humor make them captivating storytellers and conversationalists.

- **Witty:** With their quick minds and clever wordplay, Geminis are skilled at injecting humor and levity into conversations. They have an innate ability to think on their feet, making them sharp and entertaining.

- **Curious:** Their endless curiosity pushes them to explore new ideas, cultures, and experiences. This openness to learning helps them grow and evolve constantly, preventing them from becoming stagnant.

Challenges:
- **Indecisive:** Geminis' ability to see multiple sides of a situation can make decision-making difficult. They may overanalyze options, struggle to commit, or change their minds frequently, leading to frustration for themselves and those around them.
- **Restless:** The constant need for mental and physical stimulation can result in a restless nature. Geminis often start many projects at once but may struggle to see them through to completion, as their interest quickly shifts to the next exciting idea.
- **Superficial:** Their broad range of interests sometimes results in a lack of depth in any single area. They may have a tendency to skim the surface rather than delve deeply into a subject, preferring to know a little about everything rather than mastering one thing.
- **Inconsistent:** Due to their dual nature, Geminis can be inconsistent in their moods and behaviors. They may say one thing and do another, not out of malice but simply because their thoughts and feelings are constantly evolving.
- **Gossipy:** With their love of conversation and information, Geminis can sometimes veer into gossip. Their desire to share the latest news or tidbits can unintentionally lead to spreading rumors or revealing secrets.

Element: Air
Gemini is ruled by the element of Air, which represents the intellect, communication, and the exchange of ideas. Air signs are known for their curiosity, adaptability, and love for mental stimulation, and Gemini embodies these traits through its endless quest for knowledge and connection. The Air element fuels Gemini's desire to learn, explore, and engage with the world through conversation and intellectual pursuits. This element also grants Gemini the ability to think quickly, adapt to changing circumstances, and communicate effectively. However, just like the wind can shift directions unpredictably, the Air element can make Gemini prone to restlessness and inconsistency. Learning to ground their energy and focus on deeper understanding is key for Gemini's growth.

Modality: Mutable

Gemini belongs to the Mutable modality, which is associated with flexibility, adaptability, and change. Mutable signs are the editors and adjusters of the zodiac, constantly refining and evolving based on new information. For Gemini, this Mutable energy manifests in their ability to effortlessly switch between ideas, perspectives, and situations. They are highly adaptable, able to adjust to their surroundings or shift their approach depending on the context. This makes Gemini open-minded and versatile, but it can also lead to a tendency to be indecisive or inconsistent. While their Mutable nature allows them to go with the flow and embrace change, learning to stay grounded and focused is essential for Gemini's personal development.

Gemini's Lesson:

The challenge for Gemini is to learn the value of focus and depth. While their versatility and curiosity are strengths, there is also merit in committing to a single path or idea long enough to see it through. By learning to balance their need for variety with the discipline of persistence, Gemini can harness their mental energy in a more productive and fulfilling way.

Cancer (June 21 - July 22)

Symbol: ♋

Cancer, the fourth sign of the zodiac, is symbolized by the Crab, representing its protective, nurturing, and sometimes defensive nature. Ruled by the Moon, the planet of emotions, intuition, and the subconscious, Cancer is deeply connected to its feelings and is known for its empathy, sensitivity, and caring disposition. As a Water sign, Cancer navigates life through the ebb and flow of its emotional currents. Those born under this sign are often highly intuitive, compassionate, and devoted to the people and places they care about.

Symbol: The Crab

The symbol of Cancer is the Crab, representing protection, sensitivity, and a deep connection to home and family, which are central themes for this Water sign. The Crab, with its hard outer shell and soft, vulnerable interior, reflects Cancer's instinct to protect themselves and their loved ones emotionally, often retreating into their "shell" when feeling threatened or overwhelmed. This symbolism captures Cancer's nurturing nature, as they are deeply empathetic and devoted to the well-being of those they care about. Just as the Crab clings tightly with its claws, Cancer is known for their strong attachments to home, tradition, and relationships, often fiercely protective of their personal space and emotional bonds. The Crab also moves sideways, symbolizing Cancer's indirect approach to situations—they prefer to feel things out and rely on their intuition before taking action. This symbol encapsulates Cancer's dual need for security and emotional depth, as well as their natural ability to navigate the changing tides of emotion with sensitivity and care.

Ruling Planet: The Moon

The Moon rules Cancer, infusing it with nurturing qualities, emotional depth, and heightened receptivity. The Moon's phases reflect Cancer's changeable moods, as they are sensitive to the subtle energies around them. This lunar influence makes Cancer deeply connected to their instincts and feelings, often relying on their intuition to navigate life. It also fosters a protective nature, much like the Moon shelters the Earth with its gentle glow, leading Cancers to be fiercely loyal to their loved ones. However, this emotional intensity can also cause them to retreat into their shells when feeling vulnerable or threatened.

Key Traits:

- **Nurturing and Caring:** Cancer is the archetypal caretaker of the zodiac, always seeking to provide support and comfort to those they love. They have an innate desire to nurture, whether it's through cooking a meal, lending a listening ear, or offering a shoulder to cry on. This nurturing quality extends beyond people; Cancers often find themselves drawn to caring for pets, plants, or any living thing that needs love and attention. They possess a strong maternal or paternal instinct, making them naturally protective and concerned about the well-being of others.

- **Emotional and Sensitive:** As a Water sign ruled by the Moon, Cancer is highly attuned to their emotions. They feel things deeply and are empathetic, often absorbing the moods and feelings of those around them. This sensitivity allows them to connect with others on an emotional level, offering compassion and understanding. However, it also makes them susceptible to emotional fluctuations and moodiness, as they can be easily affected by the environment and the people they interact with. Cancers are like emotional sponges, soaking up energies, both positive and negative, which can sometimes lead to overwhelm.

- **Intuitive and Perceptive:** Cancers possess a strong intuition and often rely on their gut feelings when making decisions. They are perceptive, picking up on subtle cues that others might overlook, which allows them to understand people's needs and feelings without a word being spoken. This intuitive insight often makes them excellent judges of character, as they can sense when something is off. Their intuition guides them in matters of the heart and home, helping them create spaces that feel safe, welcoming, and nurturing.

- **Protective and Loyal:** Like the Crab, Cancer has a hard outershell that serves to protect its sensitive inner self. They are fiercely protective of their loved ones and will go to great lengths to ensure the safety and happiness of those they care about. Loyalty is one of Cancer's most admirable qualities; once they have formed an emotional bond, they are committed for the long haul. However, this protective nature can sometimes lead to possessiveness, as Cancers may struggle with letting go or giving others the space they need.

- **Retreating and Cautious:** When faced with emotional turmoil or when feeling threatened, Cancer tends to retreat into their shell. They value their personal space and may withdraw to process their feelings in private. This cautious nature means that they rarely rush into situations or relationships; instead, they prefer to observe and feel things out before making decisions. While this can help them avoid unnecessary risks, it can also make them appear guarded or distant to those who don't know them well.

Strengths:

- **Compassionate:** Cancer's empathy allows them to connect with others on a deep, emotional level. They are excellent listeners and are often the first to offer support when someone is in need.

- **Nurturing:** Their caring nature extends to all areas of life. Whether in relationships, work, or hobbies, Cancer seeks to create environments that are comfortable, harmonious, and supportive.

- **Loyal:** When Cancer commits, they are steadfast and loyal. They value trust and reliability, and their relationships are built on a strong foundation of emotional connection.

- **Intuitive:** Cancers have a keen sense of intuition, allowing them to perceive things beyond the surface. They are often able to sense the emotions of others and adapt their responses accordingly.

- **Protective:** Cancer's desire to care for others makes them protective. They are like a shield for their loved ones, always ready to defend and support them when needed.

Challenges:
- **Overly Sensitive:** Cancer's emotional nature means that they can take things to heart easily. They may overreact to criticism or perceived slights, which can lead to hurt feelings and withdrawal.
- **Moody:** Like the Moon's phases, Cancer's mood can change rapidly. They may go from feeling happy and content to withdrawn and melancholic without warning, making it difficult for others to keep up.
- **Possessive:** Cancer's protective instincts can sometimes manifest as possessiveness. They may become clingy or have difficulty letting go, particularly in relationships where they feel deeply invested.
- **Insecure:** Despite their nurturing qualities, Cancers often struggle with self-doubt and insecurity. They may seek constant reassurance from others, especially in their personal relationships.
- **Retreating:** When overwhelmed, Cancer tends to retreat into their shell, avoiding confrontation and shutting others out. While this self-protective mechanism helps them cope, it can also hinder communication and problem-solving.
- **Manipulative:** Their deep emotional intelligence allows Cancer to sense what others need or want, but when out of balance, they may use this awareness to subtly influence situations or people. This can manifest as guilt-tripping, passive-aggressiveness, or playing the victim to get their way.

Element: Water
Cancer is ruled by the element of Water, which represents emotions, intuition, and the subconscious. Water signs are deeply connected to their feelings, and Cancer exemplifies this through its nurturing, empathetic, and protective nature. The Water element grants Cancer the ability to navigate the emotional currents of life with sensitivity and compassion, allowing them to connect with others on a deep, emotional level. Like the ebb and flow of the tides, Cancer's moods can change rapidly, making them both intuitive and reactive to their environment. Water's influence also enhances Cancer's protective instincts, encouraging them to care for others and

create emotionally secure spaces. However, just as water can retreat into hidden depths, Cancer's challenge is learning not to retreat too far into their emotional shell when feeling vulnerable.

Modality: Cardinal

Cancer is a Cardinal sign, which means it embodies the qualities of leadership, initiation, and action. Cardinal signs are the initiators of the zodiac, and Cancer expresses this through its nurturing and protective instincts. Cancer is motivated to take the lead when it comes to caring for others, creating safe spaces, and fostering emotional connections. They are often the first to offer support, start new projects related to home or family, or take initiative in emotional matters. However, Cancer's leadership is more subtle and caring, as it revolves around emotional security rather than overt control. While this Cardinal energy helps Cancer be proactive in caring for loved ones, learning to balance this with giving others space and maintaining healthy emotional boundaries is a key part of their growth.

Cancer's Lesson:

The challenge for Cancer is to learn how to balance their emotional depth with a sense of objectivity. While their caring nature is a gift, it's important for them to recognize when to protect their own boundaries and avoid becoming overly involved in the lives of others. By learning to manage their sensitivity and nurturing qualities, Cancer can cultivate healthier relationships and environments that reflect both their compassion and their need for self-care.

Leo (July 23 - August 22)

Symbol: ♌

Leo, the fifth sign of the zodiac, is symbolized by the Lion, embodying strength, pride, and regal authority. Ruled by the Sun, the center of the solar system, Leos are born to shine and naturally draw attention with their warmth, vitality, and charisma. As a Fire sign, Leo is passionate, energetic, and full of life, often expressing themselves with confidence and flair. Those born under this sign are known for their generous spirit, creativity, and strong desire to lead and inspire others.

Symbol: The Lion

The symbol of Leo is the Lion, representing power, confidence, and a commanding presence, perfectly capturing the bold and charismatic nature of this Fire sign. The Lion, known as the "king of the jungle," represents Leo's natural leadership abilities, confidence, and desire to be at the center of attention. This symbolism reflects Leo's innate sense of pride and dignity, as they often carry themselves with a commanding presence and a generous spirit. Just as the Lion leads its pride with authority and protection, Leo is driven to inspire and uplift those around them, often taking on leadership roles in their communities or social circles. The Lion also symbolizes Leo's fierce loyalty and protective instincts—when it comes to their loved ones, Leo is both caring and fiercely protective. The sun-like radiance of the Lion matches Leo's warmth, enthusiasm, and passion for life, as they are often seen as vibrant and magnetic individuals. This symbol emphasizes Leo's desire for recognition, respect, and admiration, while also showcasing their big-hearted generosity and willingness to share the spotlight with those they care about.

Ruling Planet: The Sun

The Sun, the heart of our solar system, rules Leo, granting this sign an inherent sense of self-assurance, purpose, and the need to express its individuality. The Sun represents ego, willpower, and the essence of one's identity, which is why Leos are often seen as the epitome of confidence, pride, and self-expression. This solar influence gives them a radiant energy that draws others to their warmth and light. Just as the Sun provides life to the planets, Leo seeks to bring joy, vitality, and positivity to those around them.

Key Traits:
- **Confident and Charismatic:** Leos are natural-born leaders with a commanding presence that instantly draws people in. They carry themselves with poise and assurance, exuding a sense of self-confidence that can be inspiring to others. This charisma often places them at the center of attention, where they thrive. They are not afraid to take the spotlight and showcase their talents, making them stand out in social and professional settings. This confidence isn't just for show; it stems from an inner belief in their abilities and the value they bring to the world.

- **Generous and Warm-hearted:** Leo has a big heart and a generous spirit. They love to give, whether it's offering a helping hand, showering loved ones with gifts, or providing emotional support. Their warmth makes them incredibly loyal friends and partners, as they are deeply invested in the happiness and well-being of those they care about. Leos are protective and often take on the role of the provider or guardian, ensuring that those around them are well cared for. Their generosity is not just material; they give freely of their time, attention, and affection.

- **Creative and Expressive:** Ruled by the Sun, Leo is brimming with creative energy. They are drawn to activities that allow them to express their individuality and talents, whether it's through art, music, theater, or leadership roles. Leos are naturally imaginative and have a flair for the dramatic, often bringing a sense of drama, color, and excitement to their endeavors. They have a strong need to create and to be recognized for their contributions, which can make them successful in any field that values originality and artistic expression.

- **Proud and Ambitious:** Leos have a deep sense of pride in themselves and their accomplishments. They are driven by a desire to succeed and be admired, often setting high standards for themselves and working diligently to achieve their goals. This ambition is fueled by a need for recognition and respect, as Leos are most fulfilled when they are praised and appreciated for their efforts. However, their pride can also make them sensitive to criticism, as they have a strong desire to be seen in a positive light.

- **Dramatic and Attention-Seeking:** Leo loves to be in the spotlight and often gravitates toward roles or situations that allow them to shine. They have a natural theatricality and may be prone to dramatic displays of emotion, especially when they feel undervalued or ignored. While this need for attention can make them vibrant and entertaining, it can also lead to vanity or a tendency to dominate conversations. Leos crave admiration and affirmation, and they may sometimes struggle to share the stage with others.

Strengths:

- **Confident:** Leo's self-assured nature allows them to take on leadership roles and pursue their goals with determination. They believe in their abilities and are not easily swayed by doubts or insecurities.
- **Generous:** Leos have a generous spirit and are often willing to go out of their way to help others. They are loving, loyal, and fiercely protective of those they care about.
- **Creative:** With a natural flair for artistry and drama, Leo excels in creative endeavors. They bring passion and imagination to their work, often producing results that are both bold and innovative.
- **Optimistic:** Ruled by the Sun, Leos possess a sunny disposition. They have a positive outlook on life and the ability to uplift others with their enthusiasm and zest for life.
- **Loyal:** In relationships, Leo is deeply loyal and devoted. They are protective of their loved ones and will go to great lengths to ensure their happiness and security.

Challenges:

- **Stubborn:** Leos can be quite set in their ways, holding firmly to their opinions and beliefs. Their pride makes them reluctant to admit when they are wrong, leading to stubbornness that can create conflicts.

- **Attention-Seeking:** Leo's desire to be in the limelight can sometimes come across as self-centered. They may dominate conversations or situations, seeking constant validation and admiration from others.

- **Prideful:** While their pride is a source of strength, it can also be a weakness. Leos may struggle with criticism and may become defensive or dramatic when their ego is bruised.

- **Domineering:** In their quest to lead, Leos can sometimes become overbearing, attempting to control situations or people to ensure things go according to their plan. This can create tension in relationships, especially when others feel overshadowed or undermined.

- **Impatient:** With their natural drive to achieve, Leos can be impatient with delays or obstacles. They want to see progress quickly and may become frustrated when things do not go according to their expectations.

Element: Fire

Leo is ruled by the element of Fire, which represents passion, energy, and creativity. Fire signs are known for their dynamic and vibrant personalities, and Leo is the embodiment of this fiery spirit. The Fire element gives Leo its enthusiasm, courage, and drive to express itself fully and confidently. Like a blazing flame, Leo's energy is radiant and captivating, often drawing others into their warmth and light. The Fire element fuels Leo's desire to lead, inspire, and create, making them natural-born leaders who seek to bring joy and vitality to those around them. However, just as fire can burn out of control, Leo must learn to balance their intense need for attention and recognition with humility and understanding, ensuring their flame brightens rather than overwhelms those in their orbit.

Modality: Fixed

Leo belongs to the Fixed modality, which is associated with

stability, determination, and persistence. Fixed signs are known for their unwavering commitment and ability to follow through on their goals. For Leo, this Fixed energy manifests as an unshakable sense of purpose and loyalty to their ambitions. Once Leo sets their sights on something, they pursue it with a steadfast dedication, refusing to be easily swayed. This Fixed nature also extends to their relationships, where Leos are fiercely loyal and protective of those they love. However, while their Fixed energy helps them remain focused and determined, it can also lead to stubbornness, as they may resist change or hold on to their pride too tightly. Learning flexibility and compromise is essential for Leo's personal growth.

Leo's Lesson:

The challenge for Leo is to learn humility and the value of sharing the spotlight. While their confidence and ambition are their strengths, it's important for them to acknowledge the contributions of others and practice empathy. By balancing their need for recognition with generosity of spirit, Leos can lead not just with authority but also with kindness and warmth, truly embodying the heart of the lion.

Virgo (August 23 - September 22)

Symbol: ♍

Virgo, the sixth sign of the zodiac, is symbolized by the Maiden, representing purity, meticulousness, and a deep connection to nature and practicality. Ruled by Mercury, the planet of communication, intellect, and analytical thought, Virgo embodies a sharp, detail-oriented mindset and a desire for order. As an Earth sign, Virgo is grounded, realistic, and focused on the tangible aspects of life. Those born under this sign are known for their dedication, reliability, and methodical approach to every endeavor, constantly striving for improvement and excellence.

Symbol: The Maiden

The symbol of Virgo is the Maiden, often depicted holding a sheaf of wheat, symbolizing purity, harvest, and a deep connection to the earth and nature's cycles. This imagery reflects Virgo's focus on growth, service, and practicality. The Maiden represents Virgo's desire to nurture and care for the world through a meticulous, detail-oriented approach, much like tending to a garden with patience and precision. Virgo is known for their analytical mind and desire for order, and the Maiden symbolizes their careful, methodical way of improving and organizing their surroundings. The sheaf of wheat in the Maiden's hand symbolizes Virgo's ability to gather knowledge and resources to help others, reflecting their service-oriented nature and desire to make things better for those around them. The Maiden also represents purity, highlighting Virgo's high standards and their tendency to seek perfection in everything they do, from their work to their personal lives. This symbol embodies Virgo's connection to health, wellness, and practicality, as well as their strong sense of responsibility and dedication to refining and improving both themselves and their environment.

Ruling Planet: Mercury

Mercury's influence on Virgo is distinct from its effect on

Gemini. While Gemini is quick, versatile, and expressive, Virgo manifests Mercury's energy in a more refined, analytical, and methodical manner. This planet grants Virgo an acute attention to detail, strong communication skills, and a practical mindset that seeks to understand the world through analysis and organization. Mercury's presence in Virgo also bestows an inherent curiosity, driving them to acquire knowledge and perfect their skills. Their communication style is precise, thoughtful, and often focused on finding solutions and providing constructive criticism.

Key Traits:

- **Analytical and Detail-Oriented:** Virgos possess a sharp, analytical mind that naturally hones in on the finer details. They are observant and meticulous, with an ability to notice things that others might overlook. This trait makes them skilled problem-solvers, as they approach challenges methodically and with an eye for precision. They are often seen as the perfectionists of the zodiac, constantly seeking to refine and improve the world around them. However, this analytical nature can sometimes lead to overthinking or an inability to see the bigger picture due to their focus on the small details.

- **Practical and Reliable:** As an Earth sign, Virgo is grounded and realistic in its approach to life. They are highly practical, preferring to deal with facts, figures, and tangible outcomes rather than abstract theories or fantasies. Virgos are dependable and trustworthy, taking their commitments seriously and striving to fulfill their responsibilities to the best of their ability. Their methodical nature makes them efficient planners, organizers, and caretakers. They are the ones others turn to when a situation requires a clear-headed, well-thought-out approach.

- **Helpful and Service-Oriented:** One of Virgo's most admirable qualities is their desire to be of service to others. They are naturally inclined to help, whether it's by offering practical advice, lending a hand with tasks, or simply being a supportive presence. Virgos take great satisfaction in knowing they have contributed positively to the lives of those around them. Their service-oriented nature often extends to their work, where they thrive in roles that involve healing, teaching, or improving systems and processes.

- **Humble and Modest:** Despite their intelligence and capabilities, Virgos are often humble and modest about their achievements. They prefer to let their actions speak for themselves rather than seek the spotlight. This humility stems from their high standards; they are rarely satisfied with anything less than perfection, and they may downplay their accomplishments if they feel they could have done better. While this trait makes them approachable and relatable, it can also lead to self-criticism and a reluctance to acknowledge their own worth.

- **Critical and Self-Sacrificing:** Virgos have an innate desire for everything to be in order, both within themselves and in their environment. This pursuit of perfection can make them overly critical, not just of others but especially of themselves. They may struggle with feelings of inadequacy or self-doubt, constantly striving to meet the high standards they set. Additionally, their helpful nature can sometimes lead them to overextend themselves, sacrificing their own needs in the process of caring for others.

Strengths:

- **Detail-Oriented:** Virgos excel at paying attention to the finer details, which makes them invaluable in roles that require precision, thoroughness, and accuracy. They are natural organizers and planners, ensuring that nothing is overlooked.

- **Practical:** Their down-to-earth approach allows them to handle life's challenges with a level-headed mindset. They are adept at finding practical solutions and applying logic to solve problems.

- **Reliable:** When a Virgo commits to something, they follow through with dedication and responsibility. They are dependable friends, colleagues, and partners, always ready to lend a hand or provide support.

- **Hardworking:** Virgos are diligent workers who take pride in their work. They are willing to put in the effort to achieve their goals, often going the extra mile to ensure tasks are completed to the highest standard.

- **Helpful:** Their service-oriented nature makes them generous with their time and resources. They find fulfillment in helping others and are often the first to offer assistance when someone is in need.

Challenges:
- **Overly Critical:** Virgo's desire for perfection can make them overly critical of themselves and others. They may become fixated on flaws, which can lead to feelings of inadequacy or discontentment.
- **Worry-Prone:** Virgos tend to overanalyze situations, which can result in excessive worry and anxiety. They may struggle to relax, as their minds are often racing with thoughts about what could go wrong or how things could be improved.
- **Perfectionistic:** The pursuit of perfection can sometimes paralyze Virgo, making it difficult for them to complete tasks or be satisfied with the outcome. They may have trouble letting go of control, especially when they fear that things won't meet their high standards.
- **Reserved:** While Virgos are helpful and caring, they can also be reserved and guarded in expressing their own emotions. They prefer to keep their feelings private, which can sometimes make them seem distant or hard to read.
- **Self-Sacrificing:** Virgo's desire to help others can lead them to neglect their own needs. They may take on too many responsibilities or put others' needs before their own, resulting in burnout or resentment.

Element: Earth
Virgo is ruled by the element of Earth, which represents practicality, stability, and a focus on the material world. Earth signs are grounded, realistic, and concerned with the tangible aspects of life, and Virgo embodies these traits through its meticulous approach to tasks, its dedication to service, and its desire to create order. The Earth element gives Virgo a strong sense of responsibility and a methodical mindset, allowing them to excel in situations that require

attention to detail and careful planning. Virgos are rooted in the physical world, preferring to deal with facts and concrete outcomes rather than abstract ideas. However, the Earth element can also make Virgo prone to worry and overthinking, as they seek perfection in everything they do. Learning to balance their need for control with acceptance of life's imperfections is key to Virgo's growth.

Modality: Mutable

Virgo belongs to the Mutable modality, which is associated with adaptability, flexibility, and change. Mutable signs are the editors and refiners of the zodiac, constantly adjusting and improving their surroundings to create order and efficiency. For Virgo, this Mutable energy manifests as a natural ability to adapt to new information and circumstances, always seeking to refine and perfect processes. This makes Virgos skilled at analyzing situations and making necessary adjustments to improve outcomes. However, their Mutable nature can also make them prone to over analyzing or second-guessing themselves. While this adaptability allows Virgo to excel in problem-solving and service, learning to trust their instincts and know when to let things be is essential for their personal growth.

Virgo's Lesson:

The challenge for Virgo is to embrace imperfection and find balance. While their desire for order and excellence is admirable, it's important for them to recognize that perfection is often an unattainable goal. By learning to appreciate the beauty in imperfection and letting go of excessive self-criticism, Virgos can cultivate a more relaxed and positive outlook. This self-acceptance will allow them to use their strengths in a way that nurtures both themselves and those around them.

Libra (September 23 - October 22)

Symbol:

Libra, the seventh sign of the zodiac, is symbolized by the Scales, representing balance, harmony, and fairness. Ruled by Venus, the planet of love, beauty, and pleasure, Libra embodies grace, diplomacy, and a strong aesthetic sense. As an Air sign, Libra is intellectually driven, focused on relationships, and thrives in social settings. Individuals born under this sign are known for their charm, diplomatic nature, and desire to create harmony in all aspects of their lives. They seek balance and strive to ensure justice and equality in their relationships and environment.

Symbol: The Scales

The symbol of Libra is the Scales, representing balance, harmony, and justice, perfectly reflecting the core values of this Air sign. The Scales symbolize Libra's innate desire for equilibrium in all areas of life, whether in relationships, social settings, or decision-making. Just as scales require perfect balance to function properly, Libra seeks fairness and equality, always striving to weigh both sides of a situation before making judgments. The Scales represent Libra's deep connection to justice and morality, as they are often concerned with ensuring that everyone is treated fairly and that decisions are made with integrity. This sense of balance extends to Libra's personal life, where they seek beauty, peace, and symmetry in their relationships and environments. The Scales emphasize Libra's love of art, aesthetics, and refined taste, as they are drawn to things that reflect balance and harmony both visually and emotionally. This symbol encapsulates Libra's role as the peacemaker of the zodiac, always striving to create harmony in both personal and social spheres.

Ruling Planet: Venus

Venus, the planet of love, beauty, and harmony, exerts a powerful influence over Libra, endowing this sign with a refined sense of aesthetics, an appreciation for art, and a deep desire for meaningful connections. Venus makes Libra naturally charming, social, and focused on partnership, whether romantic, platonic, or professional. Libra's love of beauty often translates into a keen eye for fashion, art, and design, while Venus also enhances their diplomatic abilities, enabling them to navigate social dynamics gracefully. However, Venus's influence can also make Libra indecisive, as they weigh all options in their quest for balance.

Key Traits:

- **Diplomatic and Fair:** Libra is known for its strong sense of justice and fairness. They are natural mediators, always striving to create harmony and resolve conflicts. Libras have an innate ability to see multiple sides of a situation, which allows them to offer balanced perspectives and find common ground between differing viewpoints. This diplomatic nature makes them skilled in navigating complex social dynamics, as they use their charm and tact to bring people together. However, their desire for fairness can sometimes lead to indecisiveness, as they struggle to choose a side for fear of causing discord.

- **Charming and Social:** Ruled by Venus, Libra exudes charm and grace. They are social butterflies who thrive in environments where they can engage with others and share ideas. Their natural charisma draws people to them, making them popular in social circles. Libras have a talent for making others feel comfortable and appreciated, often using their humor, wit, and genuine interest in people to form meaningful connections. They value companionship and often seek out relationships that bring beauty, pleasure, and balance into their lives.

- **Idealistic and Romantic:** Libra has a strong idealistic streak, particularly when it comes to love and relationships. They are romantics at heart, seeking deep, harmonious partnerships that embody their ideals of beauty, love, and fairness. This idealism extends to their vision of the world; Libras are often driven by a desire to create a more just and balanced society. They have high standards for themselves and others, which can sometimes lead them to pursue an ideal that is difficult to achieve. However, this pursuit of perfection is what makes Libra passionate about building a world that reflects their values.

- **Indecisive and People-Pleasing:** One of Libra's most challenging traits is their indecisiveness. Their need to weigh all sides of an issue can lead to overthinking and an inability to make decisions, especially when the outcome affects others. Libras dislike conflict and will go to great lengths to avoid upsetting people, often prioritizing harmony over their own needs. This people-pleasing tendency can sometimes result in them suppressing their true feelings or agreeing to things they don't fully support in order to keep the peace.

- **Aesthetic and Refined:** With Venus as their ruling planet, Libras have a deep appreciation for beauty and art. They are drawn to environments that are aesthetically pleasing, often displaying a refined taste in fashion, design, and culture. Libras have a natural eye for balance and symmetry, which they bring into every aspect of their lives, from their homes to their personal style. This love of beauty and refinement also influences their relationships, as they seek partners who match their aesthetic values and who can share in their love of life's finer pleasures.

Strengths:

- **Charming:** Libra's warm and friendly demeanor allows them to connect with others easily. They are skilled conversationalists who know how to make people feel valued and understood.

- **Diplomatic:** Libras excel at mediating conflicts and finding solutions that satisfy all parties. Their ability to see different perspectives makes them effective at fostering cooperation and understanding.

- **Fair-Minded:** With a strong sense of justice, Libras are committed to doing what's right and ensuring equality. They strive to treat everyone with respect and fairness, making them trustworthy and reliable friends and partners.

- **Romantic:** In love, Libra is passionate, affectionate, and dedicated. They are generous with their love and seek to create a harmonious, loving atmosphere in their relationships.

- **Socially Intelligent:** Libra's social skills are unmatched. They are adept at reading people and situations, which allows them to navigate social environments with ease and grace.

Challenges:

- **Indecisive:** Libra's desire for balance can lead to excessive deliberation. They may struggle to make decisions, particularly when they fear the potential for conflict or dissatisfaction.
- **Avoidant:** In their quest for harmony, Libras may avoid difficult conversations or confrontations. This avoidance can lead to unresolved issues in their relationships, as they may prioritize peace over addressing problems.
- **People-Pleasing:** Libra's need for approval can make them overly concerned with what others think. They may suppress their own needs or go along with others' wishes to keep the peace, leading to feelings of resentment or burnout.
- **Superficial:** While their love for beauty is a strength, it can sometimes make Libras appear superficial. They may focus too much on appearances or be overly concerned with how things look, rather than how they truly are.
- **Indulgent:** Ruled by Venus, Libra has a penchant for luxury and pleasure. They may indulge in life's finer things, sometimes at the expense of practicality or moderation.
- **Flirtatious:** Charismatic and socially charming, Libras often enjoy playful interactions and lighthearted connections. However, their flirtatious nature can sometimes be misinterpreted, leading to confusion or unintended romantic expectations.

Element: Air

Libra is ruled by the element of Air, which represents intellect, communication, and the exchange of ideas. Air signs are known for their love of social interaction, their ability to see different perspectives, and their intellectual curiosity. For Libra, the Air element fuels their desire for harmony, fairness, and balanced relationships. This element gives Libra the ability to connect with others on a mental and social level, making them skilled diplomats and mediators. Air's influence enhances Libra's ability to navigate social dynamics with grace and charm, as they seek to foster understanding and cooperation. However, just like air can be difficult to grasp, Libra's tendency to weigh all sides of an issue can sometimes lead to indecisiveness. Learning to trust their intuition and make decisions with confidence is key to Libra's growth.

Modality: Cardinal

Libra is a Cardinal sign, which means it carries the energy of initiation, leadership, and action. Cardinal signs are the pioneers of the zodiac, and Libra expresses this through their ability to create harmony, build relationships, and take the lead in social and intellectual pursuits. Libra's Cardinal energy drives them to seek balance and justice, often being the first to initiate conversations or start projects that promote peace and equality. This modality gives Libra the drive to foster connections and maintain social harmony. However, while Libra excels at initiating relationships and social interactions, they may struggle with follow-through, especially when faced with difficult decisions or conflicts. Learning to embrace decisive action, even when it leads to discomfort, is essential for Libra's personal growth.

Libra's Lesson:

The challenge for Libra is to find balance within themselves and learn to assert their own needs. While their desire for harmony is a strength, it's important for them to embrace conflict when necessary and to make decisions based on their own values rather than simply trying to please others. By learning to set boundaries and trust their own judgment, Libras can create a more authentic and balanced life, both in their relationships and within themselves.

Scorpio (October 23 - November 21)

Symbol: ♏

Scorpio, the eighth sign of the zodiac, is symbolized by the Scorpion, representing intensity, depth, and a transformative nature. Ruled by Pluto, the planet of transformation and rebirth, and traditionally by Mars, the planet of action and desire, Scorpio embodies power, passion, and an unyielding drive to uncover the truth. As a Water sign, Scorpio is deeply emotional, intuitive, and perceptive, navigating life through its complex layers. Scorpios are known for their magnetic presence, resourcefulness, and a desire for profound connections that transcend the superficial.

Symbol: The Scorpion

The symbol of Scorpio is the Scorpion, representing intensity, transformation, and hidden strength, which are key traits of this powerful Water sign. The Scorpion's imagery reflects Scorpio's deeply emotional and mysterious nature, as well as their ability to navigate the complexities of life with precision and control. Known for its ability to defend itself with a sharp sting, the Scorpion symbolizes Scorpio's fierce protectiveness, particularly over their emotions and personal boundaries. This defensive nature also speaks to Scorpio's guarded personality, as they reveal their true selves only to those they trust deeply. The Scorpion's association with transformation and rebirth aligns with Scorpio's ruling planet Pluto, emphasizing their capacity for personal growth and their ability to rise stronger from difficult situations. Just as the Scorpion can shed its exoskeleton, Scorpio is adept at shedding old habits, beliefs, or attachments to evolve and regenerate. This symbolism captures Scorpio's depth, intensity, and resilience, as they are unafraid to explore life's darker, more hidden aspects. The Scorpion also highlights Scorpio's determination and focus, reflecting their all-or-nothing approach to life and their powerful drive to uncover truth and experience profound emotional connections.

Ruling Planets: Pluto and Mars

Pluto, the ruler of Scorpio, is associated with transformation, rebirth, and the subconscious. It gives Scorpio a natural affinity for delving into the depths of life, exploring hidden truths, and embracing the cycle of change. This Plutonian influence makes Scorpios drawn to the mysteries of the human psyche, often unafraid to confront the darker aspects of existence. Additionally, Mars, the planet of action and desire, contributes to Scorpio's intensity, determination, and assertiveness. Together, these planetary influences give Scorpio a powerful combination of passion, resourcefulness, and a deep, sometimes obsessive, focus on their goals.

Key Traits:

- **Intense and Passionate:** Scorpios experience life with unparalleled intensity. Their emotions run deep, and they approach everything—whether it be love, work, or personal interests—with fierce passion. This intensity makes them highly driven individuals who are unafraid to pursue what they want with unwavering focus and determination. In relationships, Scorpios are passionate lovers, seeking profound emotional connections that go beyond the surface. They do not do anything halfway; when a Scorpio commits to something, they are all in.

- **Mysterious and Reserved:** Scorpio is known for its enigmatic and secretive nature. They are not ones to reveal their thoughts and feelings easily, preferring to keep their true selves guarded. This mystery often draws people to them, as others are intrigued by the depths they sense but cannot fully understand. Scorpios have an innate ability to observe and absorb their surroundings without revealing too much in return. They are excellent at reading others, using their keen perception to navigate social dynamics while remaining elusive themselves.

- **Resourceful and Determined:** When faced with challenges, Scorpios exhibit remarkable resourcefulness. They are strategic thinkers who can adapt to changing circumstances and find solutions where others might see none. This trait, combined with their determination, allows them to overcome obstacles and achieve their goals. They do not shy away from difficult situations; instead, they tackle problems head-on, often emerging stronger and wiser. Scorpios are known for their resilience and capacity to rebuild, no matter how many times they fall.

- **Emotional and Perceptive:** As a Water sign, Scorpio is deeply emotional and sensitive, even if they do not always show it. They have a powerful intuition that allows them to sense what lies beneath the surface of situations and people. This perceptiveness makes them excellent judges of character, as they can quickly identify sincerity, deception, or hidden motives. Their emotions can be intense and all-consuming, leading them to experience both profound highs and devastating lows. Scorpios are not afraid to confront their own emotions, embracing the full spectrum of their inner experiences.

- **Transformative and Powerful:** Scorpios are the natural alchemists of the zodiac, constantly undergoing cycles of transformation and rebirth. They have an innate understanding of the power of change and are willing to shed old skin to become a more evolved version of themselves. This transformative nature makes them incredibly powerful, as they can harness the strength found in their darkest moments to fuel their growth. Scorpios seek to understand life's deeper mysteries, often delving into the realms of psychology, spirituality, and the occult.

Strengths:

- **Passionate:** Scorpio's passion is their driving force. They pursue their goals with intensity and are deeply committed to the people and causes they care about.
- **Resourceful:** Scorpios are adept at navigating complex situations and finding solutions, no matter how challenging. Their ability to adapt and strategize makes them formidable in any endeavor.
- **Loyal:** When Scorpio commits to a relationship, they are fiercely loyal and protective. They value trust and expect the same level of loyalty in return.

- **Intuitive:** Scorpio's perceptive nature allows them to see beyond appearances and grasp the underlying truths in situations. Their intuition guides them in their interactions and decision-making.
- **Resilient:** Scorpios have a remarkable capacity to recover from setbacks. They are not easily defeated and often emerge from challenges with renewed strength and insight.

Challenges:

- **Secretive:** Scorpio's reserved nature can make them appear distant or unapproachable. They may struggle to open up to others, even in close relationships, leading to misunderstandings.
- **Possessive:** In relationships, Scorpios can be intensely possessive, as they fear betrayal and loss. This possessiveness can sometimes lead to control issues or jealousy.
- **Obsessive:** Scorpio's all-or-nothing mindset can make them prone to obsession, whether it be with a person, goal, or idea. They may become fixated and struggle to let go, even when it is in their best interest.
- **Vindictive:** When wronged, Scorpio's reaction can be intense. They are known for their strong sense of justice and can hold onto grudges, seeking retribution rather than forgiveness.
- **Emotionally Intense:** Scorpio's emotions can be overwhelming, both for themselves and for those around them. Their mood swings and intense feelings can create an aura of unpredictability.
- **Deceptive:** When operating from a place of fear or self-protection, Scorpios can be highly strategic and secretive, sometimes resorting to manipulation or dishonesty to maintain control. They may withhold information, engage in covert actions, or conceal their true intentions to avoid vulnerability. This can manifest as power plays or emotional manipulation.

Element: Water

Scorpio is ruled by the element of Water, which represents emotions, intuition, and the subconscious. Water signs are deeply connected to their feelings and often navigate life through their emotional depth, and Scorpio exemplifies this with intensity and passion. The Water element gives Scorpio its profound sensitivity, allowing them to perceive what lies beneath the surface and uncover hidden truths. This element also enhances Scorpio's intuition, making them adept at understanding others on a deep emotional and psychological level. Water's influence fuels Scorpio's desire for transformation and rebirth, as they constantly seek to evolve and understand life's complexities. However, like the deep and often turbulent waters, Scorpio's emotions can run intensely, and learning to manage the ebb and flow of their inner world is crucial to their personal growth.

Modality: Fixed

Scorpio belongs to the Fixed modality, which is associated with stability, determination, and persistence. Fixed signs are known for their unwavering focus and dedication, and Scorpio expresses this through its intense emotional depth and commitment to transformation. Once Scorpio sets its mind on something, they pursue it with relentless focus, whether it's a personal goal, a relationship, or a quest for truth. This Fixed energy gives Scorpio a powerful sense of purpose and the ability to endure through difficult situations, often emerging stronger and more evolved. However, Scorpio's Fixed nature can also make them resistant to change, especially when it comes to letting go of past hurts or emotional attachments. Learning to embrace flexibility while maintaining their inner strength is essential for Scorpio's growth.

Scorpio's Lesson:

The challenge for Scorpio is to embrace vulnerability and learn to trust. While their intensity and passion are their strengths, it is important for them to open up to others and share their inner world without fear of judgment or betrayal. By learning to let go of control and accept the uncertainties of life, Scorpios can experience deeper connections and a more balanced emotional life. Understanding that transformation is not just about power but also about surrender can help Scorpio navigate their relationships and personal growth with greater ease.

Sagittarius (November 22- December 21)

Symbol: ↗

Sagittarius, the ninth sign of the zodiac, is symbolized by the Archer, embodying a sense of adventure, exploration, and the pursuit of truth. Ruled by Jupiter, the planet of expansion, growth, and optimism, Sagittarius is known for its love of freedom, philosophical nature, and insatiable curiosity about the world. As a Fire sign, Sagittarius is full of energy, enthusiasm, and an adventurous spirit. People born under this sign are often seen as fun-loving, spontaneous, and open-minded, always seeking new experiences and knowledge.

Symbol: The Archer

The symbol of Sagittarius is the Archer, represented by a centaur shooting an arrow, symbolizing the quest for knowledge, adventure, and higher purpose that defines this Fire sign. The Archer's imagery reflects Sagittarius' love of exploration and their constant pursuit of truth and wisdom. With their arrow aimed high, Sagittarius is always looking toward distant horizons, seeking new experiences, ideas, and perspectives. This symbolizes their optimistic, forward-thinking nature and their desire to expand both their physical and intellectual boundaries. The centaur, a mythological creature that is half human and half horse, emphasizes Sagittarius' dual nature—combining intellect and philosophical thought with a strong sense of adventure and action. The centaur's animalistic side symbolizes their need for freedom, spontaneity, and a connection to nature, while the human side reflects their curiosity and desire for understanding. Sagittarius is known for their adventurous spirit and open-mindedness, always ready to explore new philosophies, cultures, or faraway places. The Archer's arrow also represents Sagittarius' directness and honesty, as they are known for speaking their truth with boldness, sometimes with a sharp, straightforward edge. This symbol encapsulates Sagittarius' boundless energy, optimism, and desire to explore the world, both physically and intellectually.

Ruling Planet: Jupiter

Jupiter, the largest planet in the solar system, rules Sagittarius, imparting qualities of abundance, wisdom, and expansiveness. This planetary influence gives Sagittarius a natural inclination toward growth, exploration, and a desire to broaden their horizons, whether through travel, higher learning, or philosophical discussions. Jupiter's energy makes Sagittarians optimistic, generous, and confident, driving them to seek out new experiences and embrace life's opportunities with enthusiasm. However, this expansive nature can sometimes lead to overindulgence or a tendency to take on more than they can handle.

Key Traits:

- **Adventurous and Free-Spirited:** Sagittarius is the traveler of the zodiac, constantly seeking new horizons and experiences. They have an unquenchable thirst for adventure and are always eager to explore the unknown, whether it's through travel, learning, or new social interactions. Freedom is essential for Sagittarius, as they dislike feeling restricted or confined. This free-spirited nature makes them open to change and new perspectives, and they often thrive in environments that allow them to move, explore, and grow.
- **Optimistic and Enthusiastic:** Ruled by Jupiter, Sagittarius possesses a naturally optimistic and positive outlook on life. They are enthusiastic and full of energy, always looking for the silver lining in every situation. This upbeat attitude can be infectious, often lifting the spirits of those around them. Sagittarians approach life with a sense of wonder and excitement, eager to see what the world has to offer. Their enthusiasm extends to their projects, relationships, and ideas, making them inspiring and motivating companions.
- **Honest and Direct:** Sagittarius values honesty and is known for its straightforward, no-nonsense communication style. They speak their minds without sugarcoating their words, preferring to be open and transparent in their interactions. While their directness

can be refreshing, it can sometimes come across as blunt or tactless, especially when delivering criticism. However, their honesty stems from a genuine desire to share the truth and encourage others to see things from a broader perspective.

- Intellectual and Philosophical: Sagittarius is a seeker of knowledge and truth. They are naturally curious and often drawn to philosophical, spiritual, or cultural studies that expand their understanding of the world. Sagittarians love engaging in deep, thought-provoking conversations and exploring new ideas that challenge their beliefs. They are not afraid to question the status quo and are always on the lookout for new insights that can broaden their mental and spiritual horizons. This intellectual curiosity makes them lifelong learners who are constantly evolving in their thinking.

- Restless and Impulsive: With their boundless energy and desire for new experiences, Sagittarians can be restless and impulsive. They have a tendency to leap before they look, diving into new projects, relationships, or adventures without much forethought. While this spontaneity adds excitement to their lives, it can also lead to a lack of follow-through or unfinished plans. Sagittarians may become easily bored with routine or restrictive environments, seeking constant change and variety to keep themselves stimulated.

Strengths:

- Optimistic: Sagittarius's positive outlook helps them overcome challenges with ease. They are resilient and have a knack for finding joy and opportunity, even in difficult situations.

- Adventurous: Sagittarians are natural explorers who embrace new experiences and are not afraid to step out of their comfort zones. Their adventurous spirit makes them open-minded and adaptable.

- Honest: Sagittarius values truth and authenticity. Their directness, while sometimes blunt, ensures that they communicate openly and genuinely, building trust in their relationships.

- Intellectual: With their love of learning and exploring new

ideas, Sagittarians are often well-read and knowledgeable in a variety of subjects. They are curious thinkers who enjoy delving into philosophical and cultural topics.
- **Generous:** Ruled by Jupiter, the planet of abundance, Sagittarius is known for its generosity. They are willing to share their resources, time, and knowledge with others, often going out of their way to help those in need.

Challenges:
- **Impulsive:** Sagittarius's desire for spontaneity can lead to impulsive decisions. They may jump into situations without considering the consequences, which can result in overcommitment or unfinished projects.
- **Blunt:** While their honesty is a strength, Sagittarians can sometimes be too blunt in their communication. Their frankness, though well-intentioned, can hurt others' feelings if not delivered with tact and sensitivity.
- **Restless:** Sagittarians crave change and variety, which can make them restless in environments that are too routine or predictable. They may struggle with sticking to long-term plans or commitments.
- **Overconfident:** The optimistic nature of Sagittarius can sometimes lead to overconfidence. They may take on more than they can handle, assuming that things will work out without adequately preparing for potential obstacles.
- **Noncommittal:** Sagittarius values freedom and may resist settling down, whether in relationships, careers, or locations. Their fear of being tied down can lead to a tendency to avoid deep emotional commitments.

Element: Fire
Sagittarius is ruled by the element of Fire, which symbolizes passion, energy, and enthusiasm. Fire signs are dynamic, adventurous, and driven by their desire for action and exploration. Sagittarius exemplifies this fiery spirit through their love of freedom, adventure, and the pursuit of truth. The Fire element gives

Sagittarius a boundless sense of optimism and excitement, fueling their desire to explore new horizons, both physically and intellectually. This element also imparts a sense of spontaneity and risk-taking, making Sagittarius willing to leap into new experiences with an open heart. However, just like fire, Sagittarius's energy can be difficult to contain, and they must learn to temper their impulsive nature and channel their enthusiasm into focused pursuits for sustained growth.

Modality: Mutable

Sagittarius belongs to the Mutable modality, which is associated with adaptability, flexibility, and change. Mutable signs are known for their ability to go with the flow, embrace transitions and seek out new experiences. For Sagittarius, this Mutable energy manifests in their love of exploration and constant pursuit of knowledge. They are open to change and thrive in environments that offer variety and movement. Sagittarians are adaptable thinkers, able to shift perspectives and remain open-minded when faced with new ideas or challenges. However, their Mutable nature can also make them restless, as they may struggle to stay committed to one path or goal for too long. Learning to balance their desire for freedom with a focus on long-term growth is essential for Sagittarius' personal evolution.

Sagittarius's Lesson:

The challenge for Sagittarius is to learn the value of patience and focus. While their adventurous spirit and desire for growth are strengths, they need to find balance by considering the consequences of their actions and committing to their goals. By embracing discipline and recognizing that not every journey needs to happen all at once, Sagittarians can harness their energy in a way that leads to lasting success and fulfillment.

Capricorn (December 22 - January 19)

Symbol: ♑

Capricorn, the tenth sign of the zodiac, is known for its unwavering determination and strategic approach to success. Symbolized by the Mountain Goat, it embodies resilience, ambition, and the ability to steadily climb toward long-term goals. Ruled by Saturn, the planet of discipline, structure, and responsibility, Capricorn embodies practicality, hard work, and a strong sense of duty. As an Earth sign, Capricorn is grounded, reliable, and focused on tangible results. Those born under this sign are known for their commitment, strategic thinking, and ability to turn dreams into reality through careful planning and relentless effort.

Symbol: The Goat

The symbol of Capricorn is the Goat, representing ambition, perseverance, and the steady climb toward success. Like a mountain goat scaling steep, rocky terrains, Capricorn embodies determination, resilience, and the willingness to work hard to reach their goals. The Goat reflects Capricorn's practicality and focus on long-term achievements, as they carefully plan their steps and are undeterred by challenges along the way. This symbolism captures Capricorn's disciplined approach to life, their sense of responsibility, and their unwavering commitment to their aspirations. The Goat also symbolizes Capricorn's self-sufficiency and ability to thrive even in difficult conditions, highlighting their resourcefulness and strong work ethic. Just as the goat climbs toward the highest peaks, Capricorn is driven to attain success and security through persistence and careful planning. This symbol perfectly encapsulates Capricorn's ambition, resilience, and ability to overcome obstacles with patience and strategic effort.

Ruling Planet: Saturn

Saturn, the ruler of Capricorn, is associated with discipline, structure, time, and karma. It grants Capricorn a profound understanding of the importance of patience, hard work, and the slow and steady pursuit of goals. This planetary influence makes Capricorns highly ambitious, pragmatic, and serious about their responsibilities. Saturn's energy also teaches Capricorn the value of limitations and boundaries, helping them to develop a strong sense of self-control and endurance. While Saturn's influence can sometimes feel heavy, it is the source of Capricorn's strength, giving them the resilience to overcome challenges and achieve long-term success.

Key Traits:
- **Ambitious and Determined:** Capricorns are some of the most ambitious individuals in the zodiac. They set high goals for themselves and are willing to put in the necessary work to achieve them. Their determination is unmatched; they approach their pursuits with a steady, methodical mindset, carefully planning each step to ensure success. This ambition drives them to seek status, recognition, and material security, often motivating them to strive for leadership positions or achievements that reflect their hard work and dedication.
- **Disciplined and Responsible:** Saturn's influence makes Capricorn exceptionally disciplined and responsible. They take their obligations seriously and are known for their reliability. Whether in personal or professional matters, Capricorns can be counted on to follow through on their commitments. They possess a strong work ethic and a sense of duty that compels them to approach tasks with care and precision. This discipline extends to all areas of their life, from their career to their finances, as they value order, structure, and long-term planning.
- **Practical and Realistic:** As an Earth sign, Capricorn is grounded and realistic. They prefer to deal with facts and tangible outcomes rather than abstract theories or fantasies. Capricorns have a practical approach to life; they focus on what is achievable and are not swayed by fleeting whims or idealistic notions. This practicality makes them excellent problem-solvers, as they can assess situations objectively and devise effective, actionable plans. They are often the voice of reason in chaotic situations, providing

guidance based on logic and experience.

- **Patient and Persistent:** Capricorns understand that good things come to those who wait. They are willing to be patient and take a long-term view of their endeavors. This patience, combined with their persistence, allows them to keep moving forward, even in the face of obstacles or setbacks. They do not give up easily and are willing to put in the time and effort required to build a solid foundation for their future. This steadfastness often leads them to achieve success later in life, as they continue to climb their metaphorical mountain with quiet determination.

- **Reserved and Self-Sufficient:** Capricorn tends to be reserved and private. They are not ones to wear their hearts on their sleeves, preferring to keep their thoughts and emotions to themselves until they are sure of their surroundings and the people they are with. They are highly self-sufficient, relying on their own abilities and judgment rather than seeking help from others. While this independence is a source of strength, it can sometimes make them seem distant or unapproachable. Capricorns value control and prefer to maintain a strong sense of order in their personal lives.

Strengths:

- **Hardworking:** Capricorns are known for their remarkable work ethic. They are diligent, focused, and willing to put in the necessary effort to achieve their goals, often going above and beyond to fulfill their responsibilities.

- **Responsible:** Capricorns take their commitments seriously. They are reliable and dependable, ensuring that they follow through on their promises and obligations.

- **Strategic:** Capricorns are natural strategists. They can think long-term, carefully planning each step to ensure that they stay on course toward their objectives. This strategic mindset allows them to navigate challenges effectively.

- **Patient:** Capricorns understand that success does not happen overnight. They are willing to be patient, steadily working toward their goals without rushing or taking shortcuts.

- **Wise:** Ruled by Saturn, the planet of wisdom, Capricorns often possess a maturity beyond their years. They are thoughtful and measured in their actions, guided by experience and a deep understanding of life's complexities.

Challenges:
- **Pessimistic:** Capricorn's realistic nature can sometimes tilt toward pessimism. They may focus on potential problems or risks, which can make them seem overly cautious or negative to others.
- **Workaholic:** Capricorns can become so focused on their goals and responsibilities that they neglect other areas of their life, such as relaxation, hobbies, or social connections. This tendency can lead to burnout or a lack of work-life balance.
- **Aloof:** Capricorns' reserved nature can make them seem distant or unapproachable. They may have difficulty expressing their emotions, which can create misunderstandings in their relationships.
- **Stubborn:** Capricorns can be quite set in their ways, especially when they have committed to a plan or belief. They may struggle to adapt or be open to alternative perspectives if they feel it contradicts their carefully laid-out strategies.
- **Overly Cautious:** Capricorn's desire for security and control can lead to excessive caution. They may be hesitant to take risks or try new things, which can sometimes limit their growth or opportunities for innovation.

Element: Earth
Capricorn is ruled by the element of Earth, which represents practicality, stability, and a focus on the material world. Earth signs are grounded, reliable, and focused on tangible outcomes, and Capricorn embodies these traits through its disciplined approach to life and its determination to achieve long-term goals. The Earth element gives Capricorn a strong sense of responsibility, as well as the patience and persistence needed to build a secure foundation for the future. This element also imparts a practical mindset, allowing Capricorn to assess situations logically and make realistic plans. However, like the unyielding ground, Capricorn's Earth

element can sometimes make them resistant to change or overly cautious, as they prioritize stability over taking risks. Learning to balance their need for control with openness to new experiences is key to Capricorn's growth.

Modality: Cardinal

Capricorn belongs to the Cardinal modality, which is associated with leadership, initiation, and action. Cardinal signs are the initiators of the zodiac, and Capricorn expresses this energy through its ambitious drive and goal-oriented nature. Capricorn is a natural leader, always looking for ways to begin new projects, create structures, and set long-term plans in motion. This Cardinal energy makes Capricorns proactive and focused on achievement, often taking charge in their professional and personal lives. However, while their leadership and initiative are strong, Capricorn must learn to balance this with adaptability, as their strong attachment to their plans can make them resistant to change. Embracing flexibility while maintaining their leadership qualities is key to Capricorn's personal growth.

Capricorn's Lesson:

The challenge for Capricorn is to embrace flexibility and find balance. While their ambition and discipline are great strengths, they need to learn that not everything in life can be controlled or planned. By allowing themselves to take risks, relax, and express their emotions, Capricorns can experience a fuller, more balanced life. Understanding that success is not just about achievements but also about enjoying the journey can help them foster deeper connections and a greater sense of fulfillment.

Aquarius (January 20 - February 18)

Symbol:

Aquarius, the eleventh sign of the zodiac, is symbolized by the Water Bearer, representing the flow of ideas, knowledge, and humanitarianism. Ruled by Uranus, the planet of innovation, rebellion, and sudden change, and traditionally by Saturn, the planet of structure and discipline, Aquarius embodies progress, originality, and a strong sense of social consciousness. As an Air sign, Aquarius is intellectual, communicative, and driven by a desire to understand and improve the world around them. People born under this sign are known for their forward-thinking ideas, independence, and unconventional approach to life.

Symbol: Water Bearer

The symbol of Aquarius is the Water Bearer, representing the flow of ideas, knowledge, and humanitarianism. The Water Bearer is often depicted as a figure pouring water from a jug, symbolizing Aquarius' role as a bringer of wisdom, progress, and innovation to society. The flowing water represents the sharing of knowledge and insight, as Aquarius is known for their intellectual and forward-thinking nature. This imagery reflects Aquarius' desire to improve the world, often through unconventional or groundbreaking ideas that challenge the status quo. Though Aquarius is an Air sign, not a Water sign, the Water Bearer symbolizes their connection to the collective—pouring out wisdom, creativity, and new ways of thinking to benefit humanity. This symbol emphasizes Aquarius' humanitarian instincts, as they are often driven by a deep sense of social responsibility and a vision for a better, more just future. The Water Bearer also signifies Aquarius' independence and originality, as they march to the beat of their own drum, unafraid to be different or think outside the box. This symbol perfectly encapsulates Aquarius' progressive mindset, intellectual curiosity, and commitment to sharing knowledge for the greater good.

Ruling Planets: Uranus and Saturn

Uranus, the modern ruler of Aquarius, is associated with innovation, change, and the unexpected. It gives Aquarius its unique, visionary nature, pushing them to think outside the box and embrace the unconventional. Uranus imparts a sense of individuality and a desire for freedom, making Aquarians naturally rebellious against outdated norms and restrictions. On the other hand, Saturn, the traditional ruler of Aquarius, provides structure, discipline, and a focus on societal progress. This dual influence allows Aquarius to blend a forward-thinking mentality with a grounded sense of responsibility, making them champions of both radical ideas and social justice.

Key Traits:

- **Innovative and Visionary:** Aquarius is the thinker of the zodiac, constantly brimming with new ideas and concepts that push the boundaries of conventional wisdom. They are natural innovators who enjoy exploring new technologies, theories, and methods to solve problems. Their visionary mindset allows them to see beyond the present and imagine a future shaped by progress and change. This innovation is not limited to technology or science; it extends to social structures, art, philosophy, and nearly every facet of life. Aquarians often challenge the status quo, advocating for reforms that benefit society as a whole.

- **Independent and Unconventional:** Aquarians value their independence above all else. They are fiercely individualistic and dislike being confined by societal norms or expectations. This sense of freedom extends to their thoughts, lifestyle, and relationships, as they prefer to live on their own terms. Aquarians often adopt unconventional approaches to life, whether in their career, personal style, or beliefs. They are not afraid to be different and often take pride in standing out from the crowd. This independence makes them open-minded, welcoming new perspectives and embracing diversity in all its forms.

- **Humanitarian and Idealistic:** Ruled by Uranus and Saturn, Aquarius is deeply concerned with social issues and the well-being of humanity. They are idealistic and believe in the possibility of a better world. This humanitarian drive often leads them to advocate for causes related to equality, human rights, environmentalism, and other progressive movements. Aquarians are naturally altruistic, motivated by a desire to contribute to society and make a lasting, positive impact. They are often drawn to careers or activities that involve community service, activism, or other forms of social contribution.

- **Intellectual and Analytical:** As an Air sign, Aquarius is intellectually oriented, with a strong emphasis on logic, reason, and analysis. They are curious thinkers who love to explore abstract ideas, scientific theories, and philosophical concepts. Aquarians enjoy engaging in stimulating conversations, where they can exchange ideas and debate various viewpoints. Their analytical nature allows them to think critically and approach problems with a detached, objective mindset. However, this intellectual focus can sometimes make them seem aloof or emotionally distant, as they prefer to process feelings through the lens of logic rather than sentiment.

- **Detached and Eccentric:** Aquarius is known for its somewhat detached demeanor. They value personal space and freedom, often needing time alone to reflect on their thoughts and recharge. This emotional detachment can make them appear aloof or unfeeling to others, even though they care deeply about humanity on a broader scale. Additionally, Aquarians are known for their eccentricity; they embrace the quirky and unconventional, often charting their own unique path. They delight in being different and are not afraid to defy societal norms in pursuit of authenticity and self-expression.

Strengths:

- **Innovative:** Aquarius is naturally inventive, always coming up with creative solutions to problems. They are not afraid to experiment with new ideas and are often ahead of their time in their thinking.

- **Humanitarian:** Aquarians are deeply concerned with the welfare of others. They are passionate about social justice and are often involved in causes that aim to improve society and promote equality.

- **Intellectual:** Aquarius has a sharp, analytical mind. They are quick thinkers who enjoy learning about a wide range of subjects, often engaging in deep discussions on complex topics.
- **Open-Minded:** Aquarians are accepting of diverse perspectives and lifestyles. They are nonjudgmental and encourage others to be themselves, fostering an environment of inclusivity and understanding.
- **Independent:** Self-sufficient and autonomous, Aquarius is not reliant on others for validation. They confidently pursue their own path, free from societal constraints or expectations.

Challenges:

- **Aloof:** Aquarius's preference for intellectual processing over emotional expression can make them seem cold or detached. They may struggle to connect with others on an emotional level, even when they deeply care.
- **Unpredictable:** Ruled by Uranus, Aquarius is subject to sudden shifts in mood, interests, or direction. This unpredictability can make it difficult for others to keep up with them or understand their intentions.
- **Stubborn:** Despite their open-mindedness, Aquarians can be surprisingly stubborn, especially when it comes to their principles or ideals. They are firm in their beliefs and can resist changes that do not align with their values.
- **Detached:** Aquarius values independence and often maintains a level of emotional distance, which can lead to feelings of isolation or difficulty in forming close personal relationships.
- **Rebellious:** While their rebellious nature drives progress, it can also lead to resistance against authority or established norms, even when compromise might be beneficial.

Element: Air

Aquarius is ruled by the element of Air, which represents intellect, communication, and the exchange of ideas. Air signs are driven by curiosity, abstract thinking, and a desire for knowledge, and Aquarius exemplifies these traits through its visionary mindset and progressive ideals. The Air element gives Aquarius a strong sense of individuality and the ability to detach emotionally in order to think critically and objectively. This allows them to approach problems with an open mind, considering new perspectives and innovative solutions. Air's influence also fuels Aquarius's love for social interaction and their passion for humanitarian causes, as they seek to improve the world through intellectual discourse and collective action. However, just as air can be elusive, Aquarius's emotional detachment can sometimes make them seem aloof or distant, emphasizing the importance of balancing their intellectual pursuits with emotional connections.

Modality: Fixed

Aquarius belongs to the Fixed modality, which is associated with determination, persistence, and stability. Fixed signs are known for their unwavering focus and strong sense of commitment, and Aquarius channels this energy into their ideals and vision for the future. Once Aquarius has set their mind on a cause or idea, they pursue it with steadfast dedication, often becoming advocates for change and progress in society. This Fixed nature gives Aquarius the determination to challenge norms and work towards long-term goals, especially in humanitarian or intellectual pursuits. However, their Fixed energy can also lead to stubbornness, particularly when it comes to their ideals and personal beliefs. Learning to remain open to flexibility and compromise, while maintaining their core values, is key to Aquarius' growth.

Aquarius's Lesson:

The challenge for Aquarius is to embrace emotional vulnerability and cultivate deeper personal connections. While their intellect and independence are great strengths, it is important for them to recognize the value of empathy, warmth, and intimacy in relationships. By learning to express their emotions more openly and to connect on a personal level, Aquarians can balance their humanitarian ideals with the needs of their individual relationships. Understanding that they can genuinely care for both the collective and the personal allows them to cultivate a more fulfilling and well-rounded life.

Pisces (February 19 - March 20)

Symbol: ♓

Pisces, the twelfth and final sign of the zodiac, is symbolized by two fish swimming in opposite directions, representing the duality of their nature and their connection to both the material and spiritual worlds. Ruled by Neptune, the planet of dreams, intuition, and illusions, Pisces embodies empathy, creativity, and a deep sense of compassion. As a Water sign, Pisces is emotionally sensitive, intuitive, and receptive, often navigating life through their feelings and imagination. Those born under this sign are known for their kindness, artistic talents, and ability to empathize with others on a profound level.

Symbol: Two Fish

The symbol of Pisces is two Fish swimming in opposite directions, representing the duality of their nature and their connection to both the material and spiritual worlds. The fish symbolize Pisces' fluid, adaptable nature, as well as their deep emotional sensitivity and intuition. The two fish swimming in different directions reflect the internal struggle that Pisces often experiences between their practical, earthly concerns and their desire to escape into their imaginative, spiritual realms. This duality also represents Pisces' ability to exist in both worlds simultaneously, navigating the complexities of life while remaining deeply connected to their inner emotional and spiritual experiences. The fish are also linked to water, which symbolizes Pisces' emotional depth and capacity for empathy. As a Water sign, Pisces is intuitive, compassionate, and deeply in tune with the feelings of others, often absorbing the emotions around them. The symbolism of the fish highlights Pisces' tendency to "go with the flow," as they are adaptable and often willing to sacrifice their own needs to help those they care about. This symbol encapsulates Pisces' dreamy, creative nature, their strong connection to the spiritual world, and their ability to feel deeply while navigating life's emotional currents with grace and compassion.

Ruling Planet: Neptune and Jupiter

Neptune, the ruler of Pisces, is associated with dreams, illusions, spirituality, and the subconscious. It imbues Pisces with a strong intuition, creativity, and a vivid imagination. Neptune's influence allows Pisces to transcend ordinary reality, making them naturally drawn to the mystical, artistic, and emotional aspects of life. This planetary energy can make them deeply empathetic and compassionate, uniquely able to sense the feelings and needs of those around them. However, Neptune can also blur the lines between reality and fantasy, leading Pisces to sometimes struggle with boundaries and clarity.

Jupiter, the traditional ruler of Pisces, complements Neptune's ethereal energy by bringing a sense of growth, wisdom, and expansiveness. It encourages Pisces to seek meaning and purpose, often through spiritual exploration or acts of kindness. Jupiter's influence enhances Pisces' optimism and idealism, inspiring them to dream big and believe in a higher purpose. Together, Neptune and Jupiter create a harmonious blend of imagination and faith, empowering Pisces to connect deeply with both the mystical and the practical elements of life. However, this dual rulership can also make Pisces prone to overidealization or escapism if not balanced with grounded awareness.

Key Traits:

- **Empathetic and Compassionate:** Pisces is the most compassionate sign of the zodiac. They have an innate ability to empathize with others, often absorbing the emotions and experiences of those around them. This sensitivity allows them to offer comfort, support, and understanding to those in need, often putting others' needs before their own. Pisceans are natural healers and often drawn to roles that involve caring for others. However, their empathy can sometimes be overwhelming, causing them to take on the burdens of others to their own detriment.

- Intuitive and Spiritual: Ruled by Neptune, Pisces is deeply intuitive and in tune with the unseen realms. They rely heavily on their gut feelings and instincts when making decisions, often sensing things that others cannot. This spiritual connection gives Pisces a profound understanding of life's mysteries, making them drawn to the metaphysical, mystical, or religious aspects of existence. They often seek to explore their spirituality through meditation, art, music, or other forms of creative expression. This connection to the spiritual world makes them compassionate listeners and wise advisors, as they can see beyond the surface to the deeper truths.

- Creative and Imaginative: Pisceans are highly creative and possess a rich imagination. They are natural artists, musicians, writers, and dreamers who find solace and expression through creative pursuits. This creativity stems from their ability to tap into their inner world, drawing inspiration from their emotions, dreams, and the beauty around them. They often use art as a way to explore and convey their feelings, making them gifted storytellers who can captivate others with their visions and ideas.

- Gentle and Adaptable: Pisces is known for its gentle, kind-hearted nature. They are peaceful souls who dislike conflict and will go out of their way to avoid it. Pisceans are adaptable and open-minded, willing to go with the flow and adjust to changing circumstances. They are not rigid in their thinking or behavior, allowing them to embrace new experiences and perspectives. This flexibility makes them easy to get along with, as they can find harmony in diverse situations and relationships.

- Escapist and Elusive: One of Pisces' most complex traits is their tendency to escape reality. When faced with stress, pain, or harsh truths, Pisceans may retreat into their inner world of dreams, fantasies, or creative pursuits. They can be elusive, often slipping away when situations become too overwhelming or demanding. This escapist nature can manifest in various ways, such as daydreaming, avoiding responsibilities, or indulging in substances to numb their feelings. While this trait offers them a refuge, it can also prevent them from confronting and resolving real-life issues.

Strengths:
- **Compassionate:** Pisces' empathy makes them incredibly caring and supportive. They are quick to offer a shoulder to cry on and provide comfort to those in need, often going out of their way to help others.
- **Creative:** Pisceans have a boundless imagination and an innate talent for artistic expression. They excel in creative fields, using their emotional depth and intuition to produce art that resonates with others.
- **Intuitive:** Pisces is deeply connected to their intuition. They often have an uncanny sense of what is going on beneath the surface, allowing them to understand people and situations on a profound level.
- **Adaptable:** Pisces' fluid nature makes them open to change and willing to adapt to new environments and experiences. They are not easily confined by routines or expectations, preferring to move with the current.
- **Selfless:** Pisceans are naturally generous and selfless. They are willing to put others' needs ahead of their own, often sacrificing their comfort to ensure the well-being of those they care about.

Challenges:
- **Overly Sensitive:** Pisces' deep empathy can make them overly sensitive to criticism or negativity. They may take things to heart, leading to feelings of sadness or being easily hurt by others' words or actions.
- **Escapist:** When life becomes too difficult, Pisceans have a tendency to retreat into their fantasy world or avoid reality. This escapist behavior can prevent them from addressing their problems and achieving their goals.
- **Indecisive:** Pisces' adaptable nature can sometimes result in indecisiveness. They may struggle to make decisions, particularly when they feel torn between their emotions and the practical aspects of a situation.
- **Boundary Issues:** Due to their empathetic and giving nature, Pisces can have difficulty setting boundaries. They may absorb

others' emotions or take on their problems, leading to burnout or emotional overwhelm.

- **Idealistic:** Pisces' dreamy disposition can lead them to be overly idealistic. They may hold unrealistic expectations for themselves and others, resulting in disappointment when reality does not match their dreams.

Element: Water

Pisces is ruled by the element of Water, which represents emotions, intuition, and the subconscious. Water signs are deeply connected to their feelings and often experience life through the lens of empathy and intuition. For Pisces, the Water element enhances their sensitivity, compassion, and artistic nature, allowing them to easily tap into the emotions of others and the world around them. This emotional depth makes Pisces naturally nurturing and empathetic, as they are often attuned to the unseen and spiritual dimensions of life. Water's influence also fuels Pisces's vivid imagination and creativity, helping them express their inner world through art, music, and storytelling. However, like the ocean, which can be both calm and turbulent, Pisces's emotional sensitivity can sometimes lead to feelings of overwhelm or escapism. Learning to balance their emotional openness with practical boundaries is key to their growth.

Modality: Mutable

Pisces belongs to the Mutable modality, which is associated with adaptability, flexibility, and change. Mutable signs are known for their ability to adjust to different situations and go with the flow, and Pisces embodies this energy through their emotional fluidity and openness to new experiences. Pisceans can easily shift between the realms of reality and imagination, making them highly adaptable to change and receptive to new perspectives. This Mutable energy allows Pisces to blend in with various environments and social situations, as they are naturally empathetic and attuned to the needs of others. However, their Mutable nature can also make them indecisive or prone to escapism, as they may struggle to set boundaries or commit to one course of action. Learning to balance their adaptability with clear boundaries is essential for Pisces' personal growth.

Pisces' Lesson:

The challenge for Pisces is to learn how to set boundaries and face reality. While their compassion and creativity are great strengths, it is important for them to recognize when they are taking on too much or when they need to ground themselves in the practical aspects of life. By learning to assert their boundaries, confront their fears, and embrace the full spectrum of human experience, Pisceans can use their gifts in a way that enriches their lives and those around them. Understanding that balance between dream and reality is the key to their fulfillment can help Pisces navigate the world with both grace and strength.

4. The Houses

"I am a passionate believer in astrology, because it opens the mind to the possibilities of the universe."
- Salvador Dalí

Introduction to the Placidus House System

As mentioned in the Preface, this book uses the Placidus house system, a widely favored method in modern astrology. The Placidus system divides the birth chart into 12 segments, known as houses, based on the Earth's rotation and the observer's geographical location. Unlike some other house systems, this method results in houses of varying sizes, meaning that some signs may stretch across more than one house, while others might fully occupy a single house. This variation adds depth and detail to chart interpretation, allowing for a more dynamic and personalized understanding of how the signs influence different areas of life.

The Significance of Houses Without Planets

One key thing to remember is that you don't need a planet in a house for it to be significant in your chart. Even without planetary placements, the sign(s) that occupy each house still play a crucial role in shaping how the themes of that house are expressed in your life. The ruling sign of the house governs how you experience the energies of that area, providing insight into the underlying approach or attitude you bring to those aspects of your life.

Additionally, the ruling planet of the sign in the house plays an impactful role, as it often connects different areas of your life. For instance, the ruling planet of a sign may be located in a different house, creating a link between the two houses. This connection helps explain how the themes of one house influence or are influenced by another. We'll explore the role of ruling planets and these connections in much more depth later, so don't worry if this concept feels unfamiliar for now.

Understanding Multiple Signs in a House

When a house contains more than one sign, it creates a blend of energies that uniquely shapes that particular area of life. Each house governs different aspects, such as career, relationships, or personal values. I like to consider houses the "where" of your birth chart. They show us where in our life the energy from the signs and planets are playing out. When multiple signs occupy a single house, their characteristics mix, affecting how you experience and navigate that part of your life.

It's important to note that the sign on the cusp of the house—the sign that begins the house—typically dominates. This cusp sign sets the tone for how the house's energy is initially expressed and serves as the primary influence in that area of life. The subsequent signs add layers and subtleties, enriching the overall dynamic but not overtaking the core energy established by the cusp.

For example, if the second house, which is associated with finances and personal values, begins in Taurus but also includes a section of Gemini, the steady and practical approach of Taurus sets the foundation as the dominant influence. As the cusp sign, Taurus shapes the individual's strong preference for financial stability and grounded values. However, Gemini's curiosity and flexibility would still play a role, perhaps influencing the individual to explore diverse ways to generate income or communicate their values.

Having more than one sign in a house introduces complexity and variety to its energy. It suggests that managing this area of life may involve balancing the differing traits of each sign, adapting to changes, or handling fluctuating influences. This layered effect makes each house more dynamic, setting the stage for a richer, more nuanced interpretation of how the signs impact an individual's life. Understanding the dominant influence of the cusp sign helps provide clarity while still appreciating the subtleties added by the other signs within the house.

The First House: The House of Self

The First House begins at the Ascendant (ASC), also known as your Rising Sign, and is the most personal and individualized house in the natal chart. It marks the starting point of the zodiac wheel and represents the moment of birth—the entry of your soul into the physical world. This house is fundamentally about the self, shaping both how you perceive yourself and how others perceive you.

What the First House Represents:
- **Self-Identity:** The First House is the house of "I am." It represents your self-awareness, how you define yourself, and your sense of individuality. It is the core of your personality, the traits that define who you are at a fundamental level.
- **Physical Appearance:** This house governs your physical body, including your appearance, physique, and the overall impression you make on others. It influences your facial expressions, posture, and even the way you dress and present yourself.
- **Personal Style and Mannerisms:** The First House reflects your personal style, the way you express yourself, and how you engage with the world around you. It encompasses your demeanor, behavior, and the way you respond to external stimuli.
- **First Impressions:** The First House is about the first impression you make when you meet someone new. It's the energy and aura you project when you step into a room, the initial vibe that others pick up on before getting to know you on a deeper level.
- **Approach to Life:** This house also represents your general outlook on life and how you approach new situations. It reflects your instinctive reactions, the way you begin new ventures, and your attitude towards challenges and opportunities.
- **Beginnings and Initiatives:** The First House is linked to beginnings, symbolizing the start of your journey in this lifetime. It relates to how you initiate actions, how you set goals, and how you embark on new projects or endeavors.
- **Vitality and Health:** The First House is connected to your overall health, vitality, and physical well-being. It gives insights

into your natural energy levels, how you take care of your body, and any tendencies toward health issues.

Key Descriptive Words:
- Self-Identity
- Attitude
- Persona
- Beginnings
- Mannerisms
- Approach to Life
- Personality
- Behavior
- First Impressions
- Physical Appearance
- The Body

In essence, the First House is the most personal and immediate expression of your being. It sets the tone for how you move through the world and how you are seen by others. It is the mask you wear, the face you show to the world, and the lens through which you experience life. Understanding the First House in your natal chart provides deep insight into your core personality, your instincts, and the way you start your life journey.

The Second House: The House of Values and Possessions

The Second House is the house that governs our material world, including money, possessions, and personal resources. It follows the First House and builds upon the sense of self by exploring how we sustain and nurture ourselves in the physical world. The Second House is about what we value—both in terms of material wealth and the intangible, such as self-worth and personal values. It represents how we attract, accumulate, and manage our resources, as well as our attitudes toward wealth and possessions.

What the Second House Represents:
- **Material Wealth and Possessions:** The Second House is most commonly associated with money, finances, and material assets. It reflects your earning potential, how you handle your finances, and your relationship with wealth and possessions. This house shows your attitude towards money, whether you are inclined to save, spend, or invest.
- **Personal Values:** Beyond material wealth, the Second House represents your core values—the things you hold dear and consider essential to your well-being. This includes your moral values, ethics, and what you deem valuable in life, such as security, comfort, or freedom.
- **Self-Worth and Security:** The Second House is closely tied to self-esteem and self-worth. It reflects how you value yourself and your confidence in your abilities to generate resources. Your sense of security, both financial and emotional, is rooted in this house. It shows how secure you feel in the world based on your material and emotional resources.
- **Earning Potential and Income:** This house provides insight into how you earn your living and your approach to work and income. It reveals your natural talents and abilities that can be monetized, as well as your attitudes towards work and financial independence.
- **Material Desires and Comfort:** The Second House also

speaks to your desires for comfort, luxury, and material pleasures. It reflects what you need to feel comfortable and secure in your environment, whether that be a stable home, financial security, or physical pleasures.

- **Resource Management:** This house deals with how you manage and utilize your resources, including how you spend, save, or invest your money. It reflects your financial habits and your ability to maintain and grow your wealth over time.

Key Descriptive Words:
   - Wealth
   - Money
   - Self-Worth
   - Income
   - Priorities
   - Earning Potential
   - Work Ethic
   - Values
   - Work Habits
   - Daily Routines
   - Your Job
   - Material Possessions

In summary, the Second House is fundamentally about what you value, both materially and spiritually. It explores your relationship with money, possessions, and the things you cherish. This house also delves into your sense of self-worth and how that influences your ability to attract and maintain wealth and resources. Understanding the Second House in your natal chart provides insight into your financial behavior, your attitudes towards material success, and the foundations of your security and comfort in life.

The Third House: The House of Communication

The Third House is the realm of communication, learning, and immediate environment. It is the house that governs how we think, express ourselves, and connect with the world around us. Positioned after the Second House, which deals with material values and personal resources, the Third House shifts the focus to intellectual values and the exchange of information. It represents our early education, relationships with siblings and neighbors, and the ways in which we share ideas and knowledge.

What the Third House Represents:
- **Communication and Expression:** The Third House is primarily concerned with communication in all its forms—speaking, writing, teaching, and everyday interactions. It governs how you express your thoughts, the style of your communication, and your ability to convey ideas to others.
- **Thinking and Mental Processes:** This house reflects your thinking patterns, cognitive abilities, and intellectual interests. It reveals how you process information, whether you prefer logical reasoning or creative thinking, and your approach to learning and problem-solving.
- **Learning and Education:** The Third House is associated with early education, including the formative years of schooling and basic learning experiences. It encompasses not just formal education but also the curiosity and desire for knowledge that drive you to explore new ideas and concepts.
- **Siblings and Immediate Family:** This house also represents relationships with siblings, cousins, and extended family members, particularly those who were part of your early environment. It can indicate the dynamics of these relationships and how they influence your communication style.
- **Neighborhood and Local Environment:** The Third House governs your immediate surroundings—your neighborhood, community, and the places you frequent in your daily life. It reflects your connection to your local environment and how you

interact with your neighbors and community members.

- **Short Trips and Daily Travel:** The Third House is linked to short journeys and daily commutes, such as traveling to work, school, or running errands. It represents the movement within your local area and the experiences you gain from these everyday travels.

- **Information Exchange:** This house is about the exchange of ideas, whether through conversations, letters, emails, or social media. It reflects how you gather, share, and disseminate information, and your role in the communication networks around you.

Key Descriptive Words:
  - Communication
  - Learning
  - The Mind
  - Thinking
  - Early Education
  - Neighbors
  - Siblings
  - Short Trips
  - Local Environment
  - Social Activities/Interests
  - Daily Interactions

In summary, the Third House is the hub of communication and intellectual exchange. It governs how you think, learn, and share information with others. This house also explores your relationships with siblings and neighbors, your connection to your immediate environment, and your everyday interactions and movements. Understanding the Third House in your natal chart provides insight into your communication style, intellectual interests, and the way you connect with the world on a daily basis.

The Fourth House: The House of Home and Family

The Fourth House is one of the most personal and foundational houses in a natal chart. It is associated with home, family, roots, and the deep emotional undercurrents that shape your sense of security and belonging. The cusp of the Fourth House is marked by the Imum Coeli (IC), a critical point in the chart that represents your most private and innermost self. The Fourth House reflects your private life, the place where you feel most at home, and the influence of your family, particularly your upbringing and ancestral heritage. It is also associated with your emotional foundation, your sense of inner security, and the end of life.

What the Fourth House Represents:
- **Home and Domestic Life:** The Fourth House governs your physical home, the place where you live, and the environment that provides you with comfort and security. It reflects your relationship with your living space, your preferences in home design and atmosphere, and what makes a place feel like "home" to you.
- **Family and Ancestry:** This house represents your family of origin, particularly your parents or primary caregivers, and the influence they have had on you. It encompasses your ancestry, cultural heritage, and the traditions that have been passed down through generations. The Fourth House reveals the family dynamics and the role you play within your family.
- **Emotional Foundations:** The Fourth House is deeply connected to your inner world and emotional security. It represents the foundation of your emotional life, including your sense of belonging, your need for nurturing, and how you seek comfort and protection. This house reflects your early childhood experiences and how they have shaped your emotional landscape.
- **Roots and Heritage:** This house speaks to your roots—where you come from, both geographically and culturally. It represents the influence of your homeland, your connection to your ancestors, and the traditions that have shaped your identity. The Fourth House can also reveal how connected you feel to your past and your

sense of continuity with it.

- Private Life and Inner World: The Fourth House governs the most private aspects of your life, including your personal space and the parts of yourself that you keep hidden from the outside world. It is the house of your inner sanctum, where you retreat to recharge and reconnect with yourself.

- Security and Stability: The Fourth House is linked to your sense of security and stability, both physically and emotionally. It reflects what you need to feel safe and protected, as well as how you create a secure environment for yourself and your loved ones.

- End of Life and Legacy: Traditionally, the Fourth House is also associated with the later years of life and how you will be remembered after you are gone. It can indicate the legacy you leave behind and the final chapter of your life story.

Key Descriptive Words
- Home
- Family
- Roots
- Domestic Life
- Inner World
- Stability
- Foundation
- Upbringing
- Emotional Security
- Mother
- Children
- Femininity
- Women
- Self-Care

In summary, the Fourth House is the foundation of your natal chart, representing your home, family, and emotional roots. It delves into your private life, your relationship with your family of origin, and the traditions and heritage that have shaped who you are. This house is also about your inner security and the emotional foundations that provide you with stability and comfort. Understanding the Fourth House in your natal chart provides insight into your deepest needs for belonging, protection, and emotional sustenance, as well as your connection to your past and your legacy.

The Fifth House: The House of Pleasure and Creativity

The Fifth House is the realm of self-expression, creativity, pleasure, and joy. It governs all the activities that bring us delight and allow us to express our true selves, including romance, hobbies, and artistic pursuits. Positioned after the Fourth House, which deals with home and emotional security, the Fifth House is where we explore what makes life fun, vibrant, and fulfilling. It represents our creative potential, our approach to love and romance, and our capacity for joy and play.

What the Fifth House Represents:

- **Creativity and Self-Expression:** The Fifth House is the house of creativity and personal expression. It reflects how you channel your creative energy, whether through art, music, writing, or any form of artistic endeavor. This house reveals your unique talents, how you express your individuality, and your desire to create something that is uniquely yours.

- **Romance and Love Affairs:** This house governs romantic relationships and love affairs, particularly those that are more about enjoyment and passion than long-term commitment. It represents the fun and excitement of new love, flirtation, and the pleasure of connecting with others on a romantic level.

- **Pleasure and Enjoyment:** The Fifth House is all about what brings you joy and pleasure in life. It includes hobbies, recreational activities, and anything that allows you to unwind and have fun. This house reveals what you do for enjoyment and how you incorporate leisure into your life.

- **Children and Childlike Joy:** The Fifth House also relates to children, both your own and the concept of childhood itself. It reflects your relationship with your children, your attitudes towards parenting, and your ability to connect with the childlike joy within yourself. This house is about playfulness, spontaneity, and the ability to enjoy life with a sense of wonder.

- **Risk-Taking and Speculation:** This house governs activities that involve risk and speculation, such as gambling, investing, and entrepreneurial ventures. It reflects your willingness to take chances and your approach to activities where the outcome is uncertain but potentially rewarding.

- Entertainment and Performance: The Fifth House is linked to entertainment, performance, and anything that puts you in the spotlight. Whether it's acting, singing, dancing, or any other form of performance art, this house shows how you enjoy expressing yourself in front of an audience and your desire to be seen and appreciated for your talents.

- Passion and Enthusiasm: The Fifth House represents your passions—what excites you and makes you feel alive. It's about the things you are enthusiastic about, whether it's a creative project, a romantic relationship, or a hobby that you love. This house reveals what makes your heart race and what you pursue with zest and fervor.

Key Descriptive Words:
   - Creativity
   - Self-Expression
   - Joy
   - Pleasure
   - Romance
   - Hobbies
   - Childlike Spirit
   - Passion
   - Playfulness
   - Artistic Talent
   - Entertainment
   - Play
   - Love Affairs

   In summary, the Fifth House is the house of pleasure, creativity, and self-expression. It governs the activities that bring joy and fulfillment, from artistic pursuits and hobbies to romance and play. This house is about letting your inner child thrive, embracing your passions, and finding ways to express your true self. Understanding the Fifth House in your natal chart provides insight into how you approach love, creativity, and leisure, and what brings you the most joy and satisfaction in life.

The Sixth House: The House of Health and Service

The Sixth House is the domain of work, health, daily routines, and service to others. It is the house that governs your everyday life, including the habits you develop, the work you do, and how you take care of your physical and mental well-being. Following the Fifth House, which is about creativity and pleasure, the Sixth House brings a sense of discipline, order, and responsibility into your life. It is where you focus on the practical aspects of living and how you contribute to the well-being of yourself and others.

What the Sixth House Represents:

- **Work and Daily Responsibilities:** The Sixth House is associated with your day-to-day work, whether it's your job, chores, or any responsibilities that require consistent effort. It reflects your attitude toward work, your work ethic, and how you manage your daily tasks. This house reveals how you approach your duties and the role you play in your work environment.

- **Health and Well-Being:** This house governs your physical health and overall well-being. It reflects your approach to diet, exercise, and how you maintain your health. The Sixth House can indicate your health habits, any potential health issues, and how you take care of your body on a daily basis.

- **Service and Helping Others:** The Sixth House is also about service—how you help others and contribute to the community. It reflects your sense of duty and how you use your skills to assist those around you. This house is connected to professions in health care, service industries, and any work that involves caring for others.

- **Routines and Habits:** This house represents your daily routines, the habits you form, and the structure of your everyday life. It shows how you organize your time, how disciplined you are, and the rituals you perform regularly. The Sixth House reveals the importance of routine in your life and how it contributes to your overall sense of stability and order.

- **Skill Development:** The Sixth House is also linked to the development of skills, particularly those that require practice and precision. It reflects your ability to improve, refine, and perfect your abilities through consistent effort and attention to detail. This house can indicate areas where you have a natural talent or where you may need to focus on growth.

- **Discipline and Self-Improvement:** This house is where you work on self-improvement, not just in terms of health, but also in character and efficiency. It's about honing your abilities, creating productive habits, and striving to become the best version of yourself through discipline and hard work.

- **Pets and Small Animals:** Traditionally, the Sixth House also rules pets and small animals. It can indicate your relationship with animals and how they fit into your daily life. This house reflects the care and service you provide to these creatures and how they contribute to your sense of routine and well-being.

Key Descriptive Words:
- Work Habits
- Well-Being
- Health
- Routines
- Discipline
- Service Given
- Habits
- Self-Improvement
- Fitness
- Systems
- Analytical Nature
- Pets
- Daily Responsibilities
- Organization

In summary, the Sixth House is the house of health, work, and service, focusing on the practical and essential aspects of daily life. It governs how you approach your job, your routines, and the way you maintain your health and well-being. This house is about discipline, responsibility, and the contributions you make to your environment, both at work and in your personal life. Understanding the Sixth House in your natal chart provides insight into how you manage your day-to-day existence, how you care for your body and mind, and how you use your skills to serve others and improve yourself.

The Seventh House: The House of Partnerships

The Seventh House is the realm of relationships, partnerships, and how we connect with others on a one-on-one basis. The cusp of this house is marked by the Descendant (DSC), which represents the point in the chart where we meet others and reflects what we look for in relationships. The Seventh House directly opposes the First House, which is about the self, making it the area of the chart that focuses on others. This house governs all forms of partnerships, including marriage, business collaborations, and close friendships. It also reflects your approach to relationships, what you seek in a partner, and how you relate to those who are close to you.

What the Seventh House Represents:
- **Marriage and Long-Term Relationships:** The Seventh House is traditionally known as the house of marriage. It represents committed partnerships, particularly romantic ones, and the qualities you look for in a spouse. This house reveals your approach to long-term relationships, your needs within a partnership, and what you seek to build with another person.
- **Business Partnerships:** Beyond romantic relationships, the Seventh House also governs business partnerships and professional alliances. It reflects how you work with others in a professional context, the type of business relationships you form, and the qualities you value in a collaborator.
- **Contracts and Agreements:** This house is associated with legal matters, contracts, and formal agreements between individuals. It governs the commitments you make with others, whether in personal or professional contexts, and how you navigate the terms and conditions of these agreements.
- **Balance and Harmony:** The Seventh House is closely linked to the concept of balance and harmony in relationships. It represents the give-and-take dynamics in partnerships, the need for equality, and the pursuit of fairness. This house reflects your desire for harmony in your interactions and your ability to create balanced, mutually beneficial relationships.

- **Open Enemies:** Traditionally, the Seventh House is also the house of "open enemies"—those who oppose you or challenge you in a direct way. This can include rivals, competitors, or adversaries in both personal and professional spheres. The house reveals how you deal with conflict and opposition in relationships.

- **Public Relations and Image:** The Seventh House also influences how you relate to the public and your image in the eyes of others. It can reflect your approach to public relations, diplomacy, and how you manage your reputation within the broader community.

- **Relationship Dynamics:** This house reveals the dynamics that play out in your relationships, including how you relate to others, what you bring to the table, and what you expect in return. It shows how you navigate issues of power, control, and compromise in partnerships.

Key Descriptive Words:
- Partnerships
- Equality
- Sharing
- Public Relations
- Interpersonal Style
- Agreements
- Commitment
- Agreements
- Collaboration
- Business Partners
- Relationships
- Contracts
- Marriage

In summary, the Seventh House is the house of partnerships and relationships, focusing on how you connect with others in significant, committed ways. It governs marriage, business partnerships, legal agreements, and the dynamics of one-on-one relationships. This house is about finding balance and harmony with others, understanding your relationship needs, and navigating the complexities of close partnerships. Understanding the Seventh House in your natal chart provides insight into how you approach commitments, what you seek in a partner, and how you manage relationships in both personal and professional contexts.

The Eighth House: The House of Transformation and Shared Resources

The Eighth House is one of the most profound and mysterious houses in the natal chart, often associated with deep transformation, shared resources, and the cycles of life, death, and rebirth. It delves into the realms of intimacy, power dynamics, and the things that are hidden beneath the surface. The Eighth House also governs other people's money, such as inheritance, taxes, investments, and financial partnerships. This house is where you confront the complexities of life, experience profound change, and explore the deeper aspects of your psyche.

What the Eighth House Represents:
- **Transformation and Rebirth:** The Eighth House is the house of transformation, signifying the cycles of death and rebirth that we experience throughout life. This can be literal, such as the end of one phase and the beginning of another, or metaphorical, involving deep personal changes, psychological growth, and renewal.
- **Intimacy and Deep Connections:** This house governs the deepest forms of intimacy and bonding, particularly in relationships where there is a merging of resources or energies. It reflects your approach to sexual relationships, emotional intimacy, and how you share yourself with others on a profound level.
- **Shared Resources and Finances:** The Eighth House is closely tied to shared resources and financial matters involving others. It governs inheritances, taxes, joint finances, investments, and any situation where money or assets are shared. This house shows how you manage and are affected by financial partnerships and other people's money.
- **Power and Control:** Power dynamics are a key theme of the Eighth House. It represents how you handle power, control, and influence in relationships and situations. This house explores issues of dominance, manipulation, and the ways in which power is exchanged and exercised in your life.
- **Psychological Depth and the Unconscious:** The Eighth

House is also the gateway to your unconscious mind and the deeper layers of your psyche. It's associated with psychological exploration, shadow work, and the hidden aspects of your personality. This house encourages you to confront your fears, desires, and unresolved issues.

- **Mystery and the Occult:** This house is linked to the mystical, the occult, and the unknown. It governs your interest in astrology, tarot, magic, and other esoteric subjects. The Eighth House is where you explore the mysteries of life, death, and the unseen forces that shape your existence.

- **Endings and Beginnings:** The Eighth House deals with endings and the transitions that follow. It's about letting go, releasing what no longer serves you, and embracing the new. This house teaches you about the inevitability of change and the importance of transformation in your personal evolution.

Key Descriptive Words:
- Transformation
- Shared Resources
- Mystery
- Sexual Relations
- Inheritance
- Death and Rebirth
- Control
- Property
- Sexuality
- Power
- Merging
- Loans
- Assets
- Intimacy
- Taxes
- Partner's Resources

In summary, the Eighth House is the house of deep transformation, shared resources, and profound connections. It governs the cycles of life and death, the merging of energies and resources with others, and the exploration of the hidden and mysterious aspects of life. This house is about embracing change, understanding the power dynamics in your relationships, and delving into the depths of your psyche. Understanding the Eighth House in your natal chart provides insight into how you navigate issues of intimacy, power, and transformation, as well as your approach to shared finances and the mysteries of life.

The Ninth House: The House of Philosophy and Higher Learning

The Ninth House is the realm of exploration, both physical and intellectual. It governs long-distance travel, higher education, philosophy, religion, and the quest for truth and meaning in life. This house represents your desire to expand your horizons, seek out new experiences, and explore the world beyond your immediate environment. The Ninth House is about broadening your mind, understanding different cultures, and searching for deeper understanding through learning and spiritual growth.

What the Ninth House Represents:

- Higher Education and Learning: The Ninth House is associated with higher education, such as universities, advanced studies, and the pursuit of knowledge that goes beyond basic learning. It reflects your approach to learning, your intellectual pursuits, and your interest in gaining wisdom and understanding through study.

- Philosophy and Beliefs: This house governs your personal philosophy, religious beliefs, and moral principles. It reflects your quest for meaning in life and how you seek to understand the world through a broader, more universal perspective. The Ninth House is where you explore big ideas, question your beliefs, and develop your worldview.

- Long-Distance Travel and Exploration: The Ninth House is linked to long-distance travel, foreign cultures, and the exploration of the world beyond your immediate surroundings. It represents your desire to experience new places, meet people from different backgrounds, and learn from diverse cultures. This house reflects your wanderlust and your passion for adventure and discovery.

- Spirituality and Religion: This house is also connected to spirituality and religious practices. It reflects your relationship with the divine, your spiritual beliefs, and how you seek to connect with something greater than yourself. The Ninth House explores your spiritual journey, your quest for enlightenment, and your approach to religious or spiritual practices.

- Legal Matters and Ethics: The Ninth House is associated with law, ethics, and the principles that guide society. It governs legal matters, justice, and your sense of what is right and wrong. This house reflects your interest in the legal system, your sense of justice, and your desire to live according to ethical principles.

- Publishing and Dissemination of Ideas: This house is linked to publishing, media, and the sharing of knowledge on a broad scale. It reflects your ability to communicate big ideas, your interest in spreading knowledge, and your involvement in publishing, teaching, or broadcasting.

- Cultural Understanding and Global Awareness: The Ninth House represents your awareness of the world and your desire to understand different cultures and global issues. It reflects your interest in cultural exchange, global travel, and your openness to new ideas and perspectives.

Key Descriptive Words:
- Higher Education
- Philosophy
- Religion
- Law
- Exploration
- Wisdom
- Learning
- Cross-Cultural Relations
- Ethics
- Travel
- Quest for Truth
- Adventure
- Justice

In summary, the Ninth House is the house of philosophy, higher learning, and exploration. It governs your quest for knowledge, your pursuit of truth, and your desire to expand your horizons through travel, education, and spiritual growth. This house is about exploring the bigger picture, understanding the world from a broader perspective, and seeking deeper meaning in life. Understanding the Ninth House in your natal chart provides insight into how you approach learning, your beliefs and philosophies, and your desire to explore the world and connect with different cultures and ideas.

The Tenth House: The House of Career and Public Life

The Tenth House is one of the most significant houses in a natal chart, with the cusp often referred to as the "Midheaven" or "Medium Coeli" (MC). It represents your public life, career, reputation, and the legacy you wish to leave behind. This house governs your ambitions, achievements, and how you are perceived by society. The Tenth House is where you strive for recognition, establish your professional identity, and define your life's work.

What the Tenth House Represents:
- **Career and Profession:** The Tenth House is strongly associated with your career and professional life. It reflects your ambitions, your chosen career path, and the work you do to achieve your goals. This house reveals the type of profession you are drawn to and how you seek to establish yourself in the world.
- **Public Image and Reputation:** This house governs your public image, how others see you, and the reputation you build over time. It represents the status and recognition you achieve through your work and public actions. The Tenth House shows how you present yourself to the world and the legacy you create.
- **Authority and Leadership:** The Tenth House is linked to authority, leadership, and your relationship with power and responsibility. It reflects your ability to take charge, assume leadership roles, and navigate hierarchies. This house also indicates your relationship with authority figures and how you handle positions of power.
- **Ambition and Achievement:** This house is all about ambition and the drive to achieve your goals. It represents your long-term aspirations, the milestones you aim to reach, and your desire for success and recognition. The Tenth House shows how you set goals, work towards them, and measure your achievements.
- **Life Purpose and Legacy:** The Tenth House also reflects your life purpose and the legacy you want to leave behind. It's about the impact you wish to make on the world and how you hope to be

remembered. This house reveals the larger goals you pursue and the contributions you make to society.

- Relationship with Authority Figures: This house also governs your interactions with authority figures, such as bosses, mentors, and government officials. It reflects your attitude towards authority, your respect for societal structures, and how you navigate the expectations placed on you by those in power.

- Social Status and Recognition: The Tenth House is closely tied to social status and the recognition you receive from your peers and society at large. It represents the rewards and honors you achieve for your work and efforts, and how you seek to gain respect and admiration from others.

Key Descriptive Words:
- Career
- Masculinity
- Authority
- Recognition
- Fame
- Father
- Status
- Public Image
- Social Status
- Experts
- Men
- Structure
- Achievement
- Reputation
- Long-Term Goals
- Public Life

In summary, the Tenth House is the house of career, public life, and ambition. It governs your professional identity, the reputation you build, and the achievements you strive for. This house is about the pursuit of success, the establishment of your place in the world, and the legacy you wish to leave behind. Understanding the

Tenth House in your natal chart provides insight into your career aspirations, your approach to leadership and authority, and how you are perceived by society. It reveals your life's work, your long-term goals, and the impact you aim to have on the world.

The Eleventh House: The House of Friendships and Community

The Eleventh House is the realm of social connections, friendships, groups, and the larger community. It is associated with your social network, your involvement in groups and organizations, and your hopes and dreams for the future. This house represents how you interact with society at large, the causes you support, and the communities you align with. It also governs your long-term goals, aspirations, and the role of social support in achieving them.

What the Eleventh House Represents:

- **Friendships and Social Networks:** The Eleventh House is the house of friendships and social connections. It reflects the people you choose to surround yourself with, the friendships you form, and your ability to connect with others on a social level. This house shows the quality and nature of your friendships and how you interact within your social circles.

- **Groups and Organizations:** This house governs your involvement in groups, clubs, organizations, and any collective activities. It represents your participation in community efforts, your role within organizations, and how you contribute to group dynamics. The Eleventh House shows how you align with others to pursue common goals.

- **Hopes, Dreams, and Aspirations:** The Eleventh House is associated with your long-term goals, dreams, and aspirations. It reflects the vision you have for your future, the ideals you strive for, and your hopes for what you wish to achieve in life. This house reveals the dreams that drive you and how you seek to make them a reality.

- **Community and Social Causes:** This house is also about your connection to the broader community and your involvement in social causes. It reflects your desire to contribute to society, your interest in humanitarian efforts, and the ways in which you work to create positive change in the world.

- **Innovation and Progress:** The Eleventh House is linked to innovation, progress, and forward-thinking ideas. It represents your ability to think outside the box, your interest in new technologies, and your desire to be part of movements that push society forward. This house shows how you embrace change and seek to contribute to societal evolution.

- **Support Systems and Allies:** The Eleventh House also represents the support systems and allies that help you achieve your goals. It reflects the people who rally behind you, the networks you build, and the resources you draw upon to pursue your aspirations. This house shows the strength of your social support and how you leverage it to succeed.

- **Social Ideals and Utopian Visions:** This house is where you explore your social ideals and visions for a better world. It reflects your hopes for the future of society, your belief in collective action, and your desire to create a more just and equitable world. The Eleventh House represents your utopian dreams and the role you play in making them come true.

Key Descriptive Words:
- Friendships
- Humanitarianism
- Groups
- Social Awareness
- Dreams
- Hopes and Wishes
- Social Networks
- Collective Action
- Social Causes
- Friendships
- Aspirations
- Technology
- Organizations
- The Future

In summary, the Eleventh House is the house of friendships, community, and aspirations. It governs your social connections, your involvement in groups and organizations, and your long-term goals and dreams. This house is about how you interact with the larger community, the causes you support, and the role of social networks in achieving your aspirations. Understanding the Eleventh House in your natal chart provides insight into your social life, your approach to collective endeavors, and the dreams and ideals that drive you. It reveals how you connect with others to create positive change and how you contribute to the progress and evolution of society.

The Twelfth House: The House of the Unconscious and Secrets

The Twelfth House is the most mysterious and enigmatic house in the natal chart, often referred to as the "House of the Unseen" or the "House of the Subconscious." It governs the hidden aspects of life, including the unconscious mind, secrets, and the things that are kept out of sight. This house is associated with spirituality, karma, endings, and the things we must confront before we can move forward. The Twelfth House is where we face our fears, deal with our past, and connect with the spiritual or mystical dimensions of existence.

What the Twelfth House Represents:
- **The Unconscious Mind:** The Twelfth House is the realm of the unconscious, the part of your psyche that lies beneath the surface of awareness. It governs your dreams, intuition, and the hidden aspects of your mind that influence your thoughts, feelings, and behaviors. This house reveals the parts of yourself that you may not be fully aware of, including your deepest fears and desires.
- **Secrets and Hidden Matters:** This house is associated with secrets, things that are hidden from view, and matters that are kept private. It reflects what is concealed in your life, whether intentionally or unconsciously. The Twelfth House can indicate hidden enemies, repressed emotions, or issues that need to be brought to light for healing and resolution.
- **Spirituality and Mysticism:** The Twelfth House is deeply connected to spirituality, mysticism, and the exploration of the divine. It governs your relationship with the spiritual realm, your connection to the collective unconscious, and your quest for enlightenment. This house reflects your interest in meditation, prayer, and other spiritual practices that help you connect with higher consciousness.
- **Karma and Past Lives:** This house is linked to karma, the concept of past actions influencing the present, and the idea of past lives. It represents the karmic debts or blessings you carry with

you, the lessons you are here to learn, and the spiritual growth you are meant to achieve in this lifetime. The Twelfth House shows how you deal with the consequences of your actions and the spiritual journey you are on.

- **Endings and Closure:** The Twelfth House is associated with endings, closure, and the process of letting go. It represents the final stages of a cycle, where you must confront and release what no longer serves you. This house governs the transitions that lead to new beginnings and the process of surrendering to the flow of life.

- **Solitude and Isolation:** This house is also connected to solitude, retreat, and places of confinement, such as hospitals, prisons, or monasteries. It reflects the times when you need to withdraw from the world to reflect, heal, and regenerate. The Twelfth House can indicate periods of isolation, introspection, or seclusion, where you confront your inner world.

- **Healing and Compassion:** The Twelfth House is the house of healing, both for yourself and others. It represents the compassion you feel for those who are suffering, your ability to offer support and care, and your own need for healing and self-compassion. This house shows how you deal with emotional wounds and how you find peace and forgiveness.

Key Descriptive Words:
- Unconscious Mind
- Secrets
- Mysticism
- Spirituality
- Karma
- Past Lives
- Solitude
- Endings
- Closure
- Compassion
- Healing
- Intuition
- Old Age

- Afterlife
- What's Hidden
- Limiting Beliefs

In summary, the Twelfth House is the house of the unconscious, spirituality, and hidden aspects of life. It governs your inner world, including your dreams, fears, and the secrets you keep. This house is about confronting the past, dealing with karma, and finding spiritual enlightenment. It represents the need for solitude, healing, and introspection, and the process of letting go and moving forward. Understanding the Twelfth House in your natal chart provides insight into your spiritual journey, your unconscious mind, and the hidden forces that shape your life. It reveals the lessons you must learn, the challenges you must face, and the spiritual growth you are here to achieve.

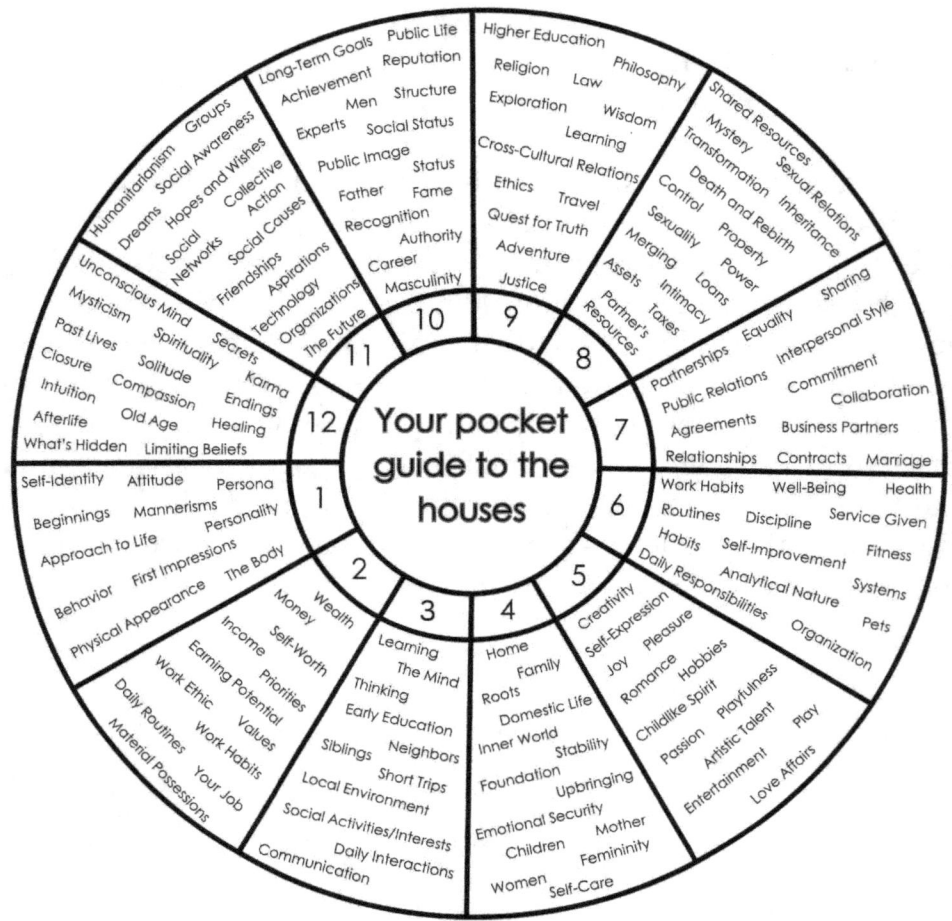

I created this graphic to serve as a quick reference for understanding the houses in astrology, making it easier to remember their core meanings. When I first began studying astrology, I relied on a similar visual guide to help solidify my knowledge of how each house governs specific areas of life. The houses represent the "where" in your chart—where the energies of the planets and signs manifest in your daily experiences. With this graphic, you'll be able to quickly recall the themes and areas of life associated with each house, from relationships and career to creativity and personal growth. It's designed to offer both clarity and convenience as you navigate your chart. I hope this helps you grasp the technicalities of the houses while keeping the learning process enjoyable and accessible.

5. The Planets, Objects & Angles

"Astrology is a language. If you understand this language, the sky speaks to you."
- Pablo Picasso

The Role of Planets, Objects, and Angles in Astrology

In astrology, each planet, object, and angle carries a unique influence that shapes your personality, behavior, and life experiences. This section delves into the characteristics of the major celestial bodies and key angles in a natal chart, explaining how they govern various aspects of life, such as communication, emotions, and responsibility. For each planet or angle, you'll learn not only what it represents but also how its placement, movement, and interactions with other elements in the chart affect your overall birth chart.

Understanding Planetary Qualities and Retrogrades

Key features include the qualities of each planet, how they express themselves in different zodiac signs, and the significance of their retrograde periods. We also explore the ruling signs for each planet, where they are most at home, as well as their exaltation, detriment, and fall—highlighting where their energies are strongest or face challenges. By understanding the role of each celestial body, you gain deeper insight into the layers of your personality and life's journey, allowing you to interpret your birth chart with greater clarity and detail.

Planetary Interactions: Aspects and Their Influence

In this section, I'll briefly touch on the importance of aspects when discussing the planets. Aspects play a significant role in weaving together the energy of different planets, signs, and houses. They help reveal the strengths, challenges, and unique qualities of your chart, forming the connections that bring the cosmic map to life. The deeper understanding of aspects will give you even more tools to interpret your natal chart as a whole. While aspects are crucial in understanding the relationships between different points in a chart, we'll only explore them lightly here to keep the focus on the planets themselves. Don't worry, though—later on, we'll dive much deeper into aspects and how they influence the dynamics between the planets, signs, and houses in your chart.

Sun: The Core of Your Identity

Symbol: ☉

The Sun in astrology is one of the most important celestial bodies, representing the core of your personality, the essence of who you are, and the driving force behind your individuality. Just as the physical Sun is the center of the solar system, your Sun sign serves as a central influence in your natal chart, shaping your identity, vitality, and overall sense of purpose. The Sun is a symbol of consciousness, vitality, purpose, and the light that you shine into the world.

What the Sun Represents

- **Core Identity and Ego:** The Sun reflects your inner self, your true identity, and the person you are at your core. It signifies your ego, willpower, and the qualities you consciously strive to express. The Sun represents the essence of your being and how you radiate your unique energy into the world.

- **Vitality and Life Force:** The Sun governs your life force and vitality. Its placement in your natal chart can indicate your overall energy level, how you recharge, and what gives you a sense of purpose and fulfillment. A well-placed Sun can suggest a strong life force and confidence, while challenging aspects may indicate struggles with self-esteem or vitality.

- **Conscious Will and Purpose:** The Sun is associated with your conscious desires, life goals, and the direction you naturally gravitate toward. It reveals what you aim for in life, how you want to be seen, and the path you seek to follow. The Sun's placement guides you toward the areas where you can best express your unique talents and fulfill your life's mission.

- **Self-Expression:** The Sun influences how you express yourself and your creativity. It symbolizes your desire to stand out, to be recognized for your unique qualities, and to leave an imprint on the world. The sign and house placement of the Sun show how you shine your light and in what areas of life you are meant to make your mark.

- Father and Authority Figures: Traditionally, the Sun is also associated with the father or dominant authority figures in your life. It can describe the relationship you have with your father or father figure and how their influence has shaped your identity and sense of self-worth.

Qualities of the Sun

- Masculine, Positive, and Active: The Sun is a masculine and active force, representing outward expression, assertiveness, and conscious action. It embodies qualities of leadership, initiative, and confidence.

- Fixed and Steady: Astrologically, the Sun is fixed in nature, symbolizing stability, consistency, and a strong sense of self. It represents the parts of you that remain constant throughout life, regardless of external changes or influences.

- Element of Fire: The Sun naturally resonates with the Fire element, signifying warmth, enthusiasm, passion, and a vibrant approach to life. It brings illumination, clarity, and inspiration, driving individuals to pursue their goals with vigor.

The Sun in the Natal Chart

- Sun Sign: The Sun sign is often what people refer to when they say, "What's your sign?" It indicates the zodiac sign in which the Sun was positioned at the time of your birth. This placement reveals your core personality traits, your overall character, and the qualities you are meant to embody.

- House Placement: The house where the Sun is located in your chart highlights the area of life where you seek to shine and express yourself most fully. It shows where your central life focus and primary life force will manifest.

The Sun and the Fifth House

The Sun has a natural affinity with the Fifth House, often called the "house of creativity and self-expression." This house governs joy, artistic pursuits, romance, and the playful spirit of life. As the ruler of the Fifth House, the Sun resonates deeply with these themes, illuminating the areas where individuals can express themselves authentically and pursue what brings them happiness.

When the Sun is in the Fifth House, individuals often possess a strong creative drive and a natural inclination to shine in activities that showcase their unique talents. They are drawn to artistic expression, hobbies, and romantic connections that bring excitement and fulfillment. This placement emphasizes confidence, playfulness, and a deep connection to personal passions, encouraging individuals to embrace their inner child and take bold risks in the pursuit of joy.

While the Sun here fosters a vibrant and expressive nature, it can also lead to a need for validation or an overemphasis on external recognition. Developing a strong sense of self-worth allows individuals to channel the Sun's energy constructively, finding fulfillment in their creativity and personal joys rather than seeking approval from others.

The Movement of the Sun

The Sun spends approximately 30 days in each sign, completing the zodiac cycle in one year.

The Sun's "Home" – Its Comfort Zone

- **Ruling Sign – Leo:** The Sun rules the zodiac sign Leo, making this sign its natural home. In Leo, the Sun is at its strongest and most expressive, emphasizing traits like creativity, warmth, generosity, confidence, and leadership. Leo embodies the Sun's qualities of self-expression and the desire for recognition. Individuals with the Sun in Leo often have a strong need to be seen, appreciated, and admired for their unique qualities. They exude charisma, radiance, and a sense of grandeur that draws others to them.

The Sun in its "Exaltation" – Aries

When a planet is in its "exaltation," it is in a sign where it expresses its natural qualities with ease and strength. The Sun is exalted in Aries, where it thrives in the sign's dynamic, bold, and pioneering nature. This placement amplifies the Sun's core energy, emphasizing self-expression, independence, and the drive to take action.

- Self-Assertion: Aries' assertive and direct qualities align perfectly with the Sun's need to express its core identity. In Aries, the Sun embodies courage, taking the initiative, and boldly pursuing personal goals. There is a strong focus on self-assertion and the drive to carve out one's own path, making individuals with this placement naturally confident and willing to take risks.

- Dynamic Energy: The Sun in Aries is fueled by the sign's fiery, energetic nature. This placement infuses the individual with enthusiasm, vitality, and an innate desire to take on challenges. The Sun in Aries feels energized by action and thrives when they are actively pursuing their passions and goals, often leading them to be pioneers and trailblazers in their endeavors.

- Independence: Aries is a sign of independence and self-sufficiency, which complements the Sun's desire to shine autonomously. The Sun in Aries does not wait for validation from others; it acts on its impulses and desires with confidence. This placement encourages a strong sense of self-reliance, inspiring individuals to embrace their unique qualities and express them without hesitation.

- Positive Aspects: The Sun in Aries shines brightly through its boldness, determination, and passion for life. This placement brings an inspiring sense of initiative, fearlessness, and the courage to embrace new beginnings. When harnessed positively, the Sun in Aries can lead individuals to become dynamic leaders, motivators, and innovators who inspire others through their sheer drive and zest for life.

The Sun in its "Fall" – Libra

When a planet is in its "fall," it is positioned in a sign where it struggles to express its natural qualities. The Sun is in its fall in Libra, which presents challenges to the Sun's core energy and expression. Libra's qualities of balance, partnership, and harmony can conflict with the Sun's need for self-expression and independence.

- Focus on Others: While the Sun naturally represents the self and ego, Libra is oriented toward relationships and the needs of others. This can create tension, as the Sun in Libra may seek validation externally rather than expressing its innate desires. There might be a tendency to prioritize others' needs over personal aspirations, affecting the Sun's ability to shine independently.

- **Need for Balance:** The Sun in Libra constantly strives for harmony and balance in relationships and life situations, which can dilute its natural confidence and boldness. The need to weigh different options and perspectives may lead to indecision or a reluctance to assert individuality.

- **Reluctance to Stand Out:** Libra energy emphasizes diplomacy and cooperation, which may cause those with the Sun in Libra to shy away from the spotlight. The Sun's drive for recognition can be subdued, as they might feel more comfortable working alongside others rather than taking the lead.

- **Positive Aspects:** Despite these challenges, the Sun in Libra can still shine through its sense of fairness, grace, and charm. Individuals can express their creativity and individuality through partnerships and the pursuit of beauty and harmony. By learning to assert their identity within relationships, they can navigate the fall placement effectively.

Summary

The Sun in astrology is the essence of who you are, representing your core identity, vitality, conscious will, and life's purpose. It shapes your personality, drives your actions, and signifies the qualities you are here to develop. As the ruler of Leo and the natural tenant of the Fifth House, the Sun thrives in environments that allow for creative self-expression, leadership, and the pursuit of personal joy. Understanding the Sun's sign, house placement, and aspects in a natal chart is key to unlocking the deeper layers of your identity and your unique path in life. Recognizing the Sun's exaltation in Aries and its fall in Libra provides further insight into the strengths and challenges of its expression in different signs.

Moon: The Emotional Core

Symbol: ☾

The Moon in astrology is one of the most crucial celestial bodies, representing your emotions, instincts, subconscious, and inner self. It reflects your emotional nature, your needs, and how you respond to life's experiences. The Moon governs your habits, moods, and intuition, serving as the counterpart to the Sun by symbolizing your inner world. It is a guide to your feelings and reveals how you nurture and protect both yourself and others.

What the Moon Represents

- **Emotional Nature:** The Moon reveals how you process and express your emotions. It shows what makes you feel secure, how you respond to emotional experiences, and the way you instinctively react to different situations. Your Moon sign colors your emotional makeup and influences your inner world.

- **Subconscious and Habits:** The Moon governs the subconscious mind, encompassing deep-rooted habits, instincts, and behaviors developed over time. It guides your automatic responses and reflects the things that you do without conscious thought, often linked to your childhood and past experiences.

- **Needs and Comfort:** The Moon indicates what you need to feel safe, comfortable, and nurtured. It reflects the areas of life where you seek emotional fulfillment and security. Understanding your Moon sign can provide insight into what brings you inner peace and a sense of belonging.

- **Nurturing and Care:** Traditionally associated with the mother and maternal figures, the Moon describes how you give and receive care. It can reveal your nurturing qualities, how you provide comfort to others, and the nature of your relationship with your mother or primary caregivers.

- **Intuition:** The Moon is connected to intuition and psychic sensitivity. It represents your ability to sense things on a deeper, non-rational level, highlighting how you pick up on the emotional atmosphere around you.

Qualities of the Moon
- **Feminine, Receptive, and Passive:** The Moon is a feminine force in astrology, symbolizing receptivity, sensitivity, and the capacity to reflect and absorb. It embodies the qualities of nurturing, empathy, and inner reflection.
- **Mutable and Changeable:** The Moon's nature is changeable, reflecting its phases and cycles in the sky. Astrologically, it symbolizes moods, fluctuations, and the waxing and waning of emotions. Its influence can feel different from day to day, depending on the experiences and situations you encounter.
- **Element of Water:** The Moon resonates with the Water element, emphasizing feelings, emotions, and the subconscious. It brings a deep connection to intuition, creativity, and the ebb and flow of emotional experiences.

The Moon in the Natal Chart
- **Moon Sign:** Your Moon sign indicates the zodiac sign in which the Moon was positioned at the time of your birth. It reveals your emotional nature, instinctual reactions, and the way you nurture and seek comfort.
- **House Placement:** The house where the Moon is located in your chart points to the area of life where your emotional experiences, instincts, and need for security manifest most strongly. It shows where you might be most reactive, intuitive, or nurturing.

The Moon and the Fourth House
The Moon has a natural affinity with the Fourth House, often referred to as the "house of home and family." This house governs your emotional foundation, sense of security, and connection to your roots. As the ruler of Cancer, the Moon resonates deeply with the Fourth House's themes of nurturing, comfort, and the past, shaping your emotional instincts and inner world.

When the Moon is in the Fourth House, individuals often have strong emotional ties to their home, family, and upbringing. Their early experiences play a significant role in shaping their emotional responses and sense of security. They are deeply connected to their personal sanctuary, seeking comfort in familiar surroundings and desiring a stable, nurturing environment. This placement enhances emotional sensitivity and intuition, making home life a crucial aspect of well-being.

While the Moon here fosters deep emotional connections, it can also lead to heightened mood fluctuations or an over-reliance on the past for comfort. Developing emotional resilience and creating a secure, supportive home environment allows individuals to embrace the Moon's nurturing energy while maintaining balance and personal growth.

The Movement of the Moon

The Moon changes signs every 2.5 days and completes a full cycle through the zodiac in about 28 days.

The Moon's "Home" – Its Comfort Zone

- **Ruling Sign – Cancer:** The Moon rules the zodiac sign Cancer, where it is at home and most comfortable. In Cancer, the Moon's nurturing, sensitive, and protective qualities are fully expressed. Individuals with the Moon in Cancer have strong emotional instincts, a deep connection to their feelings, and an intuitive approach to life. They possess a natural ability to nurture and create a sense of security for themselves and others, often finding comfort in home and family.

The Moon in its "Exaltation" – Taurus

When a planet is in its "exaltation," it expresses its natural qualities with ease and strength. The Moon is exalted in Taurus, where its need for emotional stability and comfort aligns with Taurus's grounded and steady nature.

- **Emotional Stability:** Taurus's fixed and earthy qualities provide the Moon with a stable environment. The Moon in Taurus is less prone to emotional fluctuations, offering a steady and calm approach to feelings. There is an inherent need for security and consistency, allowing emotions to be expressed in a balanced and measured way.

- **Sensual Comfort:** The Moon in Taurus finds comfort in sensual pleasures and the physical world. There is a deep appreciation for beauty, nature, and tactile experiences, such as good food, cozy surroundings, and material comforts that provide a sense of well-being.
- **Dependability:** The Moon in Taurus emphasizes reliability and steadfastness in nurturing. These individuals are deeply caring and devoted to those they love, providing a solid and dependable source of emotional support.
- **Positive Aspects:** The Moon in Taurus can bring a sense of emotional resilience, warmth, and an ability to enjoy life's simple pleasures. This placement encourages a nurturing approach that is practical, consistent, and rooted in the physical world, making it a source of strength and calm in times of turmoil.

The Moon in its "Fall" – Scorpio

When a planet is in its "fall," it struggles to express its natural qualities. The Moon is in its fall in Scorpio, where its need for security and comfort meets Scorpio's intensity and emotional depth, often creating an internal conflict.

- **Intensity and Depth:** Scorpio's nature brings a deep emotional intensity to the Moon. This placement may result in powerful, sometimes overwhelming emotions that are hard to control or express. Feelings can run deep, leading to a complex inner life that craves emotional transformation and depth.
- **Struggles with Vulnerability:** The Moon in Scorpio often struggles to show vulnerability and may guard emotions tightly. There is a tendency to keep feelings private and hidden, resulting in a reserved or secretive demeanor. This need to protect oneself can make it challenging to find emotional security and trust in others.
- **Control and Power:** Scorpio's desire for control can influence the Moon's emotional nature, leading to an internal struggle between the need to feel and the need to maintain power.

Emotional experiences can be intense and transformative, but also difficult to navigate, as the individual may resist letting go or fully expressing their feelings.

- Positive Aspects: Despite these challenges, the Moon in Scorpio can bring immense emotional strength, resilience, and the capacity for profound transformation. Those with this placement often possess a powerful intuition and a deep understanding of the complexities of human emotions, allowing them to nurture others with insight and empathy.

Summary

The Moon in astrology represents your emotional core, subconscious habits, nurturing qualities, and intuitive responses. It shapes how you experience and express emotions, highlighting the areas in life where you seek comfort and security. As the ruler of Cancer and the natural tenant of the Fourth House, the Moon thrives in environments that allow for emotional connection, security, and care. Understanding the Moon's sign, house placement, and aspects in a natal chart is key to uncovering your emotional needs and nurturing instincts. Recognizing the Moon's exaltation in Taurus and its fall in Scorpio provides further insight into the strengths and challenges of its expression in different signs.

Mercury: The Messenger of the Mind

Symbol: ☿

Mercury in astrology represents communication, intellect, thought processes, and how you exchange information. It governs the mind, learning, perception, and all forms of expression, including writing, speaking, and even body language. Mercury's placement in your natal chart reveals how you think, process information, learn, and interact with your environment.

What Mercury Represents

- **Communication:** Mercury is the planet of communication. It governs how you express your thoughts and ideas, how you convey messages, and your style of speaking and writing. It reflects how you interact with others, whether you are direct, articulate, reserved, or lively in conversation.

- **Intellect and Thought Processes:** Mercury represents your mental processes, including how you think, analyze, and solve problems. It indicates whether you are more logical, practical, curious, imaginative, or detail-oriented. The sign and aspects of Mercury in your chart influence your mindset, learning style, and intellectual strengths.

- **Learning and Curiosity:** Mercury rules learning and information gathering. It reveals what subjects pique your curiosity and how you approach the process of learning. A strong Mercury placement suggests an active mind that seeks knowledge and enjoys mental stimulation.

- **Decision-Making:** As the planet of reasoning, Mercury influences how you make decisions. It shows whether you rely on intuition, facts, logic, or instinct. It also highlights how quickly you come to conclusions and whether you are flexible or fixed in your thinking.

- **Travel and Movement:** Mercury is associated with short-distance travel, movement, and how you navigate your surroundings. It governs daily activities, routines, and how you adapt to changes in your immediate environment.

Qualities of Mercury
- **Neutral and Adaptive:** Mercury is neutral in nature, neither inherently masculine nor feminine. It is adaptable, taking on the qualities of the sign it occupies. This flexibility allows Mercury to shift its expression depending on its placement and aspects in a chart.
- **Mutable and Changeable:** Reflecting its ruling signs of Gemini and Virgo, Mercury is mutable and quick. It represents mental agility, adaptability, and the ability to think on one's feet. It thrives in environments that require versatility and a dynamic exchange of ideas.
- **Element of Air and Earth:** Mercury resonates with both Air and Earth elements. Its Air qualities (through Gemini) highlight communication, intellectual pursuits, and social interaction, while its Earth qualities (through Virgo) emphasize practicality, analysis, and attention to detail.

Mercury in the Natal Chart
- **Mercury Sign:** The sign Mercury occupies in your natal chart indicates your communication style, thought processes, and how you learn and express yourself.
- **House Placement:** The house where Mercury is located in your chart points to the area of life where your mental focus, communication, and intellectual activities are most prominent. It highlights where you seek to exchange information and connect with others.

Mercury and the Third House
Mercury has a natural affinity with the Third House, often called the "house of communication and learning." This house governs the exchange of ideas, early education, and connections with siblings and neighbors. As the planet of intellect and expression, Mercury thrives here, shaping how individuals think, speak, write,

and process information.

When Mercury is in the Third House, individuals often possess a sharp mind and a natural curiosity about the world. They are quick learners, adaptable communicators, and thrive in environments that encourage dialogue and intellectual exploration. This placement emphasizes mental agility and versatility, fostering a love for learning and an ease in forming connections.

While Mercury here enhances communication skills, it can also lead to restlessness or a tendency to become easily distracted. Developing focus and deepening intellectual pursuits allows individuals to channel Mercury's energy productively, making the most of their natural talents in conversation and learning.

Mercury and the Sixth House

Mercury has a strong connection to the Sixth House, often referred to as the "house of work and daily routines." This house governs organization, problem-solving, health, and service, aligning closely with Mercury's analytical and detail-oriented nature. It reflects how individuals approach their responsibilities, manage tasks, and maintain well-being.

When Mercury is in the Sixth House, individuals often excel in roles that require precision, critical thinking, and organization. They are methodical in their approach to work, enjoy structured routines, and have a strong focus on efficiency. This placement enhances problem-solving abilities, making them skilled at finding practical solutions to everyday challenges.

While Mercury here strengthens productivity, it can also lead to overanalyzing or becoming overly focused on minor details. Learning to balance efficiency with flexibility allows individuals to use Mercury's energy effectively, creating a structured yet adaptable approach to work and wellness.

The Movement of Mercury

Mercury typically spends about 14-21 days in each sign during its direct motion. However, when retrograde, it can remain in the same sign for up to 6-8 weeks, depending on whether it retrogrades entirely in one sign or moves between two. Mercury completes its journey through all 12 zodiac signs in approximately 88 days, aligning with its swift orbital period around the Sun.

Mercury Retrograde

Mercury retrograde occurs three to four times per year, lasting approximately three weeks each time, and is one of the most widely recognized retrograde periods in astrology. It is often associated with communication breakdowns, technological glitches, and travel delays, as well as misunderstandings and the need to revise plans. This period invites introspection, encouraging individuals to review past decisions, resolve unfinished business, and approach challenges with a reflective mindset. In a natal chart, Mercury retrograde often signifies a tendency toward introspective thinking and unique communication styles. Individuals with this placement might feel misunderstood or process information internally before expressing their thoughts outwardly. They may revisit ideas or rethink decisions more frequently, approaching communication and thought processes with a reflective and analytical perspective. This placement can also suggest early challenges in education or learning, which often lead to greater mastery and insight over time. Rather than causing constant delays, Mercury retrograde in a birth chart can highlight a deep intellectual strength, as these individuals learn to navigate the world in their own thoughtful and considered way.

Mercury's "Home" – Its Comfort Zone
- **Ruling Signs – Gemini and Virgo:** Mercury rules both Gemini and Virgo, making these signs its natural homes. In Gemini, Mercury expresses its qualities of communication, curiosity, and adaptability. Those with Mercury in Gemini are typically quick-minded, versatile, and skilled at multitasking, thriving on intellectual exchange and constant learning. In Virgo, Mercury embodies its analytical, practical side. Here, it brings a methodical, detail-oriented approach to thinking and problem-solving, emphasizing precision, organization, and a critical eye for improvement.

Mercury in its "Exaltation" – Virgo

When a planet is in its "exaltation," it expresses its natural qualities with ease and strength. Mercury is exalted in Virgo, where its analytical, logical, and detail-focused nature is fully realized.

- **Analytical Thinking:** In Virgo, Mercury excels in critical thinking and analysis. It processes information efficiently, breaking down complex topics into manageable parts. This placement allows for an organized, methodical approach to problems, making individuals with Mercury in Virgo highly perceptive and skilled at discerning details.

- **Practical Communication:** Mercury in Virgo is characterized by clear, precise, and practical communication. These individuals convey their thoughts in a straightforward, efficient manner, often avoiding ambiguity and focusing on facts and useful information.

- **Attention to Detail:** Virgo's earthy nature provides Mercury with a grounding influence, enhancing its ability to focus on the finer points. This placement indicates an individual who is meticulous, thorough, and diligent in both thought and speech, making them excellent at research, editing, and analytical work.

- **Positive Aspects:** The exaltation of Mercury in Virgo highlights qualities such as precision, intellectual depth, and a strong sense of responsibility in communication. It fosters a highly adaptable mindset that excels in environments requiring accuracy, organization, and critical evaluation.

Mercury in its "Detriment" and "Fall" – Sagittarius and Pisces

When a planet is in its "detriment" or "fall," it struggles to express its natural qualities. Mercury is in its detriment in Sagittarius and in its fall in Pisces. Both placements present challenges to Mercury's logical, analytical nature.

- **Mercury in Sagittarius (Detriment):** Sagittarius' expansive, big-picture focus can clash with Mercury's preference for details and facts. Here, Mercury's communication becomes broad, philosophical, and often opinionated. While it can inspire grand ideas and a love of learning, it may struggle with details,

126

consistency, or precision in its thinking. There is a tendency to focus on ideals and future possibilities, sometimes overlooking the practical aspects.

- Mercury in Pisces (Fall): Pisces' dreamy, intuitive nature contrasts with Mercury's desire for clarity and logical analysis. In Pisces, Mercury operates through intuition, imagination, and abstract thinking rather than logic and precision. This placement can result in a more poetic, creative way of thinking and communicating, but it may also lead to difficulties in focusing, organizing thoughts, or expressing ideas clearly.

Despite these challenges, both placements can offer unique strengths. Mercury in Sagittarius brings a visionary perspective and a passion for truth-seeking, while Mercury in Pisces offers deep empathy, imagination, and the ability to think beyond conventional boundaries.

Summary

Mercury in astrology governs communication, intellect, learning, and the way you process information. It shapes your thinking style, decision-making processes, and how you express your ideas. As the ruler of Gemini and Virgo and the natural tenant of the Third and Sixth House, Mercury thrives in environments that require adaptability, critical thinking, and intellectual exchange. Understanding Mercury's sign, house placement, and aspects in a natal chart provides insight into your mental habits, communication style, and areas of intellectual interest. Recognizing Mercury's exaltation in Virgo and its challenges in Sagittarius and Pisces adds depth to how this planet influences your unique way of thinking and interacting with the world.

Venus: The Planet of Love and Beauty

Symbol: ♀

Venus in astrology represents love, beauty, harmony, and the ways you express affection and attract what you desire. It governs your approach to relationships, art, aesthetics, values, and pleasures. Venus influences your sense of attraction, how you relate to others, and the things that bring you joy and comfort. It embodies the principle of harmony, balance, and what you find beautiful in the world around you.

What Venus Represents

- **Love and Relationships:** Venus is the planet of love and romance, reflecting your approach to relationships and how you express affection. It shows what you seek in a partner, how you create harmony in relationships, and your style of loving. Venus's placement in your chart reveals your romantic inclinations, whether you are nurturing, passionate, playful, or reserved in love.

- **Attraction and Magnetism:** Venus governs what you are naturally attracted to and how you attract others. It signifies your charm, grace, and the qualities you find appealing. Venus's energy can make you alluring, highlighting how you draw people, experiences, and pleasures into your life.

- **Beauty and Aesthetics:** Venus rules over beauty, art, and aesthetics. It represents your sense of style, tastes, and what you consider beautiful. Your Venus sign influences how you express yourself through fashion, art, and design, and what kind of environments and experiences you find pleasurable and comforting.

- **Pleasure and Comfort:** Venus is connected to sensual pleasures and the things that bring you comfort and joy. It reveals what you enjoy indulging in, from food to music to physical touch. Venus shows where and how you seek relaxation, comfort, and satisfaction in life.

- **Values and Material Wealth:** Venus also governs your values and how you perceive worth, including money and material possessions. It indicates your relationship with wealth, luxury, and how you use resources to create a life of beauty and ease.

Qualities of Venus

- **Feminine, Receptive, and Passive:** Venus embodies feminine energy, symbolizing receptivity, grace, and the capacity to give and receive love. It represents qualities of softness, tenderness, and a harmonious approach to both relationships and life.
- **Fixed and Steady:** Venus has a fixed nature, representing stability and a deep appreciation for consistency and beauty. It enjoys creating and maintaining harmony, seeking comfort and security in relationships and surroundings.
- **Element of Earth and Air:** Venus resonates with both the Earth and Air elements. Through Taurus (Earth), Venus expresses sensuality, practicality, and the enjoyment of physical pleasures. Through Libra (Air), it embodies intellectual connections, aesthetics, and the pursuit of balance in relationships.

Venus in the Natal Chart

- **Venus Sign:** The sign Venus occupies in your natal chart indicates how you love, what you value, and your style of relating to others.
- **House Placement:** The house where Venus is located in your chart points to the area of life where you seek harmony, beauty, and pleasurable experiences. It highlights where your romantic and aesthetic tendencies manifest most strongly.

Venus and the Seventh House

Venus has a natural affinity with the Seventh House, known as the "house of partnerships." This house focuses on relationships, love, and the dynamics of balance and harmony in one-on-one connections. As the ruler of Libra, Venus naturally aligns with the Seventh House's themes of cooperation and beauty.

When Venus is in the Seventh House, relationships often play a central role in the individual's life. These people value harmony and seek partnerships that are loving, supportive, and aesthetically pleasing. They are naturally diplomatic and have a strong appreciation for balance in their connections.

This placement highlights a desire for meaningful companionship, but it can also indicate a tendency to idealize relationships. Striking a balance between personal independence and partnership is key for those with Venus in the Seventh House.

Venus and the Second House

Venus has a natural affinity with the Second House, often referred to as the "house of values and possessions." This house focuses on finances, material wealth, self-worth, and the things that bring comfort and beauty into life. As the ruler of Taurus, Venus aligns with the Second House's themes of stability and sensual pleasures.

When Venus is in the Second House, material and emotional security often take center stage. These individuals value comfort, beauty, and high-quality experiences, and they have a natural talent for attracting abundance. Their sense of self-worth is closely tied to what they value, whether it's material possessions, financial stability, or meaningful relationships.

This placement highlights a love of luxury and an appreciation for life's pleasures, but it can also indicate a tendency to seek validation through external means. Striking a balance between enjoying material comfort and cultivating inner worth is key for those with Venus in the Second House.

The Movement of Venus

Venus usually spends 23-40 days in each sign during direct motion. However, during retrograde periods, which occur approximately every 18 months, Venus can linger in a single sign for up to four months. Venus completes its journey through all 12 zodiac signs in about 7.5 months, though this timeline can extend due to retrograde motion.

Venus Retrograde

Venus retrograde occurs approximately every 18 months and lasts for about six weeks, influencing love, relationships, beauty, and values. During this time, it often prompts re-evaluations of romantic partnerships, financial matters, and self-worth. Old lovers or unresolved romantic issues may resurface, encouraging reflection on the balance of give-and-take in relationships. It is generally advised to avoid starting new relationships or making significant aesthetic changes during Venus retrograde, as the energy is more suited to introspection and reassessment. In a natal chart, Venus retrograde suggests a unique and deeply personal approach to love, relationships, and self-worth. Individuals with this placement may feel more introspective about their desires and values, often taking longer to form close bonds or to open up in relationships. They may revisit or question past relationships and feelings, seeking deeper, more meaningful connections over superficial ones. Financial matters and self-image may also become areas of reflection, with an emphasis on understanding one's intrinsic value beyond material possessions or outward appearances. Over time, this placement fosters profound personal growth in love and self-acceptance, as individuals learn to align their inner desires with the external world.

Venus's "Home" – Its Comfort Zone

- **Ruling Signs – Taurus and Libra:** Venus rules both Taurus and Libra, making these signs its natural homes. In Taurus, Venus expresses its sensual, earthy nature, focusing on physical pleasures, comfort, and material beauty. It values stability, loyalty, and the enjoyment of life's simple pleasures. In Libra, Venus embodies harmony, balance, and intellectual beauty. Here, Venus emphasizes relationships, social interactions, and a refined aesthetic, seeking to create beauty in all forms and maintain peaceful, loving connections.

Venus in its "Exaltation" – Pisces

When a planet is in its "exaltation," it expresses its natural qualities with ease and strength. Venus is exalted in Pisces, where its loving, compassionate, and creative nature can flourish.

- **Unconditional Love:** Venus in Pisces is characterized by its capacity for unconditional love and deep empathy. This placement suggests a boundless, selfless approach to relationships, where love is felt on a spiritual and emotional level. There is a natural inclination toward forgiveness, compassion, and seeing the beauty in every situation.

- **Romantic Idealism:** In Pisces, Venus expresses romance through dreams, imagination, and fantasy. This placement brings a dreamy, poetic quality to love, creating a desire for deep, soulful connections. There is an innate ability to experience joy and beauty in the ethereal and mystical aspects of life.

- **Creativity and Art:** Venus in Pisces heightens artistic and creative abilities. It inspires a love for music, art, and beauty that transcends the physical world. Individuals with this placement are often drawn to creative endeavors and find joy in expressing themselves through art, music, and other imaginative pursuits.

- **Positive Aspects:** Venus in Pisces shines through its gentleness, compassion, and intuitive understanding of love. This placement fosters an open heart and the ability to experience beauty on a spiritual level. When expressed positively, it leads to a rich inner life filled with love, creativity, and a deep sense of connection with the universe.

Venus in its "Detriment" and "Fall" – Aries and Virgo

When a planet is in its "detriment" or "fall," it struggles to express its natural qualities. Venus is in its detriment in Aries and in its fall in Virgo, presenting challenges to Venus's harmonious, receptive nature.

- **Venus in Aries (Detriment):** Aries' assertive, direct qualities can clash with Venus's preference for harmony and receptivity. In Aries, Venus expresses love impulsively, passionately, and sometimes aggressively. This placement suggests a desire for excitement and challenge in relationships, but it can also lead to impatience and a lack of subtlety in matters of love. While this can bring passion and a fearless approach to romance, it may struggle with maintaining the harmony and patience Venus naturally seeks.

- Venus in Virgo (Fall): Virgo's analytical, detail-focused nature contrasts with Venus's desire for relaxation and enjoyment. In Virgo, Venus expresses love through service, practicality, and a desire for perfection. This placement can lead to a critical or reserved approach to relationships, with a tendency to overanalyze emotions. While Venus in Virgo can be incredibly loyal and caring, it may struggle with embracing the spontaneity and ease that Venus traditionally enjoys in other signs.

Despite these challenges, both placements have their unique strengths. Venus in Aries brings excitement, courage, and a willingness to pursue love passionately, while Venus in Virgo offers a caring, dedicated approach to relationships, emphasizing growth, service, and mutual improvement.

Summary

Venus in astrology governs love, relationships, beauty, and the things that bring you pleasure. It shapes how you express affection, what you find attractive, and how you seek comfort and harmony in life. As the ruler of Taurus and Libra and the natural tenant of the Seventh and Second House, Venus thrives in environments that allow for the creation of beauty, balance, and meaningful connections. Understanding Venus's sign, house placement, and aspects in a natal chart reveals how you relate to others, what you value, and the ways you experience joy and satisfaction. Recognizing Venus's exaltation in Pisces and its challenges in Aries and Virgo adds depth to how this planet influences your love life, values, and pursuit of beauty.

Mars: The Planet of Action and Drive

Symbol: ♂

Mars in astrology represents drive, action, energy, and the way you assert yourself. It governs your physical vitality, determination, passion, and the nature of your desires. Mars embodies the principle of action, showing how you pursue goals, express anger, and take initiative. It's the planet that fuels your motivation, courage, and willingness to take risks.

What Mars Represents

- **Drive and Ambition:** Mars is the planet of drive and ambition. It represents how you pursue your goals and the level of energy you put into achieving them. Your Mars sign and its placement in your chart reveal whether you are assertive, competitive, patient, or impulsive in your endeavors.

- **Action and Initiative:** Mars governs the way you take action and assert yourself. It indicates how you respond to challenges and how you initiate new projects. This planet influences your fighting spirit, showing whether you confront obstacles head-on or prefer a more strategic, cautious approach.

- **Physical Vitality and Energy:** Mars is associated with physical energy and stamina. It reflects how you channel your physical vitality, whether through sports, exercise, or other dynamic activities. A well-placed Mars can indicate high energy levels, while challenging aspects may suggest fluctuations in physical strength or a tendency toward overexertion.

- **Desire and Sexuality:** Mars rules desire, passion, and sexuality. It reveals what fuels your passions, how you express your sexual nature, and what you find attractive. Mars' placement in your chart can indicate whether you approach intimacy with boldness, caution, or playfulness.

- **Aggression and Anger:** Mars also governs aggression, anger, and how you deal with conflict. It indicates your temper and how you assert your boundaries. Some Mars placements suggest a fiery, direct expression of anger, while others might indicate a more controlled or passive-aggressive approach to conflict.

Qualities of Mars

- **Masculine, Active, and Dynamic:** Mars embodies masculine energy, symbolizing assertiveness, action, and the drive to conquer. It is the force that propels you forward, urging you to take risks and fight for what you want. Mars represents the part of you that is fearless, bold, and unafraid to initiate change.
- **Cardinal and Fiery:** Astrologically, Mars has a cardinal, initiating quality and is associated with the Fire element. It represents spontaneity, courage, and the willingness to take charge. Mars thrives in situations that require quick decision-making and decisive action.
- **Impetuous and Independent:** Mars is impulsive and independent, preferring direct action over contemplation. It doesn't wait for permission; it moves with confidence and a clear sense of purpose. This planet's energy can be both inspiring and challenging, as it urges you to take action without hesitation.

Mars in the Natal Chart

- **Mars Sign:** The sign Mars occupies in your natal chart indicates how you assert yourself, pursue your desires, and express anger.
- **House Placement:** The house where Mars is located in your chart highlights the area of life where you channel your energy, initiative, and drive. It shows where you are most inclined to take action and where your passions are likely to manifest.

Mars and the First House

Mars has a natural affinity with the First House, often called the "house of self." This house governs your identity, physical energy, and how you assert yourself in the world. As the planet of action and drive, Mars resonates strongly with the First House's themes of initiative and personal power.

When Mars is in the First House, individuals often display a bold, dynamic presence. They are action-oriented, assertive, and unafraid to take charge. This placement emphasizes physical energy and a direct approach to challenges, often making these individuals natural leaders.

While this energy fosters courage and independence, it can also lead to impulsiveness or a quick temper. Learning to channel Mars's assertiveness constructively helps those with this placement achieve their goals effectively without unnecessary conflict.

The Movement of Mars

Mars typically spends about 6-7 weeks in each sign during direct motion. However, when retrograde—which occurs approximately every two years—it can stay in a single sign for up to six months. Mars completes its full journey through all 12 zodiac signs in about two years.

Mars Retrograde

Mars retrograde occurs about once every two years and lasts approximately ten weeks, influencing action, energy, and ambition. During this period, people may experience delays or frustration in their efforts to assert themselves or make progress. Motivation might wane, conflicts could arise more easily, and suppressed anger may become a challenge. This time is ideal for reflecting on how you pursue goals and manage conflict, encouraging a more thoughtful approach rather than aggressive action. In a natal chart, Mars retrograde suggests that a person's drive, ambition, and expression of anger are often channeled in a more internal or reflective manner. Individuals with this placement might find it difficult to assert themselves directly or feel hesitant to act impulsively in pursuit of their goals. There may be a tendency to suppress anger or frustration, which could build up over time and lead to occasional outbursts. These individuals often take more time to assess situations before acting, favoring a deliberate and thoughtful approach. This placement fosters the development of inner strength, teaching individuals to navigate challenges with patience and to reconsider their methods of handling conflict and ambition.

Mars's "Home" – Its Comfort Zone

- **Ruling Sign – Aries:** Mars rules Aries, making this sign its natural home. In Aries, Mars expresses its full, dynamic potential. It becomes bold, courageous, and impulsive, embodying the pioneering spirit of Aries. Individuals with Mars in Aries have a direct, assertive way of pursuing their desires and are unafraid to take risks. They are quick to take action, often driven by instinct and a need to conquer new challenges. This placement emphasizes independence, spontaneity, and a fearless approach to life.

Mars in its "Exaltation" – Capricorn

When a planet is in its "exaltation," it expresses its natural qualities with ease and strength. Mars is exalted in Capricorn, where its fiery energy meets Capricorn's disciplined, goal-oriented nature.

- **Strategic Action:** In Capricorn, Mars channels its energy into focused, strategic efforts. This placement suggests a methodical, patient approach to achieving goals, where actions are carefully planned and executed. Mars in Capricorn excels in situations that require endurance, persistence, and a practical outlook.

- **Ambition and Drive:** Capricorn's influence gives Mars a strong sense of ambition and the determination to succeed. Individuals with Mars in Capricorn are willing to work hard, often dedicating themselves to long-term projects. They possess a natural drive for achievement and are disciplined in their pursuit of success.

- **Controlled Energy:** Mars in Capricorn is characterized by its ability to control and direct energy efficiently. Unlike more impulsive Mars placements, it prefers to take measured steps, focusing on tangible results and steady progress. This placement indicates a resilient, hardworking nature, capable of overcoming obstacles with persistence.

- **Positive Aspects:** The exaltation of Mars in Capricorn brings qualities like patience, discipline, and a strong work ethic. It fosters a pragmatic approach to challenges, enabling individuals to take on difficult tasks and see them through to completion. This placement can lead to significant achievements and mastery in chosen fields.

Mars in its "Detriment" and "Fall" – Libra and Cancer

When a planet is in its "detriment" or "fall," it struggles to express its natural qualities. Mars is in its detriment in Libra and in its fall in Cancer, presenting challenges to its assertive, direct nature.

- **Mars in Libra (Detriment):** Libra's focus on harmony, balance, and relationships can clash with Mars' desire for direct action. In Libra, Mars expresses itself diplomatically, often preferring negotiation and compromise over confrontation. This placement suggests a more thoughtful, balanced approach to pursuing desires but may struggle with indecision or hesitance in asserting itself. While this can result in a fair, cooperative attitude, it may sometimes dilute Mars' natural drive and boldness.

- **Mars in Cancer (Fall):** Cancer's emotional, protective nature contrasts with Mars' fiery, assertive energy. In Cancer, Mars expresses its drive through nurturing and protecting loved ones, often focusing on home and family. This placement can lead to indirect or passive-aggressive ways of dealing with anger and conflict, as Cancer prefers to avoid direct confrontation. While Mars in Cancer can be fiercely protective, it may struggle with expressing desires openly and confidently.

Despite these challenges, both placements offer unique strengths. Mars in Libra brings a diplomatic, fair-minded approach to action, while Mars in Cancer offers emotional depth, nurturing qualities, and the ability to defend and protect what they care about.

Summary

Mars in astrology governs action, drive, ambition, and the way you assert your desires. It shapes how you pursue goals, express anger, and take initiative in life. As the ruler of Aries and the natural tenant of the First House, Mars thrives in environments that require courage, independence, and dynamic action. Understanding Mars's sign, house placement, and aspects in a natal chart reveals how you express your energy, pursue your passions, and deal with challenges. Recognizing Mars's exaltation in Capricorn and its challenges in Libra and Cancer adds depth to how this planet influences your assertiveness, ambition, and ability to navigate conflict and obstacles.

Jupiter: The Planet of Expansion and Growth

Symbol: ♃

Jupiter in astrology represents expansion, growth, abundance, and the pursuit of knowledge. It governs optimism, faith, philosophy, and your ability to embrace new experiences. Jupiter is the planet that symbolizes the search for meaning, truth, and purpose, guiding you to broaden your horizons, seek wisdom, and explore the world around you. It is often associated with luck, prosperity, and a sense of generosity.

What Jupiter Represents

- **Expansion and Growth:** Jupiter is the planet of expansion, symbolizing the desire to grow, both intellectually and spiritually. It urges you to go beyond your current limits, explore new possibilities, and seek out broader perspectives. Jupiter's placement in your chart indicates areas where you naturally experience growth, success, and opportunities for personal and spiritual development.

- **Optimism and Faith:** Jupiter governs optimism, hope, and the belief in positive outcomes. It represents your faith in life, your philosophical outlook, and your ability to see the bigger picture. When well-placed, Jupiter inspires confidence and encourages a positive attitude, even in challenging situations.

- **Wisdom and Knowledge:** As the planet of wisdom, Jupiter rules higher learning, philosophy, religion, and the quest for truth. It represents the pursuit of knowledge and your desire to understand the deeper aspects of existence. Jupiter's placement in your chart reveals the areas where you seek wisdom, expand your mind, and develop a more profound understanding of life.

- **Generosity and Prosperity:** Jupiter is associated with generosity, abundance, and the flow of prosperity. It represents the areas in your life where you are inclined to be giving, benevolent, and open-hearted. Jupiter's influence often brings a sense of luck

and fortunate opportunities, promoting growth and abundance.
- **Adventure and Exploration:** Jupiter embodies the spirit of adventure and exploration. It governs travel, new experiences, and the pursuit of the unknown. Jupiter encourages you to venture beyond your comfort zone, explore different cultures, and embrace diverse perspectives.

Qualities of Jupiter
- **Masculine, Positive, and Active:** Jupiter embodies a masculine energy that is positive, active, and outgoing. It represents enthusiasm, expansion, and a desire to grow. Jupiter's influence encourages you to take risks, explore new ideas, and trust in the journey.
- **Mutable and Generous:** Jupiter has a mutable quality, indicating flexibility, adaptability, and an openness to change. It is naturally generous, promoting a spirit of giving, kindness, and optimism. Jupiter's energy is about spreading joy, knowledge, and abundance.
- **Element of Fire:** Jupiter resonates with the Fire element, highlighting qualities of enthusiasm, inspiration, and a zest for life. It brings warmth, excitement, and an expansive vision, driving individuals to pursue their ideals and dreams.

Jupiter in the Natal Chart
- **Jupiter Sign:** The sign Jupiter occupies in your natal chart reveals how you seek growth, express optimism, and pursue knowledge.
- **House Placement:** The house where Jupiter is located in your chart points to the area of life where you experience expansion, opportunities, and a sense of abundance. It shows where you are inclined to seek wisdom, embrace optimism, and manifest prosperity.

Jupiter and the Ninth House
Jupiter has a natural affinity with the Ninth House, often called the "house of expansion." This house governs higher learning,

philosophy, travel, and the search for meaning in life. As the planet of growth and abundance, Jupiter aligns perfectly with the Ninth House's themes of exploration and broadening horizons.

When Jupiter is in the Ninth House, individuals often possess a strong desire for knowledge, adventure, and personal growth. They are naturally curious and drawn to experiences that expand their understanding of the world, such as travel, education, or spiritual pursuits.

This placement emphasizes optimism and a belief in endless possibilities. However, there can be a tendency toward overindulgence or taking on too much at once. Finding balance helps these individuals maximize Jupiter's expansive energy while maintaining focus on their goals.

The Movement of Jupiter

Jupiter spends approximately 12 to 13 months in each sign, moving at a steady pace that makes it one of the slower planets in astrology. It completes a full cycle through the zodiac in about 12 years, marking significant phases of growth and expansion.

Jupiter Retrograde

Jupiter retrograde occurs about once a year and lasts for approximately four months, influencing growth, expansion, philosophy, and opportunities. During this period, the focus shifts from external expansion to inner growth and spiritual reflection. It is a time to revisit personal development goals, higher learning, or long-term plans, encouraging refinement of one's vision and goals rather than actively pursuing them. In a natal chart, Jupiter retrograde indicates that an individual's path to growth, expansion, and wisdom often takes a more inward and personal route. Rather than seeking external validation or following conventional definitions of success, these individuals turn to introspection and spiritual exploration to find their sense of purpose and fulfillment. They may feel the need to redefine their personal philosophies and goals over time, often prioritizing a deep understanding of life's meanings before taking significant leaps. This placement supports personal development through self-awareness and encourages finding opportunities for growth in unconventional or internal ways, aligning ambitions with one's inner truths.

Jupiter's "Home" – Its Comfort Zone
- **Ruling Sign – Sagittarius:** Jupiter rules Sagittarius, making this sign its natural home. In Sagittarius, Jupiter expresses its full potential for exploration, optimism, and philosophical thinking. Individuals with Jupiter in Sagittarius are adventurous, open-minded, and have a thirst for knowledge. They are driven to seek the truth, expand their horizons, and explore different cultures and belief systems. This placement emphasizes a love for travel, a free-spirited attitude, and a deep sense of faith in life's journey.
- **Co-Ruler of Pisces:** Jupiter is also the traditional co-ruler of Pisces, sharing rulership with Neptune. In Pisces, Jupiter expresses its qualities of compassion, spiritual growth, and intuitive wisdom. It highlights the expansive nature of the imagination, creativity, and the ability to connect with the unseen realms of existence.

Jupiter in its "Exaltation" – Cancer
When a planet is in its "exaltation," it expresses its natural qualities with ease and strength. Jupiter is exalted in Cancer, where its nurturing, generous nature aligns with Cancer's focus on care, protection, and emotional growth.
- **Emotional Growth:** In Cancer, Jupiter expands emotional depth, compassion, and the desire to nurture others. This placement suggests a strong capacity for empathy and a need to create a sense of emotional security and comfort. Individuals with Jupiter in Cancer find personal growth through family, home life, and nurturing relationships.
- **Generosity and Nurturing:** Jupiter in Cancer is characterized by a generous spirit, particularly in matters related to family, home, and close relationships. This placement promotes giving and caring for others, often bringing a sense of abundance and luck in domestic affairs. There is a natural inclination toward hospitality, nurturing, and creating a warm, comforting environment.

- Intuitive Wisdom: Cancer's intuitive nature complements Jupiter's philosophical qualities, enhancing the individual's ability to understand and connect with others on a deep emotional level. This placement fosters spiritual growth and a profound appreciation for the emotional aspects of life.

- Positive Aspects: The exaltation of Jupiter in Cancer brings a combination of emotional warmth, generosity, and an intuitive approach to growth. It encourages a nurturing mindset, where growth is achieved through emotional support, empathy, and creating a safe, caring environment.

Jupiter in its "Detriment" and "Fall" – Gemini and Capricorn

When a planet is in its "detriment" or "fall," it struggles to express its natural qualities. Jupiter is in its detriment in Gemini and in its fall in Capricorn, presenting challenges to its expansive, optimistic nature.

- Jupiter in Gemini (Detriment): Gemini's intellectual, detail-oriented focus can clash with Jupiter's preference for broad, philosophical thinking. In Gemini, Jupiter expresses itself through curiosity and a desire to gather information, but it may struggle with consistency or depth. This placement can result in a more scattered or restless approach to growth, as the individual seeks knowledge in many directions. While it fosters adaptability and a quick mind, it may lack the deeper wisdom or long-term vision that Jupiter traditionally embodies.

- Jupiter in Capricorn (Fall): Capricorn's disciplined, practical nature contrasts with Jupiter's expansive, optimistic energy. In Capricorn, Jupiter's growth is channeled through hard work, responsibility, and careful planning. This placement can bring a more cautious, realistic approach to optimism, emphasizing structure and discipline over blind faith. While it can result in significant achievements through perseverance, it may struggle with embracing risk, spontaneity, and the easy flow of abundance that Jupiter usually represents.

Despite these challenges, both placements offer unique

strengths. Jupiter in Gemini brings intellectual curiosity and the ability to explore diverse ideas, while Jupiter in Capricorn offers disciplined ambition and a structured path to success and growth.

Summary

Jupiter in astrology governs expansion, growth, wisdom, and the pursuit of knowledge. It shapes your optimism, philosophical outlook, and how you seek to broaden your horizons. As the ruler of Sagittarius, the co-ruler of Pisces and the natural tenant of the Ninth House, Jupiter thrives in environments that allow for exploration, adventure, and the search for deeper meaning. Understanding Jupiter's sign, house placement, and aspects in a natal chart reveals how you embrace growth, where you find abundance, and how you express generosity and faith. Recognizing Jupiter's exaltation in Cancer and its challenges in Gemini and Capricorn adds depth to how this planet influences your quest for wisdom, optimism, and the pursuit of life's opportunities.

Saturn: The Planet of Discipline and Responsibility

Symbol: ♄

Saturn in astrology represents structure, discipline, responsibility, and the lessons learned through challenges. It governs the boundaries, limitations, and rules that shape our lives. Saturn embodies the principles of hard work, perseverance, maturity, and the pursuit of long-term goals. Often seen as the "taskmaster" of the zodiac, Saturn teaches patience, diligence, and the rewards of enduring effort.

What Saturn Represents

- **Discipline and Responsibility:** Saturn is the planet of discipline and responsibility. It indicates where you need to exercise control, set boundaries, and take responsibility for your actions. Its placement in your chart reveals the areas where you need to work hard, show commitment, and develop a sense of duty.

- **Limitations and Boundaries:** Saturn represents limitations, restrictions, and the obstacles that you encounter in life. It defines the boundaries of what is possible, highlighting areas where you may feel confined or challenged. Saturn's energy often teaches the importance of boundaries, whether physical, emotional, or mental, encouraging you to respect limits and learn through experiences.

- **Structure and Order:** Saturn governs structure, order, and organization. It shows how you create stability in your life through planning, rules, and structure. This planet's influence promotes a sense of order, urging you to approach situations methodically and systematically. Saturn helps you build solid foundations that can withstand the test of time.

- **Patience and Endurance:** Saturn is associated with patience, endurance, and the ability to overcome challenges. It represents the process of maturation, emphasizing that growth takes time and effort. Saturn's placement indicates where you may face delays, difficulties, or obstacles that, when overcome, lead to lasting success and personal growth.

- Karma and Life Lessons: Saturn is often linked to karma and the life lessons you need to learn. It brings experiences that test your resolve, forcing you to confront fears, limitations, and areas that require improvement. The challenges presented by Saturn serve as catalysts for personal development, helping you achieve mastery and wisdom over time.

Qualities of Saturn

- Masculine, Restrictive, and Steady: Saturn embodies masculine energy and is characterized by restraint, stability, and a sense of duty. It represents the part of you that is serious, cautious, and focused on achieving results through hard work. Saturn's influence is often associated with authority, discipline, and the willingness to take on responsibilities.

- Fixed and Determined: Saturn has a fixed quality, emphasizing perseverance and determination. It represents the need for consistency, patience, and adherence to rules. Saturn's energy is not about quick results but about building long-lasting structures and achieving success through dedication and hard work.

- Element of Earth: Saturn resonates with the Earth element, highlighting practicality, realism, and a focus on tangible results. It encourages a grounded, methodical approach to life, where success is earned through effort, planning, and careful management of resources.

Saturn in the Natal Chart

- Saturn Sign: The sign Saturn occupies in your natal chart indicates how you approach discipline, structure, and the pursuit of goals.

- House Placement: The house where Saturn is located in your chart points to the area of life where you encounter limitations, responsibilities, and the need for discipline. It shows where you are likely to face challenges that require patience, structure, and steady effort to overcome.

Saturn and the Tenth House

Saturn has a natural affinity with the Tenth House, often referred to as the "house of career and reputation." This house governs your ambitions, public image, and long-term goals. As the planet of discipline and responsibility, Saturn aligns closely with the Tenth House's themes of structure and achievement.

When Saturn is in the Tenth House, individuals are often highly driven to succeed and build a lasting legacy. They value hard work, perseverance, and the respect that comes with accomplishment. This placement emphasizes the importance of setting goals and steadily working toward them.

While Saturn here fosters ambition and resilience, it can also bring challenges, such as fear of failure or an overly serious approach to life. Balancing discipline with self-compassion helps these individuals achieve their goals while maintaining personal fulfillment.

The Movement of Saturn

Saturn typically spends about 2.5 years in each sign, making it one of the slower-moving planets in astrology. It completes its full journey through all 12 zodiac signs approximately every 29-30 years.

Saturn Retrograde

Saturn retrograde occurs about once a year, lasting approximately four and a half months, and influences discipline, structure, and responsibility. This period is a time for rethinking long-term commitments, reviewing responsibilities, and addressing areas where unnecessary restrictions may have been established. It encourages introspection about the foundations of your life and whether your personal, professional, or financial structures need reworking or refinement. In a natal chart, Saturn retrograde often suggests that lessons related to discipline, responsibility, and boundaries are approached in a more introspective and self-directed manner. Individuals with this placement may question traditional forms of authority and structure, seeking to create their own sense of responsibility rather than conforming strictly to societal expectations. They may experience an inner struggle with self-doubt or feelings of being overly burdened by external or internal expectations, prompting a need for careful self-evaluation in handling commitments and limitations. This placement fosters personal growth through reassessing life's foundations and encourages the development of a unique, internally driven approach to achieving long-term goals with reflection and patience.

Saturn's "Home" – Its Comfort Zone

- **Ruling Signs – Capricorn and Aquarius:** Saturn rules Capricorn and is the traditional ruler of Aquarius, making these signs its natural homes. In Capricorn, Saturn expresses its qualities of discipline, ambition, and the pursuit of goals through hard work. Individuals with Saturn in Capricorn are often diligent, responsible, and focused on achieving success through perseverance and careful planning. In Aquarius, Saturn's influence is channeled into the realm of intellect, innovation, and societal structures. This placement encourages disciplined thinking, a commitment to progress, and the development of unique, yet practical, solutions to problems.

Saturn in its "Exaltation" – Libra

When a planet is in its "exaltation," it expresses its natural qualities with ease and strength. Saturn is exalted in Libra, where its disciplined nature aligns with Libra's focus on balance, fairness, and relationships.

- **Balance and Justice:** In Libra, Saturn emphasizes the importance of fairness, justice, and responsibility in relationships. This placement suggests a strong sense of duty toward creating balance and harmony in partnerships, often leading to a diplomatic and measured approach to handling conflicts.
- **Commitment in Relationships:** Saturn in Libra is characterized by a serious, committed approach to relationships. It values long-term, stable partnerships and is willing to work through challenges to maintain harmony. Individuals with this

placement are often reliable, loyal, and considerate, seeking to build partnerships based on mutual respect and balance.

- **Structured Diplomacy:** Libra's diplomatic nature complements Saturn's desire for structure, promoting a strategic, methodical approach to problem-solving and decision-making. This placement fosters a careful, thoughtful approach to relationships, emphasizing the importance of boundaries and clear agreements.

- **Positive Aspects:** The exaltation of Saturn in Libra brings qualities like patience, fairness, and the ability to build stable, enduring relationships. It encourages a balanced approach to responsibility, where discipline and harmony coexist, leading to success in areas that require collaboration and mutual effort.

Saturn in its "Detriment" and "Fall" – Cancer and Aries

When a planet is in its "detriment" or "fall," it struggles to express its natural qualities. Saturn is in its detriment in Cancer and in its fall in Aries, presenting challenges to its structured, disciplined nature.

- **Saturn in Cancer (Detriment):** Cancer's emotional, nurturing focus can clash with Saturn's preference for structure and boundaries. In Cancer, Saturn's energy is directed toward emotional security, often leading to fears of vulnerability or difficulties expressing emotions. This placement suggests a need to work on building emotional resilience, learning to set healthy boundaries, and creating a secure, supportive home environment. While it can result in strong protective instincts, it may struggle with balancing emotional needs and responsibilities.

- **Saturn in Aries (Fall):** Aries' impulsive, action-oriented nature contrasts with Saturn's methodical, disciplined energy. In Aries, Saturn's influence can lead to challenges in asserting oneself or acting decisively. This placement often requires learning how to balance caution with courage, developing the patience needed to pursue goals steadily. While it can foster a pioneering spirit with careful planning, it may struggle with the impulsiveness and impatience that Aries naturally embodies.

Despite these challenges, both placements offer unique strengths. Saturn in Cancer brings deep emotional strength and the ability to nurture and protect loved ones, while Saturn in Aries offers courage, determination, and the potential for pioneering new paths with careful planning.

Summary

Saturn in astrology governs discipline, structure, responsibility, and the lessons learned through overcoming obstacles. It shapes how you approach challenges, set boundaries, and work toward long-term goals. As the ruler of Capricorn, the traditional ruler of Aquarius and the natural tenant of the Tenth House, Saturn thrives in environments that require perseverance, structure, and commitment to achieving results. Understanding Saturn's sign, house placement, and aspects in a natal chart reveals where you face restrictions, how you exercise discipline, and the life lessons you need to learn. Recognizing Saturn's exaltation in Libra and its challenges in Cancer and Aries adds depth to how this planet influences your approach to responsibility, relationships, and the development of inner strength.

Uranus: The Planet of Innovation and Change

Symbols: ♅ ⛢

Uranus in astrology represents innovation, change, liberation, and the unexpected. It governs rebellion, individuality, originality, and the drive to break free from conventions. Uranus embodies the principles of sudden change, awakening, and disruption, urging you to explore new ways of thinking and to embrace your uniqueness. It is the planet of surprises, revolutions, and insights that push you beyond the boundaries of the known.

What Uranus Represents

- **Innovation and Change:** Uranus is the planet of innovation and radical change. It signifies the drive to explore new possibilities, challenge the status quo, and bring about revolutionary ideas. Its placement in your chart indicates where you seek to innovate and where you are willing to take risks to bring about significant transformations.

- **Freedom and Independence:** Uranus represents the desire for freedom and independence. It influences how you express your individuality and resist limitations or restrictions. This planet's energy often leads to a need for personal space and autonomy, highlighting where you wish to break free from societal norms and traditional expectations.

- **Sudden Insights and Awakenings:** Uranus governs sudden insights, revelations, and flashes of genius. It symbolizes moments of awakening that can radically shift your perspective and understanding. Uranus' placement reveals the areas of life where you may experience sudden changes, breakthroughs, and moments of clarity that challenge old ways of thinking.

- **Rebellion and Unconventionality:** Uranus is associated with rebellion, eccentricity, and a desire to go against the grain. It represents the part of you that is unafraid to stand out, challenge conventions, and embrace your unique qualities. Its influence can lead to a strong sense of nonconformity and the urge to pursue a path that is distinctly your own.

- Technology and Progress: Uranus also governs technology, science, and futuristic thinking. It is connected to advances in technology, innovation in communication, and the pursuit of progress. This planet encourages you to explore new realms, both intellectually and scientifically, and to embrace the future with an open mind.

Qualities of Uranus

- Masculine, Active, and Electric: Uranus embodies a masculine, active energy characterized by an electric, dynamic quality. It represents the part of you that seeks excitement, adventure, and the thrill of the unknown. Uranus' energy is disruptive, breaking through limitations to reveal new possibilities.

- Fixed and Unpredictable: Uranus has a fixed quality, often indicating a strong commitment to individuality and the desire for personal freedom. However, its energy is also unpredictable, creating sudden shifts and changes that can alter the course of events unexpectedly.

- Element of Air: Uranus resonates with the Air element, highlighting qualities of intellectual exploration, communication, and forward-thinking. It brings an analytical, abstract approach to life, favoring ideas that challenge conventional thinking and encourage growth and expansion.

Uranus in the Natal Chart

- Uranus' Sign: The sign Uranus occupies in your natal chart indicates how you express your individuality, embrace change, and seek freedom. Since Uranus spends about 7 years in each sign, it influences entire generations, indicating broader societal shifts and changes.

- House Placement: The house where Uranus is located in your chart points to the area of life where you experience disruption, innovation, and the need for independence. It highlights where you are likely to encounter sudden changes, unexpected events, and where you can best express your unique qualities.

Uranus and the Eleventh House

Uranus has a natural affinity with the Eleventh House, often called the "house of community and innovation." This house governs friendships, social networks, and aspirations for the future. As the planet of change and originality, Uranus aligns with the Eleventh House's themes of progress and collective growth.

When Uranus is in the Eleventh House, individuals often bring unique, forward-thinking energy to their social circles and long-term goals. They value independence and may seek friendships that inspire creativity and unconventional ideas. This placement highlights a desire to challenge societal norms and contribute to change on a larger scale.

While Uranus here fosters innovation and individuality, it can also create unpredictability in relationships or difficulty adhering to group norms. Learning to balance personal freedom with collaboration can help these individuals thrive in both personal and collective pursuits.

The Movement of Uranus

Uranus typically spends about 7 years in each zodiac sign, making it the third slowest-moving planet in astrology. It takes approximately 84 years to complete a full cycle through all 12 signs.

Uranus Retrograde

Uranus retrograde occurs once a year and lasts for about five months, influencing themes of innovation, rebellion, and change. During this time, the energy for outward transformation may slow, encouraging a more introspective focus on the desire for freedom and sudden shifts. It becomes a period for reflecting on where old patterns need to be broken and for preparing for future change. Personal revolutions or sudden insights often emerge during this time, reshaping one's perspective. In a natal chart, Uranus retrograde indicates that the individual's drive for innovation, rebellion, and personal freedom is often expressed inwardly. These individuals may feel a strong internal urge for change but take a more deliberate or subtle approach to manifesting it externally. They frequently experience profound insights or breakthroughs that first transform their inner world before leading to external actions. This placement fosters a unique sense of independence and a preference for unconventional paths, often resisting societal norms through quiet reflection or behind-the-scenes changes. It encourages internal revolutions, leading to gradual but deeply transformative growth over time.

Uranus' "Home" – Its Comfort Zone
- **Ruling Sign – Aquarius:** Uranus rules Aquarius, making this sign its natural home. In Aquarius, Uranus expresses its full potential for innovation, independence, and futuristic thinking. Individuals with Uranus in Aquarius often possess a strong sense of individuality, a drive for social reform, and a unique perspective on life. They are natural rebels, drawn to technology, science, and new ideas that challenge conventional wisdom. This placement emphasizes a humanitarian approach to change, with a desire to use innovation and unconventional thinking to benefit society as a whole.

Uranus in its "Exaltation" – Scorpio
When a planet is in its "exaltation," it expresses its natural qualities with ease and strength. Uranus is exalted in Scorpio, where its revolutionary energy aligns with Scorpio's intensity, depth, and transformative nature.
- **Deep Transformation:** In Scorpio, Uranus brings a powerful drive for deep, radical transformation. This placement suggests an intense desire to explore the unknown, uncover hidden truths, and challenge existing power structures. It provides the courage to dive into taboo subjects and confront societal or personal limitations head-on.
- **Passion for Change:** Scorpio's passionate, focused nature complements Uranus's need for change, resulting in a strong drive to reform and transform. This placement often indicates an

individual who is unafraid to face upheaval to achieve a greater understanding of themselves and the world around them. They can be catalysts for profound changes in society, especially in areas that involve power dynamics, secrets, and the human psyche.

- **Intuitive Insights:** Uranus in Scorpio heightens intuitive insights and the ability to perceive beyond the surface. This placement fosters a deep, psychological understanding of change, encouraging breakthroughs that lead to personal and collective evolution.

- **Positive Aspects:** The exaltation of Uranus in Scorpio brings qualities like fearlessness, intensity, and the ability to facilitate deep transformations. It encourages a transformative mindset, where disruption and change are embraced as pathways to greater truth and understanding.

Uranus in its "Detriment" and "Fall" – Leo and Taurus

When a planet is in its "detriment" or "fall," it struggles to express its natural qualities. Uranus is in its detriment in Leo and in its fall in Taurus, presenting challenges to its free-spirited, unconventional nature.

- **Uranus in Leo (Detriment):** Leo's focus on self-expression, pride, and the need for admiration can clash with Uranus' desire for individuality and rebellion. In Leo, Uranus may express its need for change in dramatic or attention-seeking ways. This placement can lead to a tendency to rebel for the sake of standing out or to resist conforming to traditional roles of leadership and creativity. While it can inspire original self-expression and bold creativity, it may struggle with balancing the need for freedom with the desire for recognition.

- **Uranus in Taurus (Fall):** Taurus' fixed, practical nature contrasts with Uranus's drive for change and unpredictability. In Taurus, Uranus challenges the desire for stability and routine, often bringing sudden changes in areas related to material security, values, and the physical world. This placement can lead to disruptions in financial matters, personal values, or physical environments. While it encourages innovative thinking regarding resources and security, it may struggle with the tension between the need for stability and the desire for radical change.

Despite these challenges, both placements have unique strengths. Uranus in Leo brings originality and a bold approach to creativity and self-expression, while Uranus in Taurus offers innovative thinking in relation to material resources, values, and the natural world.

Summary

Uranus in astrology governs innovation, change, rebellion, and the drive for freedom. It shapes how you break free from conventions, embrace originality, and pursue radical change in your life. As the ruler of Aquarius and the natural tenant of the Eleventh House, Uranus thrives in environments that encourage individuality, progressive thinking, and social reform. Understanding Uranus's sign, house placement, and aspects in a natal chart reveals where you seek independence, experience sudden changes, and express your unique qualities. Recognizing Uranus's exaltation in Scorpio and its challenges in Leo and Taurus adds depth to how this planet influences your journey toward liberation, transformation, and the pursuit of a future that defies limitations.

Neptune: The Planet of Dreams and Illusions

Symbol: ♆

Neptune in astrology represents dreams, intuition, spirituality, and the realm of the unseen. It governs imagination, mysticism, illusion, and the dissolution of boundaries. Neptune embodies the principles of inspiration, compassion, and the longing to transcend the mundane reality. It guides you toward exploring the deeper, more spiritual aspects of existence, often through creativity, dreams, and a connection to the collective unconscious.

What Neptune Represents

- **Dreams and Imagination:** Neptune is the planet of dreams and imagination. It inspires creativity, fantasy, and a rich inner world. Its placement in your chart reveals how you connect with your dreams, how you express creativity, and where you might escape from reality into the realms of imagination.

- **Spirituality and Mysticism:** Neptune governs spirituality, mysticism, and the search for a deeper connection with the universe. It symbolizes the longing to understand the spiritual mysteries of life and to connect with something greater than the self. Neptune's influence can guide you toward exploring spiritual practices, meditation, and the pursuit of divine truth.

- **Intuition and Psychic Sensitivity:** Neptune enhances intuition and psychic sensitivity, representing your ability to perceive subtle energies and understand things beyond the logical mind. Its placement indicates where you may experience heightened intuition, empathy, and an innate understanding of the interconnectedness of all life.

- **Illusion and Deception:** Neptune also rules illusion, deception, and confusion. It blurs boundaries, making it difficult to see things clearly. This planet can create foggy perceptions, fantasies, and idealizations that may lead to misunderstandings, unrealistic expectations, or escapism. Its influence can show where you might be prone to delusions or where things are not as they seem.

- Compassion and Selflessness: Neptune embodies compassion, selflessness, and the desire to dissolve personal boundaries to connect with others. It represents unconditional love and the urge to help those in need. Neptune's placement in your chart reveals how you express compassion and where you are most likely to sacrifice for the sake of others.

Qualities of Neptune

- Feminine, Receptive, and Fluid: Neptune embodies a feminine, receptive energy that is fluid, changeable, and boundless. It represents the part of you that is sensitive, empathetic, and open to the mysteries of life. Neptune's energy is gentle, mysterious, and all-encompassing, often leading to experiences that transcend ordinary reality.

- Mutable and Uncertain: Neptune has a mutable quality, indicating flexibility, adaptability, and a tendency to flow with the currents of life. Its influence is often elusive and hard to grasp, bringing uncertainty and the dissolution of clear boundaries. Neptune's energy is like water, constantly changing form and difficult to contain or define.

- Element of Water: Neptune resonates with the Water element, highlighting emotions, intuition, and the subconscious. It brings a deep connection to feelings, dreams, and the unseen realms, encouraging empathy, creativity, and the desire to merge with something greater than oneself.

Neptune in the Natal Chart

- Neptune Sign: The sign Neptune occupies in your natal chart indicates how you express your imagination, spirituality, and ideals. Since Neptune spends about 14 years in each sign, it influences entire generations, reflecting broader trends in spirituality, creativity, and cultural ideals.

- House Placement: The house where Neptune is located in your chart points to the area of life where you are most likely to experience dreams, illusions, spiritual insights, and heightened intuition. It shows where you may encounter confusion, sacrifice, or inspiration and where you may seek to transcend ordinary reality.

Neptune and the Twelfth House

Neptune has a natural affinity with the Twelfth House, often called the "house of the subconscious and spirituality." This house governs dreams, intuition, hidden aspects of the self, and connection to the unseen. As the planet of imagination and transcendence, Neptune resonates deeply with the Twelfth House's themes of mysticism and introspection.

When Neptune is in the Twelfth House, individuals often possess heightened intuition and a deep connection to their inner world. They are drawn to spirituality, creativity, and helping others in unseen or subtle ways. This placement emphasizes compassion, empathy, and the potential for profound spiritual growth.

While Neptune here fosters a rich inner life, it can also lead to escapism or difficulty distinguishing reality from fantasy. Developing grounding practices helps individuals channel Neptune's energy constructively, allowing them to embrace their sensitivity and imagination without losing touch with the material world.

The Movement of Neptune

Neptune typically spends about 14 years in each zodiac sign, making it the second slowest-moving planet in astrology. It takes approximately 165 years to complete a full cycle through all 12 signs.

Neptune Retrograde

Neptune retrograde occurs once a year, lasting about five months, and influences themes of dreams, intuition, spirituality, and illusions. During this period, the boundary between reality and fantasy becomes thinner, making it easier to see through illusions or false narratives. It offers an opportunity for clarity, particularly in areas where self-deception or overly idealistic thinking may have clouded judgment. This time is ideal for deep spiritual reflection, meditation, and grounding, allowing for a more realistic understanding of one's aspirations and beliefs. In a natal chart, Neptune retrograde indicates that an individual's connection to intuition, spirituality, and imagination tends to be more internalized or subtle. These individuals often possess a heightened awareness of the fine line between reality and illusion, leading them to question idealistic dreams or fantasies they hold. They may undergo profound internal exploration of their spiritual beliefs, striving to discern what is real versus what is rooted in escapism or wishful thinking. Over time, this placement fosters self-reflection and growth, helping individuals cultivate a grounded yet spiritual perspective that aligns their ideals with a more realistic and balanced approach to life.

Neptune's "Home" – Its Comfort Zone

- **Ruling Sign – Pisces:** Neptune rules Pisces, making this sign its natural home. In Pisces, Neptune expresses its full potential for empathy, imagination, and spiritual connection. Individuals with Neptune in Pisces often possess deep compassion, psychic sensitivity, and an inclination toward exploring spiritual or mystical realms. They may experience an intense connection to the collective unconscious and are often drawn to artistic, musical, or healing pursuits that allow them to express their inner visions and emotions. This placement emphasizes a desire for unity, transcendence, and the dissolution of boundaries between self and others.

Neptune in its "Exaltation" – Cancer

When a planet is in its "exaltation," it expresses its natural qualities with ease and strength. Neptune is exalted in Cancer, where its compassionate, nurturing nature aligns with Cancer's focus on home, family, and emotional security.

- **Emotional Depth:** In Cancer, Neptune enhances emotional sensitivity, empathy, and the ability to connect with others on a deep, nurturing level. This placement suggests a strong capacity for compassion and the desire to care for those around you. It promotes an intuitive understanding of others' feelings and a natural inclination toward providing comfort and support.

- **Creative Imagination:** Cancer's connection to the inner emotional world complements Neptune's imaginative qualities, fostering creativity, especially in areas related to the arts, home life, and family traditions. This placement encourages you to create a nurturing environment filled with beauty, love, and an appreciation for the mystical aspects of life.

- **Spiritual Connection to Home:** Neptune in Cancer emphasizes a spiritual approach to family and home, highlighting the importance of creating a sanctuary that reflects your inner emotional world. This placement fosters a strong sense of emotional safety and the use of intuition in caring for loved ones.

- **Positive Aspects:** The exaltation of Neptune in Cancer brings qualities like deep compassion, intuitive nurturing, and a heightened capacity for emotional expression. It encourages the blending of spiritual and emotional aspects of life, resulting in a profound understanding of the importance of unconditional love and care.

Neptune in its "Detriment" and "Fall" – Virgo and Aquarius

When a planet is in its "detriment" or "fall," it struggles to express its natural qualities. Neptune is in its detriment in Virgo and in its fall in Aquarius, presenting challenges to its mystical, idealistic nature.

- **Neptune in Virgo (Detriment):** Virgo's focus on practicality, order, and details can clash with Neptune's preference for dreams, imagination, and fluidity. In Virgo, Neptune's energy is directed toward service, health, and the mundane aspects of life, which can lead to confusion between reality and idealism. This placement suggests a struggle to balance the desire for perfection with the acceptance of life's imperfections. While it fosters a compassionate, service-oriented mindset, it may also lead to disillusionment when reality does not meet idealistic expectations.

- **Neptune in Aquarius (Fall):** Aquarius' focus on intellectual detachment, logic, and progress contrasts with Neptune's emotional, intuitive nature. In Aquarius, Neptune may express its spirituality in unconventional, abstract ways, often leading to a desire for universal connection without the deep emotional involvement Neptune typically embodies. This placement can result in an intellectualized approach to spirituality and idealism, emphasizing collective ideals over personal emotional experiences. While it encourages innovative thinking in spiritual or humanitarian matters, it may struggle with the emotional depth and compassion that Neptune naturally seeks.

Despite these challenges, both placements offer unique strengths. Neptune in Virgo brings a compassionate, detail-oriented approach to helping others and finding spirituality in daily life, while Neptune in Aquarius fosters visionary thinking, humanitarian ideals, and a desire for social change.

Summary

Neptune in astrology governs dreams, intuition, spirituality, and the boundaries between reality and illusion. It shapes how you connect with your inner world, express creativity, and pursue the deeper meaning of life. As the ruler of Pisces and the natural tenant of the Twelfth House, Neptune thrives in environments that encourage imagination, empathy, and spiritual exploration. Understanding Neptune's sign, house placement, and aspects in a natal chart reveals how you experience inspiration, where you might face illusions or confusion, and how you seek to transcend ordinary reality. Recognizing Neptune's exaltation in Cancer and its challenges in Virgo and Aquarius adds depth to how this planet influences your dreams, ideals, and the journey toward spiritual understanding and compassion.

Pluto: The Planet of Transformation and Power

Symbol: ♇

Pluto in astrology represents transformation, power, rebirth, and the depths of the subconscious. It governs the forces of change, destruction, and regeneration, pushing you to confront your fears and embrace profound personal growth. Pluto embodies the principles of death and rebirth, encouraging you to let go of what no longer serves you and to rise stronger and more empowered from the ashes. It rules over the hidden aspects of life, including secrets, taboos, and the mysteries of the psyche.

What Pluto Represents
- **Transformation and Rebirth:** Pluto is the planet of transformation and rebirth. It symbolizes the process of shedding old layers to reveal a more authentic self. Pluto's placement in your chart indicates where you are likely to experience deep personal transformation, often through intense challenges, crises, or powerful emotional experiences. It represents the areas of life where you must let go to grow.
- **Power and Control:** Pluto governs power, control, and the dynamics of dominance and submission. It reveals where you seek power or where power struggles may occur in your life. Pluto's influence can teach you how to reclaim your personal power, confront issues of control, and transform situations where you feel powerless.
- **The Subconscious and Shadow:** Pluto represents the subconscious mind and the shadow self. It delves into the hidden aspects of your psyche, bringing to light fears, desires, and suppressed emotions. Pluto's placement highlights areas where you may need to confront deep-seated fears, obsessions, or unresolved issues that reside in your subconscious.
- **Intimacy and Shared Resources:** Pluto is associated with intimacy, shared resources, and the merging of energies. It governs

deep connections, such as those found in close relationships, sexuality, and financial partnerships. Pluto's influence indicates where you experience intense, transformative connections with others and how you handle shared resources, power, and trust.

- **Destruction and Renewal:** Pluto also represents destruction, decay, and the cycle of death and rebirth. It breaks down what is outdated or corrupt, clearing the way for new growth and renewal. This planet's energy often brings endings that lead to new beginnings, helping you evolve and transform through the process of letting go.

Qualities of Pluto

- **Masculine, Powerful, and Intense:** Pluto embodies a masculine energy that is powerful, intense, and unyielding. It represents the force within you that confronts challenges head-on and the drive to dig deep into the core of your being to find the truth. Pluto's influence is magnetic, drawing you toward intense experiences and transformations.

- **Fixed and Unrelenting:** Pluto has a fixed quality, emphasizing endurance and the capacity to undergo radical change. Its energy is unrelenting and uncompromising, often manifesting through a slow but powerful process of transformation that requires persistence, resilience, and an unwavering will.

- **Element of Water:** Pluto resonates with the Water element, highlighting emotional depth, intuition, and the power of the subconscious. It brings a penetrating understanding of emotions and an intense focus on the underlying motives, desires, and truths that shape your experiences.

Pluto in the Natal Chart

- **Pluto Sign:** The sign Pluto occupies in your natal chart indicates how you approach transformation, power, and control. Since Pluto spends about 12 to 30 years in each sign, it influences entire generations, reflecting broader societal changes and shifts in collective consciousness.

- **House Placement:** The house where Pluto is located in your chart points to the area of life where you are likely to experience deep transformation, power struggles, and the need to confront your fears. It reveals where you may encounter profound changes, intense emotional experiences, and the potential for rebirth.

Pluto and the Eighth House

Pluto has a natural affinity with the Eighth House, often referred to as the "house of transformation and shared resources." This house governs deep emotional bonds, personal transformation, power dynamics, and matters of life, death, and rebirth. As the planet of intensity and renewal, Pluto aligns powerfully with the Eighth House's themes of profound change and hidden depths.

When Pluto is in the Eighth House, individuals often experience transformative growth through their relationships, emotional connections, and challenges. They possess a natural ability to delve into the unseen, uncovering hidden truths and finding strength through adversity. This placement emphasizes resilience and the potential for personal empowerment.

While Pluto here fosters depth and regeneration, it can also bring struggles with control, fear of vulnerability, or difficulty letting go. Learning to embrace change and trust the process of transformation allows these individuals to harness Pluto's power for healing and growth.

The Movement of Pluto

Pluto spends approximately 12 to 30 years in each zodiac sign, depending on its elliptical orbit, making it the slowest-moving planet in astrology. It takes about 248 years to complete a full cycle through all 12 signs.

Pluto Retrograde

Pluto retrograde occurs once a year and lasts for about five to six months, focusing on themes of transformation, power, control, and deep psychological change. During this time, Pluto's intense energy turns inward, encouraging self-reflection and a confrontation with fears, shadows, and issues related to power and control. It is a period for inner transformation, allowing for the release of old patterns and the embrace of personal evolution. In a natal chart, Pluto retrograde signifies that transformation, power, and control are experienced more internally, often taking longer to manifest outwardly. Individuals with this placement are drawn to explore their inner world, uncovering hidden fears, desires, and suppressed emotions. They tend to be introspective about how power and control operate in their lives, leading to profound inner transformations over time. This placement fosters personal evolution by encouraging individuals to confront their shadows, work through past traumas, and release outdated patterns, ultimately paving the way for deep and lasting change. Those with Pluto retrograde often experience quiet but significant personal growth throughout their lives.

Pluto's "Home" – Its Comfort Zone
- **Ruling Sign – Scorpio:** Pluto rules Scorpio, making this sign its natural home. In Scorpio, Pluto expresses its full potential for intensity, depth, and transformation. Individuals with Pluto in Scorpio are often drawn to explore the mysteries of life, such as psychology, spirituality, and the hidden forces that drive human behavior. They possess a strong will, a desire for deep emotional experiences, and the courage to confront their fears. This placement emphasizes a passion for exploring taboo topics, a profound understanding of power dynamics, and the capacity for significant personal transformation.

Pluto in its "Exaltation" – Aries
When a planet is in its "exaltation," it expresses its natural qualities with ease and strength. Pluto is considered exalted in Aries, where its transformative energy aligns with Aries' courage, initiative, and drive for change.
- **Bold Transformation:** In Aries, Pluto enhances the drive to break through obstacles and initiate profound transformations. This placement suggests a fearless approach to change, where the individual is unafraid to confront challenges head-on. There is a willingness to take the necessary risks to pursue personal power

and self-mastery.

- **Empowerment through Action:** Aries' dynamic nature complements Pluto's intensity, resulting in a powerful drive to take action and assert control over one's life. This placement fosters a strong sense of personal empowerment, urging the individual to confront their fears and pursue their goals with determination and passion.

- **Positive Aspects:** The exaltation of Pluto in Aries brings qualities like courage, initiative, and the ability to embrace transformation with enthusiasm. It encourages a proactive approach to dealing with life's challenges, where obstacles are seen as opportunities for growth and self-discovery.

Pluto in its "Detriment" and "Fall" – Taurus and Libra

When a planet is in its "detriment" or "fall," it struggles to express its natural qualities. Pluto is in its detriment in Taurus and in its fall in Libra, presenting challenges to its intense, transformative nature.

- **Pluto in Taurus (Detriment):** Taurus' focus on stability, comfort, and the material world can clash with Pluto's desire for deep, transformative change. In Taurus, Pluto's energy may manifest as a strong attachment to possessions, values, or routines, making it difficult to embrace change. This placement suggests a struggle between the desire for security and the need for transformation. While it can foster the power to manifest tangible results through persistence, it may also lead to resistance against necessary change and an intense fear of loss.

- **Pluto in Libra (Fall):** Libra's focus on harmony, balance, and relationships contrasts with Pluto's intensity and desire for control. In Libra, Pluto's energy is directed toward transforming relationships, often bringing challenges related to power dynamics, control, and trust within partnerships. This placement can indicate a tendency to experience power struggles in close relationships or an inclination to avoid confronting the darker aspects of connections for the sake of maintaining peace. While it encourages the pursuit of deep, transformative connections, it may struggle with balancing the desire for harmony with the need to confront difficult truths.

Despite these challenges, both placements have unique strengths. Pluto in Taurus brings a powerful, enduring energy that can create lasting changes in the material realm, while Pluto in Libra fosters a deep understanding of relationships and the complexities of human connections.

Summary

Pluto in astrology governs transformation, power, rebirth, and the depths of the subconscious. It shapes how you experience intense changes, reclaim personal power, and confront hidden aspects of yourself. As the ruler of Scorpio and the natural tenant of the Eighth House, Pluto thrives in environments that encourage deep exploration, emotional intensity, and the embrace of life's cycles of death and rebirth. Understanding Pluto's sign, house placement, and aspects in a natal chart reveals where you face profound transformation, the areas where power dynamics are at play, and how you connect with the deeper, hidden forces of life. Recognizing Pluto's exaltation in Aries and its challenges in Taurus and Libra adds depth to how this planet influences your journey toward self-mastery, empowerment, and embracing the process of continual growth and renewal.

Part of Fortune: The Point of Prosperity and Joy

Symbol: ⊗

The Part of Fortune in astrology represents the areas of life where you are likely to find joy, success, and a sense of fulfillment. Unlike planets, the Part of Fortune is a sensitive point in the natal chart, calculated using the positions of the Sun, Moon, and Ascendant. It symbolizes the harmony between your inner self, emotions, and outer expression, providing insights into where your efforts can bring you prosperity and happiness.

What the Part of Fortune Represents

- **Path to Prosperity:** The Part of Fortune is often associated with fortune, luck, and prosperity. Its placement in your natal chart reveals where you can naturally find success and where you might encounter opportunities for abundance. It indicates how you can harness your talents, skills, and resources to create a life of well-being.

- **Harmony and Fulfillment:** The Part of Fortune reflects the harmony between your Sun (conscious self), Moon (emotional self), and Ascendant (outer expression). When these elements are balanced, you are more likely to experience a sense of inner satisfaction and fulfillment. The Part of Fortune points to areas in life where you can align your true nature with the world around you, leading to a greater sense of happiness and purpose.

- **Joy and Well-Being:** This point in the chart symbolizes where you find joy, contentment, and a sense of peace. It represents the pursuits and activities that naturally bring you happiness. The Part of Fortune indicates how you can achieve a sense of inner balance and harmony, allowing you to thrive in different aspects of life.

- **Success and Growth:** The Part of Fortune guides you toward personal growth by highlighting where your natural abilities and efforts can lead to success. It shows where you are likely to overcome obstacles and find a rewarding path forward. By focusing on the qualities and areas associated with your Part of Fortune, you can unlock your potential for success and growth.

Qualities of the Part of Fortune
- **Neutral and Harmonizing:** The Part of Fortune is neutral in nature, embodying both masculine and feminine qualities. It does not exert influence like a planet but rather acts as a guiding point that harmonizes the energies of the Sun, Moon, and Ascendant. Its energy is receptive and works best when you are in tune with your inner self and outer circumstances.
- **Reflective and Revealing:** The Part of Fortune reveals insights into your potential for happiness, success, and the pursuit of your true path. It reflects where you can achieve balance between your conscious desires, emotional needs, and outward personality. This point encourages you to explore the areas of life that align with your true nature and where you can express your gifts fully.
- **Personalized:** The significance of the Part of Fortune varies for each individual, as it is calculated based on your unique planetary and point positions. Therefore, it provides a highly personalized indication of the areas in life that are most likely to bring you joy and prosperity.

The Part of Fortune in the Natal Chart
- **Sign Placement:** The sign in which the Part of Fortune is placed in your natal chart indicates the qualities you need to cultivate to find success and fulfillment.
- **House Placement:** The house where the Part of Fortune is located reveals the area of life where you are most likely to find joy, success, and a sense of well-being. It points to the domain in which you can naturally align your inner self with your outer circumstances.

The Movement of the Part of Fortune
The Part of Fortune is a calculated point in the birth chart, derived from the positions of the Sun, Moon, and Ascendant. Its movement is directly tied to these three celestial points, meaning it shifts dynamically as they do. Specifically, the Part of Fortune moves

through the zodiac in alignment with the daily rotation of the Earth, completing a full cycle through all 12 signs roughly every 24 hours. This rapid movement ensures that its placement is highly sensitive to the time and location of birth.

The Part of Fortune's "Home" – Comfort and Alignment

- **Harmony with the Sun, Moon, and Ascendant:** The Part of Fortune feels "at home" when there is alignment between the Sun, Moon, and Ascendant in your chart. This alignment creates a flow of energy that supports your pursuit of happiness, success, and inner harmony. When you express the qualities of the sign and house of your Part of Fortune, you align with the path of least resistance and unlock the potential for prosperity.

- **Integration of Your Chart:** Since the Part of Fortune is calculated using the positions of the Sun, Moon, and Ascendant, it represents the synthesis of these key aspects of your chart. When you integrate the energies of your conscious desires (Sun), emotional needs (Moon), and outward expression (Ascendant) in the area indicated by the Part of Fortune, you find a sense of ease, balance, and joy.

The Part of Fortune in Challenging Placements

While the Part of Fortune does not have traditional exaltations, detriments, or falls like the planets, its placement can present challenges depending on the sign and house it occupies, as well as the aspects it forms.

- **Difficult Aspects:** When the Part of Fortune forms challenging aspects (e.g., squares or oppositions) with planets such as Saturn or Pluto, it may indicate obstacles on your path to success. These aspects suggest that you may need to work through certain fears, limitations, or deep-seated issues before finding prosperity in the area it represents. For example, a square with Saturn might indicate that hard work, patience, and discipline are necessary to achieve the joy and fulfillment the Part of Fortune promises.

- **Challenging Houses:** If the Part of Fortune is in houses associated with difficulties (e.g., the 8th or 12th house), the path to joy and success may involve overcoming deep psychological challenges, transformations, or sacrifices. In these placements, the Part of Fortune indicates that true prosperity comes through facing and integrating hidden aspects of yourself, such as exploring your subconscious (12th house) or navigating intense emotional experiences (8th house).

Summary

The Part of Fortune in astrology represents the areas of life where you are likely to find joy, prosperity, and fulfillment. It highlights the path to success by revealing where you can harmonize your inner desires, emotions, and outward expression. Understanding the Part of Fortune's sign, house placement, and aspects in your natal chart provides insights into how you can align with your true nature to unlock abundance and well-being. While it does not have traditional exaltations or detriments, challenging aspects or placements can indicate areas that require deeper work to achieve the joy and success that the Part of Fortune offers. By embracing the qualities of this point in your chart, you can navigate life with a sense of purpose, harmony, and fulfillment.

Vertex: The Point of Fate and Destiny

Symbol: Vx

The Vertex in astrology represents significant encounters, fated events, and pivotal turning points in your life. It is often referred to as the "Destiny's Gate" or "Fated Point" and is located on the western side of the chart, typically in the 5th, 6th, 7th, or 8th houses. The Vertex indicates experiences that come from outside your control, usually involving other people, relationships, or life-changing events that alter your path.

What the Vertex Represents

- **Fated Encounters:** The Vertex is associated with meetings and relationships that feel destined. It highlights people and situations that have a profound impact on your life, often occurring unexpectedly and bringing a sense of inevitability. These encounters are often transformative, forcing you to grow and adapt in ways you hadn't anticipated.

- **Turning Points:** The Vertex marks turning points or significant moments that can alter your life direction. It can indicate times when you face crucial choices, life-changing events, or circumstances that push you toward a new path. These experiences are often beyond your control and feel as though they are guided by a higher force.

- **Karmic Connections:** This point in the chart is linked to karmic relationships and experiences. It suggests that certain people or situations are meant to come into your life to fulfill a deeper purpose or lesson. The Vertex's placement provides insight into the types of experiences that will challenge you, expand your perspective, and contribute to your personal evolution.

- **Personal Growth and Self-Realization:** The Vertex symbolizes situations that lead to self-discovery and personal growth. It often involves interactions that push you out of your comfort zone and encourage you to explore aspects of yourself that you may have previously overlooked. These encounters often

173

highlight hidden potentials and aspects of your personality that need to be developed.

Qualities of the Vertex
- **Neutral and Receptive:** The Vertex is a neutral point in the chart; it doesn't emit energy like a planet but rather acts as a doorway through which significant events and people enter your life. Its energy is receptive, indicating that these fated experiences come to you from external sources rather than being actively sought.
- **Reflective and Relational:** The Vertex is most often associated with relationships and interpersonal dynamics. Its position can reveal what types of relationships or encounters will be most transformative for you, often involving themes of partnership, cooperation, and shared experiences.
- **Catalyst for Change:** Encounters related to the Vertex often act as catalysts for change, pushing you to grow and adapt in ways that align with your deeper life purpose. It represents circumstances that challenge your existing beliefs, encouraging you to explore new perspectives and evolve.

The Vertex in the Natal Chart
- **Sign Placement:** The sign in which the Vertex is placed indicates the qualities you need to develop or the type of energy you will encounter in your fated experiences.
- **House Placement:** The house where the Vertex is located reveals the area of life where you are likely to experience significant encounters, turning points, and life-changing events. It points to the domain in which these transformative experiences are most likely to manifest.

The Movement of the Vertex
The Vertex is a calculated point in the birth chart that moves with the Earth's rotation, completing a full cycle through the zodiac approximately every 24 hours. Its position is determined by the intersection of the ecliptic (the Sun's apparent path) and the prime

vertical (a vertical circle that splits the chart into eastern and western hemispheres). Because the Vertex is location-specific, its placement varies significantly based on geographic location and the exact time of birth. This makes the Vertex highly sensitive and unique to each individual.

The Vertex's "Home" – Its Comfort Zone
- **Connection with the Descendant:** The Vertex is always located on the right side of the chart, opposite the Ascendant, near the Descendant. This placement naturally links the Vertex to relationships and interactions with others. Its comfort zone is found in experiences that involve connecting, cooperating, and relating to others. It encourages openness to the unknown, where growth occurs through fated encounters and interpersonal dynamics.
- **Integration of Your Personal and External Worlds:** The Vertex represents a point where your internal desires and the external world meet. It reflects the integration of your personal path (Ascendant) with the experiences brought by others (Descendant). When the energy of the Vertex is activated through encounters, it allows you to discover hidden aspects of your personality and to align with a more authentic expression of yourself.
- **Vertex in the 5th House:** Fated encounters often revolve around creativity, romance, and self-expression. Relationships may feel destined, and personal growth comes through embracing joy, spontaneity, and taking risks in love. Significant events may involve children, artistic pursuits, or recognizing the importance of following your passions.
- **Vertex in the 6th House:** Life-changing moments occur through work, service, and daily routines. Encounters with others may push you toward self-improvement, discipline, or healing. Fate may place you in situations where your skills and service to others play a crucial role in shaping your destiny.
- **Vertex in the 7th House:** Major turning points come through partnerships, whether romantic, business, or close friendships.

Fated relationships feel deeply significant, and important people enter your life to teach you about balance, compromise, and connection. This placement emphasizes the transformative power of one-on-one relationships.

- **Vertex in the 8th House:** Profound, fated experiences often involve deep emotional, financial, or spiritual transformations. Encounters may be intense, pulling you into themes of power, rebirth, or shared resources. Relationships may feel karmic, pushing you toward psychological growth and personal evolution.

The Vertex in Challenging Placements

While the Vertex does not have traditional exaltations, detriments, or falls like planets, its placement and aspects can indicate where you might experience challenges or growth through unexpected circumstances.

- **Difficult Aspects:** When the Vertex forms challenging aspects (e.g., squares or oppositions) with planets like Saturn or Pluto, it may indicate encounters that are difficult or involve intense personal growth. For example, a square with Saturn suggests that fated experiences may involve lessons in patience, responsibility, or dealing with authority figures, often requiring perseverance and self-discipline.

- **Karmic Lessons:** The Vertex's connection with fated events means that its placement may point to karmic lessons you need to learn in this lifetime. Challenging aspects or placements can indicate areas where you are meant to confront deep-seated patterns, release attachments, or embrace a new way of being.

Summary

The Vertex in astrology represents significant encounters, turning points, and fated events that shape your life path. It highlights where you are likely to meet people or experience situations that feel destined and that contribute to your personal growth. By embracing the lessons and transformations that the Vertex brings, you can align more deeply with your life's purpose and the unique path set out for you.

North Node: The Path of Growth and Destiny

Symbol: ♌

The North Node in astrology represents your life's purpose, karmic path, and the qualities you are meant to develop in this lifetime. It is a point of growth, guiding you toward experiences and characteristics that help you fulfill your destiny. The North Node indicates where you need to step out of your comfort zone, embrace new challenges, and evolve toward a more authentic and fulfilling expression of your potential.

What the North Node Represents

- **Life's Purpose:** The North Node points to the lessons and areas of growth that your soul seeks in this incarnation. It represents the direction you are meant to move toward, providing clues about the life path that leads to personal fulfillment and spiritual growth. It highlights the qualities, traits, and experiences that you need to embrace to become the best version of yourself.

- **Karmic Lessons:** The North Node is often linked to karma, symbolizing the lessons you are meant to learn in this lifetime. It draws you toward new experiences that push you out of your comfort zone and challenge you to let go of familiar patterns. By working with the energies of the North Node, you can release past habits (represented by the South Node) and move toward a more balanced and fulfilling life.

- **Growth and Evolution:** The North Node is about growth and evolution. It shows the areas where you need to develop new skills, attitudes, and ways of being. It may feel uncomfortable or unfamiliar, especially in the beginning, but by embracing the qualities of your North Node, you open yourself up to new possibilities, relationships, and experiences that align with your higher self.

- **Future Orientation:** While the South Node represents past experiences and habits, the North Node is future-oriented. It guides you to look forward and focus on what you can become rather than what you have been. It acts as a beacon, lighting the way toward your potential and the life that aligns with your soul's purpose.

Qualities of the North Node

- **Challenging yet Rewarding:** The North Node's path is not always easy. It often involves stepping into the unknown and confronting fears or insecurities. However, the more you pursue the lessons of the North Node, the more rewarding your life becomes. This point encourages you to stretch beyond your limits, develop new strengths, and grow in ways that bring fulfillment.
- **Transformative:** The North Node's energy is transformative, urging you to let go of outdated habits and embrace new ways of thinking, feeling, and acting. It catalyzes deep personal change, helping you break free from the past and move toward a future that resonates with your true purpose.
- **Integrative:** The North Node is most beneficial when you integrate its lessons with the gifts and experiences of your South Node. By combining the strengths of the South Node (past) with the potential of the North Node (future), you can create a more balanced and holistic approach to life.

The North Node in the Natal Chart

- **Sign Placement:** The sign in which the North Node is placed indicates the qualities you need to develop and embody in this lifetime.
- **House Placement:** The house where the North Node is located reveals the area of life where you are likely to encounter your most significant growth, challenges, and karmic lessons. It highlights the domain in which you are meant to explore new experiences and develop the qualities of your North Node sign.

The Movement of the North Node

The North Node, also known as the True Node, moves retrograde (backward) through the zodiac, traveling in the opposite direction of most planets. It spends approximately 18 months in each sign and takes about 18.6 years to complete a full cycle through all 12 zodiac signs. This retrograde motion is due to the North Node's calculation, which is based on the intersection of the Moon's orbit and the ecliptic (the Sun's apparent path).

Because of its retrograde nature, the North Node progresses backward through your chart, marking key life themes and karmic lessons related to the sign and house it occupies. Its movement is mirrored by the South Node, which is always directly opposite the North Node, forming a polarity that highlights areas of growth (North Node) and areas to release or transform (South Node). This unique motion reflects the Nodes' symbolic role in guiding personal and spiritual evolution over time.

The North Node's "Home" – Moving Toward Your Destiny

- **Opposition to the South Node:** The North Node is always directly opposite the South Node in the natal chart. The South Node represents your comfort zone, past habits, and qualities you have already mastered. The North Node, on the other hand, represents the qualities you need to develop to create balance and harmony in your life. Your North Node's "home" is in embracing the unknown and evolving beyond the familiar tendencies of the South Node.

- **A Journey of Self-Development:** The North Node represents an ongoing journey rather than a destination. Its "home" is in the process of learning, growing, and becoming. By working toward the qualities of your North Node, you align with your soul's true purpose and find deeper fulfillment. It encourages you to take steps that may feel daunting but ultimately lead to self-discovery and a more authentic expression of who you are.

The North Node in Challenging Placements

The North Node does not have traditional exaltations, detriments, or falls, as it is not a planet but a point related to the Moon's orbit. However, its placement and aspects can indicate challenges in embracing its lessons.

- **Challenging Aspects:** When the North Node forms difficult aspects (e.g., squares or oppositions) with planets like Saturn, Pluto, or Mars, it may indicate that your path involves overcoming significant obstacles or facing inner conflicts. For example, a square with Pluto suggests that embracing your North Node path may involve confronting deep fears, power struggles, or transformative experiences.

- **Integrating the South Node:** One of the primary challenges of the North Node is the tendency to fall back on the habits and characteristics of the South Node, where you feel comfortable and safe. Growth occurs when you actively work to integrate the strengths of the South Node with the lessons of the North Node, using past experiences as a foundation to build a new, more balanced approach to life.

Summary

The North Node in astrology represents your life's purpose, karmic lessons, and the qualities you are meant to develop in this lifetime. It guides you toward new experiences and challenges that push you out of your comfort zone and lead to personal growth and fulfillment. Understanding the North Node's sign, house placement, and aspects in your natal chart provides insights into how and where you can embrace your potential, move toward your destiny, and achieve balance. While it does not have traditional exaltations or detriments, the aspects it forms can indicate the nature of the challenges or growth you will encounter on your path. By embracing the lessons and qualities of the North Node, you align with your soul's purpose and find a more rewarding and authentic way of being.

South Node: The Point of Past Experiences and Comfort Zones

Symbol: ☋

The South Node in astrology represents your past experiences, ingrained habits, and the qualities you have already mastered in previous lifetimes or earlier in your current life. It symbolizes your comfort zone and the tendencies you naturally fall back on. While the South Node reflects strengths and familiarity, it can also indicate areas where you may feel stuck or limited if over-relied upon. Balancing the South Node with the lessons of the North Node is essential for growth and fulfilling your life's purpose.

What the South Node Represents

- **Past Experiences:** The South Node is often associated with past lives, inherited karma, or early life conditioning. It reflects the experiences, skills, and characteristics that you have brought into this lifetime. These qualities may come naturally to you and can represent areas of expertise or comfort. However, they can also signify patterns that are no longer beneficial to your growth.

- **Comfort Zone:** The South Node represents your comfort zone, where you feel safe and at ease. It shows the behaviors and attitudes you instinctively revert to, particularly in times of stress or uncertainty. While it offers a sense of security, it can also keep you from exploring new experiences and embracing the challenges needed for personal evolution.

- **Ingrained Habits:** This point symbolizes ingrained habits, tendencies, and responses that you have developed over time. The South Node indicates the familiar patterns that may provide a sense of stability but can become restrictive if you cling to them. To grow, you need to consciously work on breaking free from these habitual ways of being and moving toward the lessons of the North Node.

- **Strengths and Talents:** While the South Node often highlights areas where you might feel stuck, it also represents strengths and talents that you have cultivated over lifetimes. These qualities can serve as a foundation for your journey toward the North Node, providing you with skills and insights to help you navigate new challenges. The key is to use the gifts of the South Node without becoming overly dependent on them.

Qualities of the South Node

- **Familiar yet Limiting:** The South Node's energy is familiar and comfortable, but it can also be limiting if relied on exclusively. It represents qualities and behaviors that you may use as a "crutch," preventing you from stepping into the unknown and pursuing growth. While it provides a sense of ease, the South Node's influence can hold you back from reaching your full potential.

- **Receptive to Release:** The South Node indicates areas of life that are ripe for release. It points to patterns, habits, and attitudes that need to be left behind or transformed to achieve balance and evolve. Working with the South Node involves recognizing these ingrained tendencies and consciously choosing to move beyond them, using its strengths as a foundation for your growth.

- **Balanced with the North Node:** The South Node is most beneficial when balanced with the lessons of the North Node. By integrating the strengths and experiences of the South Node while striving toward the qualities of the North Node, you create a harmonious path that combines your past expertise with future growth.

The South Node in the Natal Chart

- **Sign Placement:** The sign in which the South Node is placed indicates the qualities, tendencies, and traits that come naturally to you. These are characteristics you may have developed in past lives or early in this life.

- **House Placement:** The house where the South Node is located reveals the area of life where you are most likely to encounter familiar patterns, habits, and experiences. It shows where you may feel most comfortable and where you have already developed certain skills or expertise.

The Movement of the South Node

The South Node moves in tandem with the North Node, traveling retrograde (backward) through the zodiac. It spends approximately 18 months in each sign and completes a full cycle through all 12 signs every 18.6 years. The South Node is always positioned directly opposite the North Node in the natal chart, creating a polarity that reflects the balance between past tendencies (South Node) and future growth (North Node).

Its retrograde motion is based on the intersection of the Moon's orbit with the ecliptic (the Sun's apparent path). As it moves backward through your chart, the South Node highlights areas of life connected to past experiences, innate talents, and karmic patterns that may need transformation or release. Together with the North Node, it forms a dynamic axis that guides personal evolution and spiritual alignment throughout a lifetime.

The South Node's "Home" – Familiar Territory

- **Opposition to the North Node:** The South Node is always directly opposite the North Node in the natal chart. This opposition highlights the contrast between your comfort zone (South Node) and your path of growth (North Node). The South Node's "home" is in the familiar patterns and tendencies that feel safe and easy. While these qualities provide a foundation, growth involves moving toward the North Node, using the strengths of the South Node to support your journey.

- **A Space for Release:** The South Node represents a space for releasing what no longer serves your highest purpose. It is "at home" when you acknowledge its lessons and allow its energy to transform into a supportive foundation for your North Node journey. By recognizing when you are falling back into South Node habits, you can consciously choose to move forward toward the unknown, embracing the challenges of the North Node.

The South Node in Challenging Placements

The South Node does not have traditional exaltations, detriments, or falls like planets. However, its aspects and placements can indicate where you might encounter challenges or resistance to growth.

- **Challenging Aspects:** When the South Node forms difficult aspects (e.g., squares or oppositions) with planets like Saturn, Pluto, or Mars, it may indicate that certain ingrained patterns are particularly strong and challenging to release. For example, a square with Saturn suggests that you may feel a sense of duty or responsibility to old habits, making it harder to break free and move toward your North Node's lessons.

- **Overemphasis on Comfort:** One of the primary challenges of the South Node is the temptation to overemphasize comfort and familiarity. This can lead to stagnation, where you avoid the unknown and miss out on the growth opportunities presented by the North Node. Recognizing when you are overly relying on your South Node qualities is key to shifting toward a more balanced, forward-moving path.

Summary

The South Node in astrology represents your past experiences, comfort zone, and the qualities you have already mastered. It highlights the patterns, habits, and strengths that come naturally to you but may limit your growth if over-relied upon. Understanding the South Node's sign, house placement, and aspects in your natal chart provides insights into where you tend to fall back into familiar patterns and where you need to release old habits to embrace new growth. While it does not have traditional exaltations or detriments, its aspects can indicate the nature of the challenges you face in moving toward your North Node's lessons. By acknowledging the strengths of your South Node while striving toward the qualities of the North Node, you can find balance and evolve on your life's path.

Chiron: The Wounded Healer

Symbol: ⚷

Chiron in astrology represents the "Wounded Healer," symbolizing your deepest wounds and the path to healing them. Although Chiron is not a planet but rather a celestial body classified as a centaur—an object with characteristics of both an asteroid and a comet—it holds significant astrological influence. It governs the areas of life where you experience pain, insecurities, or a sense of inadequacy, but also where you have the potential to achieve profound personal growth and wisdom. Chiron highlights both the parts of you that are wounded and the unique gifts you can develop through working with those wounds, eventually turning your pain into a source of healing for yourself and others.

What Chiron Represents

- **Deep Wounds:** Chiron indicates your core wounds—the emotional, psychological, or physical injuries that shape your sense of self. These wounds often stem from early life experiences, past lives, or inherited family dynamics. They are areas where you may feel vulnerable, unworthy, or inadequate, and where healing requires facing and acknowledging the pain.
- **Healing and Transformation:** While Chiron points to where you feel wounded, it also reveals the path to healing. It represents the journey of transforming pain into wisdom, compassion, and strength. Chiron's placement in your chart shows how you can overcome your wounds and, in the process, develop the capacity to heal and guide others through similar challenges.
- **Wisdom and Empathy:** Chiron teaches that through embracing your wounds, you gain a deeper understanding of the human condition and develop empathy for others. It represents the wisdom that comes from experience, turning past pain into insights that can benefit yourself and those around you. Chiron's energy encourages you to share your healing journey, using your

experiences to help others navigate their own paths.

- The Teacher and Healer: Chiron is often associated with the role of the teacher and healer. Its placement indicates where you are likely to become a source of guidance, wisdom, and support for others, especially in areas related to your own wounds. By working through your Chiron-related challenges, you develop unique healing abilities that allow you to contribute positively to the world.

Qualities of Chiron

- Vulnerable Yet Strong: Chiron's energy is both vulnerable and strong, representing the paradox of being wounded while also possessing the potential to heal and grow. It teaches that true strength arises from embracing your vulnerabilities and using them as a source of wisdom and compassion.

- Transformative: Chiron has a transformative quality, urging you to confront your pain and transmute it into strength. It encourages you to face your wounds directly, fostering personal growth and the development of healing abilities that can be used to support others.

- Integrative: Chiron seeks integration of the wounded and healed aspects of the self. It promotes a holistic approach to life, where you acknowledge your imperfections, accept your vulnerabilities, and use your experiences to build a more balanced and authentic way of being.

Chiron in the Natal Chart

- Sign Placement: The sign in which Chiron is placed indicates the nature of your wounds and the qualities you need to embrace to heal.

- House Placement: The house where Chiron is located reveals the area of life where your wounds and healing journey are most prominently experienced. It points to the domains in which you are likely to encounter pain, challenges, and the need for growth.

The Movement of Chiron

Chiron spends approximately 2 to 8 years in each zodiac sign, with the duration varying due to its highly elliptical orbit. When Chiron is closer to the Sun (perihelion), it moves more quickly, spending less time in each sign. Conversely, when it is farther from the Sun (aphelion), it slows down significantly. It takes about 50 years for Chiron to complete its journey through all 12 zodiac signs.

Chiron Retrograde

Chiron retrogrades occur once a year for about five months, bringing a focus on deep emotional wounds and the healing process. Chiron in retrograde encourages inner reflection on areas where you've been hurt and how you can work through these pains to grow stronger. This period is ideal for emotional healing, therapy, and addressing past traumas. In a natal chart, Chiron retrograde suggests that the individual's journey of healing is deeply internalized, often involving a reflective and introspective process. These individuals may struggle with unresolved pain and find themselves revisiting these wounds throughout life, but this inner focus also grants them a unique ability to understand their healing process. Rather than relying on external solutions, they learn to draw strength from within, integrating their wounds into their personal growth. Over time, Chiron retrograde individuals often transform their experiences into wisdom and resilience, enabling them to become healers for themselves and others.

Chiron's "Home" – The Bridge Between the Wounded and Healed Self

- **Embracing Vulnerability:** Chiron's "home" is found in the acceptance of your vulnerabilities and the courage to face your wounds. Its energy encourages you to explore the areas where you feel inadequate or hurt and to use these experiences as a pathway to wisdom, empathy, and personal growth. Chiron is "at home" when you allow yourself to be both the wounded and the healer, recognizing that your imperfections are part of your unique journey.

- **A Journey of Healing:** Chiron's true "home" is not tied to any particular sign or house but rather to the ongoing process of healing and integration. It represents the bridge between your wounds and your capacity for healing, urging you to embrace the entire spectrum of your experiences. By working with Chiron's energy, you can transform your pain into a source of strength, developing the ability to guide and support others on their paths.

Chiron in Challenging Placements

Chiron does not have traditional exaltations, detriments, or falls, as it is a centaur. However, its placement and aspects can indicate the nature of the wounds you face and the challenges on your path to healing.

- **Difficult Aspects:** When Chiron forms challenging aspects (e.g., squares or oppositions) with planets like Saturn, Pluto, or Mars, it may indicate that your wounds are deep and complex, requiring significant effort and self-reflection to heal. For example, a square with Saturn suggests that you may feel restricted or burdened by your wounds, potentially leading to feelings of inadequacy or self-doubt. Overcoming these challenges often involves developing patience, self-discipline, and a compassionate understanding of your limitations.

- **Potential for Avoidance:** Chiron's wounds can be painful to confront, leading to a tendency to avoid or suppress them. However, true healing requires acknowledging these wounds and actively working through them. The challenge lies in facing your pain with honesty and openness, allowing it to become a source of growth and empowerment.

Summary

Chiron in astrology represents the "Wounded Healer," symbolizing your deepest wounds and the potential for profound healing and wisdom. It highlights the areas of life where you experience pain, insecurity, and challenges, but also where you have the capacity to transform these experiences into strengths. Understanding Chiron's sign, house placement, and aspects in your natal chart provides insights into the nature of your wounds, the path to healing, and how you can use your experiences to guide and support others. While Chiron does not have traditional exaltations or detriments, its aspects indicate the nature of the challenges or opportunities for growth you encounter. By embracing Chiron's energy, you can transform your pain into a source of compassion, wisdom, and the ability to heal both yourself and others.

Lilith: The Dark Feminine and Shadow Self

Symbol: ☽

Lilith in astrology, also known as the "Black Moon," is not a planet but a calculated point in the Moon's orbit, specifically the apogee, which is the farthest point from Earth. It represents the wild, untamed, and primal aspects of the psyche, embodying the shadow side of the self and bringing to light themes of raw sexuality, power, rebellion, independence, and deep-seated desires. Lilith is linked to the inner truths that society often represses or stigmatizes, highlighting areas where you assert your personal power, seek freedom, and confront societal taboos.

What Lilith Represents

- **Primal Desires:** Lilith symbolizes your deepest desires and urges, particularly those that lie outside the boundaries of social norms. It reveals the parts of you that crave independence, freedom, and authenticity, even if they go against conventional expectations. Lilith's placement in your chart points to where you may experience an intense need to break free from restrictions and live according to your own terms.

- **Raw Sexuality:** One of the primary themes associated with Lilith is sexuality, especially the aspects that are considered taboo, hidden, or rejected. It governs raw, unapologetic sexual energy and the ways in which you express or suppress your desires. Lilith's influence can bring up issues related to power dynamics, sexual autonomy, and the acceptance or rejection of your own sexual nature.

- **Rebellion and Independence:** Lilith represents the part of you that resists conformity and fights for autonomy. It signifies the drive to assert yourself, stand up for your beliefs, and refuse to be dominated or suppressed. This point in the chart highlights where you may experience conflicts around power, control, and the desire to assert your independence in the face of authority or societal expectations.

- **Shadow Self and the Forbidden:** Lilith embodies the shadow self—the parts of your personality that you may fear, reject, or keep hidden. It reveals where you grapple with issues of shame, guilt, or rejection, often due to societal conditioning. By working with Lilith's energy, you can confront these aspects of your psyche, embrace your full complexity, and find empowerment in your authenticity.

Qualities of Lilith

- **Dark and Empowering:** Lilith carries a dark, potent energy that is both empowering and unsettling. It represents the aspects of the psyche that are raw, instinctual, and untamed. Lilith encourages you to embrace your power, assert your autonomy, and confront the parts of yourself that you may have repressed or denied.

- **Rebellious and Fierce:** Lilith's energy is fierce and rebellious, often challenging authority, control, and conventional norms. It represents a refusal to be dominated or confined, urging you to explore your desires and assert your individuality, even if it means facing opposition or controversy.

- **Liberating and Transformative:** Working with Lilith's energy can be deeply liberating, as it involves confronting your shadow and integrating the parts of you that are wild, free, and unashamed. This process is transformative, leading to a deeper understanding of your true nature and the courage to live authentically.

Lilith in the Natal Chart

- **Sign Placement:** The sign in which Lilith is placed indicates the nature of your primal instincts, desires, and the ways you assert your independence.

- **House Placement:** The house where Lilith is located reveals the area of life where you experience challenges related to independence, power, and personal authenticity. It points to where you may encounter conflicts around control, desire, or societal expectations.

The Movement of Lilith

Lilith, or Black Moon Lilith, is a calculated point in astrology representing the Moon's apogee, the farthest point in its orbit from Earth. It spends about 9 months in each zodiac sign and takes approximately 9 years to complete a full cycle through the zodiac. Unlike planets, Lilith's movement is steady and does not experience retrograde motion.

Lilith's "Home" – The Realm of Authenticity and Rebellion

- **Shadow and Light:** Lilith's "home" is found in the acceptance of your shadow self. It embodies the parts of you that seek to live authentically, free from societal or internal constraints. Lilith encourages you to confront your darkest desires, embrace your raw power, and stand firm in your truth, even when it goes against societal norms.

- **Integration of the Untamed Self:** Lilith represents the integration of the untamed aspects of your psyche. By acknowledging and accepting these parts of yourself, you find a sense of empowerment and liberation. Lilith is "at home" when you explore and express your individuality without fear, shame, or the need for approval.

Lilith in Challenging Placements

Lilith does not have traditional exaltations, detriments, or falls, as it is not a physical body but rather a symbolic point. However, its placement and aspects can indicate the nature of the challenges you face in embracing your raw power and desires.

- **Challenging Aspects:** When Lilith forms difficult aspects (e.g., squares or oppositions) with planets like Saturn, Pluto, or Mars, it may indicate intense inner conflicts, struggles with control, or societal rejection. For example, a square with Saturn suggests that you may experience guilt, restriction, or suppression of your desires, leading to internal conflict around expressing your true self.

- **Facing Repression:** One of the primary challenges of Lilith is facing societal repression or internalized shame around your desires, sexuality, and independence. Confronting these issues involves acknowledging where you may feel judged, constrained, or fearful of being your authentic self. Lilith's placement often indicates the areas of life where you need to assert your power and embrace your desires without apology.

Summary

Lilith in astrology represents the wild, untamed aspects of your psyche, highlighting themes of raw sexuality, power, rebellion, and independence. It symbolizes the shadow self and the areas where you experience a struggle for autonomy and authenticity. Understanding Lilith's sign, house placement, and aspects in your natal chart provides insights into the nature of your desires, where you may experience power struggles, and how you can embrace your full complexity. While Lilith does not have traditional exaltations or detriments, its aspects can indicate the nature of the challenges you face in asserting your power and independence. By embracing Lilith's energy, you confront your shadow, embrace your true desires, and find empowerment in living authentically.

Ascendant (ASC): The Mask and First Impressions

Symbol: ASC

The Ascendant, or Rising Sign, in astrology represents the façade you present to the world, your physical appearance, and the way you interact with your environment. It is the sign that was rising on the eastern horizon at the exact time of your birth. The Ascendant is one of the most crucial components of the natal chart, as it influences how others perceive you and sets the tone for your approach to life.

What the Ascendant Represents
- **Outer Personality:** The Ascendant is often described as the "mask" you wear in public or the first impression you make on others. It governs your outer personality, demeanor, and the way you project yourself in social situations. While the Sun represents your core self and the Moon your emotions, the Ascendant reflects your outward behavior and immediate responses to the world around you.
- **Physical Appearance:** The Ascendant is also associated with physical traits and body language. The sign on the Ascendant and the planets near it can influence your appearance, facial expressions, style, and mannerisms. For example, an Aries Ascendant might have a more athletic build, a strong jawline, or a confident stride, while a Libra Ascendant might present with a more balanced, graceful posture.
- **Approach to Life:** The Ascendant defines your approach to new experiences and how you start things in life. It represents the lens through which you view the world and the strategies you use to navigate life's challenges. Your Ascendant colors how you respond to new situations, how you assert yourself, and the general attitude you adopt when facing the unknown.
- **Your Personal Identity:** While the Sun sign represents your inner self, the Ascendant shapes your personal identity and how you differentiate yourself from others. It sets the scene for how the

other planetary energies in your chart express themselves. In many ways, the Ascendant acts as a bridge between your inner world and the outer world, translating your inner desires and emotions into outward actions and behavior.

Qualities of the Ascendant

- **Expressive and Dynamic:** The Ascendant is dynamic and constantly in motion, as it represents the way you express yourself in various situations. It influences how you adapt to changing environments and how you choose to present yourself. The Ascendant's energy is about outward expression, showing how you reveal your character, temperament, and personality to the world.

- **Adaptable:** The Ascendant is adaptable, shifting depending on the environment and social setting. While it remains consistent in its overall influence (through its ruling sign), it also reflects how you change your behavior and demeanor depending on your surroundings. This adaptability is why some people may seem different in various situations, reflecting different facets of their Ascendant's energy.

- **Filtering Mechanism:** The Ascendant acts as a filtering mechanism, influencing how you perceive and interpret experiences. It colors your perception of reality, shaping how you approach relationships, handle challenges, and pursue opportunities. This filtering mechanism is essential for understanding your motivations and reactions, as it sets the stage for how you express your inner self in the outer world.

The Ascendant in the Natal Chart

- **Sign Placement:** The sign of your Ascendant indicates how you project yourself, your physical appearance, and your overall demeanor. For example, a Scorpio Ascendant suggests a mysterious, intense approach to life, often with a magnetic presence and a deeply perceptive nature. A Cancer Ascendant may indicate a nurturing, sensitive demeanor, often with a protective and intuitive approach to situations.

- **Chart Ruler:** Each Ascendant sign is associated with a ruling planet, which plays a significant role in your chart. The position and aspects of this ruling planet provide deeper insights into how your Ascendant energy is expressed. For example, if you have a Leo Ascendant, the Sun is your chart ruler. The Sun's placement in your chart will further color how you express your outward personality. If the Sun is in the 10th house, for instance, you might project a strong, authoritative presence, particularly in your public and professional life.

- **Aspects to the Ascendant:** The aspects that the Ascendant forms with other planets in your chart influence how its energy is expressed. For example, a conjunction between the Ascendant and Venus may give you a charming, attractive demeanor, while a square with Mars might indicate a more assertive or even confrontational outward personality. These aspects shape the way you present yourself and interact with others.

The Movement of the Ascendant

The Ascendant changes signs approximately every 2 hours as the Earth rotates on its axis, completing a full cycle through the zodiac in 24 hours. Its rapid movement means the Ascendant is highly time-sensitive, making an accurate birth time crucial for determining its placement. The Ascendant represents the eastern horizon at the moment of birth and serves as a key point in the natal chart, shaping the chart's structure.

The Ascendant's "Home" – The Self and Personal Expression

- **Connection to the First House:** The Ascendant marks the cusp of the first house in the natal chart, which is the house of self, personal identity, and physical appearance. This connection makes the Ascendant the "home" of your outward expression and the foundation of how you navigate life. It sets the stage for the entire birth chart by determining how the houses are structured and which signs govern each one. The sign of your Ascendant starts the sequence of the zodiac signs across the 12 houses, creating a unique blueprint for your life. For instance, if your Ascendant is in Leo,

Virgo will follow as the ruler of your second house, Libra will rule your third house, and so on, continuing in the order of the zodiac. This progression means the Ascendant plays a critical role in shaping how you experience the energies of each house and sign in your chart. By setting the framework, the Ascendant provides a personalized structure that influences how the planets and other celestial points express themselves across different areas of life.

- **Integration of Inner and Outer Worlds:** The Ascendant serves as the meeting point between your inner world (Sun, Moon, and other personal planets) and the outer world (your interactions and experiences). It integrates your personal desires, emotions, and values into a form that can be communicated and understood by others. The Ascendant is "at home" when you are able to express your true self while adapting to different environments and relationships.

The Ascendant in Challenging Placements

The Ascendant itself does not have traditional exaltations, detriments, or falls like planets, but its sign, ruler, and aspects can present challenges in expressing its energy.

- **Challenging Aspects:** When the Ascendant forms difficult aspects (e.g., squares or oppositions) with planets like Saturn, Pluto, or Mars, it may indicate struggles in how you project yourself or interact with the world. For example, an opposition between the Ascendant and Saturn might suggest a reserved or serious demeanor, possibly indicating insecurities about how you present yourself. Overcoming these challenges often involves developing self-awareness and finding a way to assert your personality authentically.

- **Balancing Inner and Outer Worlds:** One of the primary challenges of the Ascendant is balancing the outward projection with your inner self. While it's important to adapt and present yourself in ways that suit different situations, it's equally essential to remain true to your core values and desires. When the Ascendant's energy becomes overly focused on external validation, it can lead to an identity that feels disconnected from your true self.

Summary

The Ascendant in astrology represents your outer personality, physical appearance, and the way you approach life. It influences how others perceive you, how you present yourself, and how you filter your experiences. Understanding the Ascendant's sign, ruling planet, and aspects in your natal chart provides insights into your outward demeanor, your initial reactions to life's events, and how you bridge your inner world with the external environment. While the Ascendant does not have traditional exaltations or detriments, its aspects can indicate challenges in self-expression or interactions with the world. By embracing the energy of your Ascendant, you create a harmonious balance between your inner desires and your outward behavior, allowing you to navigate life with authenticity and confidence.

Imum Coeli (IC): The Foundation and Inner World

Symbol: IC

The Imum Coeli (IC), also known as the "Nadir" or "Lowest Point of the Sky," represents the roots of your being, your inner foundation, and the private aspects of your life. Located at the bottom of the natal chart, the IC marks the cusp of the fourth house and is opposite the Midheaven (MC). It symbolizes your home environment, family dynamics, childhood experiences, and the emotional underpinnings that shape your sense of inner security and personal identity.

What the Imum Coeli (IC) Represents

- **Inner Foundation:** The IC represents your internal foundation, reflecting your deepest emotional core and the hidden aspects of your psyche. It is the place in the chart where you find your sense of comfort, safety, and inner stability. The IC points to what you need at a fundamental level to feel secure and grounded.

- **Home and Family:** The IC is strongly associated with your home environment, family life, and early childhood experiences. It reveals the qualities and dynamics of your upbringing, including the values, traditions, and emotional atmosphere you were exposed to in your formative years. It also speaks to your relationship with your parents, particularly the nurturing parent.

- **Roots and Ancestry:** This point symbolizes your roots, including your family heritage, ancestry, and cultural background. It reflects how these roots influence your sense of identity, shaping your attitudes, behaviors, and emotional responses. The IC holds clues to the subconscious patterns you inherit from your family line.

- **Private Self:** The IC represents the most private, hidden parts of yourself that you may not readily show to the outside world. It describes your inner sanctuary, where you retreat to find solitude, peace, and emotional replenishment. It highlights the side of you that emerges when you are alone or in the safety of your home.

Qualities of the Imum Coeli (IC)

- **Deep and Private:** The IC is deep and private, representing the aspects of yourself that lie beneath the surface. It governs the emotional foundation that supports your outer persona (Ascendant) and public life (Midheaven). The energy of the IC is often quiet, subtle, and not always consciously recognized, but it plays a crucial role in shaping who you are.

- **Nurturing and Reflective:** The IC is reflective, pointing to the qualities you develop through your family, upbringing, and personal history. It represents the nurturing aspect of your chart, showing how you nurture yourself and others. The IC's energy is often associated with the way you create a sense of home, both physically and emotionally.

- **Stabilizing:** The IC provides a sense of stability and grounding. It represents your emotional roots, acting as an anchor in times of change or uncertainty. A well-supported IC can give you a strong inner foundation, helping you navigate life's challenges with a sense of security and self-assurance.

The Imum Coeli (IC) in the Natal Chart

- **Sign Placement:** The sign of your IC indicates the qualities you associate with home, family, and emotional security. It describes the kind of environment that nurtures you and provides a sense of comfort. For example, an IC in Cancer suggests that you find security in a nurturing, family-oriented environment, while an IC in Capricorn may indicate that you seek stability, structure, and a sense of responsibility within your home life.

- **Ruling Planet:** Each sign is associated with a ruling planet, which plays a significant role in your chart. The position and aspects of this ruling planet provide deeper insights into how your IC energy is expressed, particularly in matters of home, family, and emotional security. For example, if you have a Pisces IC, Neptune is the ruling planet of your IC. The placement of Neptune in your chart will further influence your inner world and foundational experiences. If Neptune is in the 2nd house, for instance, you might find emotional security through creativity, spiritual values, or a fluid relationship with material resources, with your home and family life reflecting these themes.

- **Aspects to the IC:** The aspects that the IC forms with other planets in your chart reveal the dynamics of your inner life and family experiences. For example, a conjunction between the IC and the Moon can indicate a strong emotional connection to your family or childhood home, while a square with Pluto may suggest intense, transformative experiences related to family dynamics, power struggles, or deep emotional issues rooted in the past.

The Movement of the Imum Coeli (IC)

The IC is the lowest point in the natal chart and is directly opposite the Midheaven (MC). It changes signs approximately every 2 hours, moving in tandem with the Ascendant as the Earth rotates. This movement allows the IC to complete a full cycle through all 12 zodiac signs in 24 hours.

The Imum Coeli's (IC) "Home" – The Roots of Your Being

- **Connection to the Fourth House:** The IC is intrinsically linked to the fourth house, the house of home, family, roots, and inner emotional life. This connection makes the IC the "home" of your personal sanctuary, reflecting the qualities you need to feel secure and at peace. It provides a base from which you build your sense of identity and navigate the outer world (Midheaven).

- **Your Inner World:** The IC represents your inner world, where you retreat to reconnect with your core self. It serves as the foundation of your chart, providing the emotional support necessary to pursue your outer ambitions. When the IC is well integrated, it creates a strong inner foundation, helping you to maintain emotional balance and resilience.

The Imum Coeli (IC) in Challenging Placements

The IC does not have traditional exaltations, detriments, or falls like planets, but its placement and aspects can present

challenges related to your inner world and family dynamics.
   - **Challenging Aspects:** When the IC forms difficult aspects (e.g., squares or oppositions) with planets like Saturn, Pluto, or Uranus, it may indicate struggles in your home life, emotional foundation, or family relationships. For example, a square with Saturn might suggest a childhood marked by emotional restrictions, a lack of nurturing, or a strong sense of responsibility within the family. Working through these challenges often involves confronting unresolved family issues, redefining your concept of home, and building a sense of inner security.
   - **Balancing Public and Private Life:** One of the challenges of the IC is balancing your private, inner world with your public life, represented by the Midheaven. You may feel tension between the demands of your outer ambitions and the need for inner peace and emotional stability. Finding harmony between these areas involves creating a solid personal foundation that supports your public endeavors.

Summary

The IC in astrology represents your roots, home, family dynamics, and the inner foundation of your being. It influences your emotional life, sense of security, and the hidden aspects of your psyche that shape your approach to the world. Understanding the IC's sign, house influence, and aspects in your natal chart provides insights into your family background, emotional needs, and the qualities you associate with a sense of inner stability. While the IC does not have traditional exaltations or detriments, its aspects can indicate challenges in your relationship with your inner world, family, and sense of self. By embracing the energy of the IC, you cultivate a strong foundation that supports your personal growth and outer ambitions, creating a harmonious balance between your private and public selves.

Descendant (DSC): The Point of Partnerships and Projection

Symbol: DSC

The Descendant in astrology represents your approach to relationships, partnerships, and the qualities you seek in others. Located on the western horizon of the natal chart, it directly opposes the Ascendant and marks the cusp of the seventh house. The Descendant symbolizes the "other" in your life, highlighting how you connect with people, the dynamics of your close relationships, and what you are drawn to in others to achieve balance and growth.

What the Descendant Represents

- **Relationships and Partnerships:** The Descendant is closely linked to the nature of your personal relationships, particularly long-term partnerships such as marriage, close friendships, and business collaborations. It shows the qualities you are attracted to in others and the types of people you are likely to form deep, committed relationships with. The Descendant can reveal the kinds of partnerships that challenge, support, or complement your own personality.

- **Projected Qualities:** The Descendant represents the traits and characteristics that you may project onto others or seek out in your relationships. These are often qualities that you might not readily recognize or embody within yourself, and thus you attract others who exhibit these characteristics to bring balance into your life. For example, if your Descendant is in Libra, you may seek partners who are diplomatic, harmonious, and focused on balance, even if you don't always display these qualities yourself.

- **Balance and Growth:** The Descendant highlights qualities that complement your own, guiding you toward personal development through your relationships. While the Ascendant describes your outward persona and how you express yourself, the Descendant reveals traits you may not fully embrace within yourself but can cultivate through interactions with others. It represents the lessons you learn from relationships and how these experiences help you grow and become more well-rounded as an individual.

- Your Shadow Side: In Jungian terms, the Descendant can be seen as a part of the "shadow self." It represents aspects of your psyche that you may not fully accept or acknowledge, which you encounter through interactions with others. By facing these traits in your partners, you have the opportunity to understand and integrate them, leading to greater self-awareness and inner harmony.

Qualities of the Descendant

- Relational and Reflective: The Descendant is inherently relational, governing how you approach interactions and the dynamics you experience in partnerships. Its energy is reflective, acting like a mirror that shows you parts of yourself through your relationships. The qualities of your Descendant sign often appear in the people you are drawn to, serving as a reflection of the traits you need to develop or integrate within yourself.

- Complementary: The Descendant complements the Ascendant, creating a balance between your outward persona and the qualities you seek in others. While the Ascendant represents how you express yourself, the Descendant shows what you are drawn to in order to feel complete. This dynamic is central to understanding your relational patterns and the type of energy that helps you grow through partnerships.

- Transformative: The Descendant can be a source of transformation, as it highlights the qualities and lessons you encounter through others. Your relationships serve as a catalyst for growth, helping you explore parts of your personality that may be underdeveloped. By engaging with the energy of your Descendant, you can evolve your understanding of yourself and your approach to relationships.

The Descendant in the Natal Chart

- Sign Placement: The sign on the Descendant describes the qualities you are naturally attracted to in partners and the traits you need to integrate into your life. For example, a Descendant in Aries indicates that you are drawn to bold, assertive, and independent individuals who encourage you to take action and stand up for yourself. A Descendant in Pisces suggests that you are attracted to compassionate, sensitive, and spiritual partners who bring a sense of emotional depth and intuition into your life.

- **Ruling Planet:** Each sign is associated with a ruling planet, which plays a significant role in your chart. The position and aspects of this ruling planet provide deeper insights into how your Descendant energy is expressed, particularly in relationships and partnerships. For example, if you have a Taurus Descendant, Venus is the ruling planet of your Descendant. The placement of Venus in your chart will further influence the qualities you seek in relationships and how you interact with others. If Venus is in the 1st house, for instance, you might attract partners who admire your charm and personal style, and your relationships may reflect a focus on beauty, harmony, and self-expression.

- **Aspects to the Descendant:** The aspects that the Descendant forms with other planets in your chart influence your relational dynamics and the types of partners you attract. For example, a conjunction between the Descendant and Venus can indicate a natural charm and attraction to beauty and harmony in relationships, while a square with Saturn may suggest challenges in forming committed partnerships, possibly due to fears of intimacy or feelings of inadequacy.

The Movement of the Descendant

The Descendant is the point in the natal chart that marks the cusp of the seventh house. It is directly opposite the Ascendant and changes signs approximately every 2 hours as the Ascendant moves. This movement allows the Descendant to complete a full cycle through all 12 zodiac signs in 24 hours, reflecting the dynamic interplay between the self (Ascendant) and others (Descendant).

The Descendant's "Home" – The Realm of Partnership and Reflection

- **Connection to the Seventh House:** The Descendant is inherently linked to the seventh house, the house of partnerships, marriage, and one-on-one relationships. This connection makes the Descendant the "home" of relational dynamics, reflecting the qualities and traits that you are drawn to in others. It represents the part of your chart that balances the self-oriented nature of the Ascendant, guiding you toward interactions that help you grow and evolve.

- **Integration of Opposites:** The Descendant serves as the point of integration between the self (Ascendant) and the other. It invites you to explore relationships as a means of understanding and embracing the complementary qualities that lie within your shadow self. By engaging with the energy of your Descendant, you create a space for mutual growth, understanding, and the blending of different aspects of your personality.

The Descendant in Challenging Placements

The Descendant does not have traditional exaltations, detriments, or falls, as it is a point rather than a planet. However, its placement and aspects can indicate challenges in your approach to relationships and partnerships.

- **Challenging Aspects:** When the Descendant forms difficult aspects (e.g., squares or oppositions) with planets like Pluto, Mars, or Saturn, it may indicate struggles in relationships. For example, a square with Pluto could suggest intense power dynamics, control issues, or deep transformations within partnerships. Navigating these challenges often involves learning to understand and balance your own needs with those of others.

- **Projecting onto Others:** One of the main challenges of the Descendant is the tendency to project your shadow traits onto others. You may attract partners who exhibit qualities you subconsciously reject or deny within yourself. Recognizing this projection is key to developing self-awareness and embracing the qualities of the Descendant within your own personality.

Summary

The Descendant in astrology represents your approach to relationships, the qualities you seek in others, and the dynamics of your partnerships. It reflects the traits that balance and complement your Ascendant, revealing the "other half" of your personality. Understanding the Descendant's sign, house influence, and aspects in your natal chart provides insights into the types of partners you attract, your relationship patterns, and the qualities you need to integrate for growth and balance. While the Descendant does not have traditional exaltations or detriments, its aspects can indicate challenges in relationships and the process of self-reflection. By embracing the energy of the Descendant, you can deepen your understanding of yourself through partnerships, achieve inner harmony, and evolve in your approach to connection and collaboration.

Midheaven (MC): The Point of Public Life and Career

Symbol: MC

The Midheaven (MC), also known as the "Medium Coeli," represents your public image, career aspirations, and life's direction. It is located at the top of the natal chart, marking the cusp of the tenth house. The MC reflects your highest ambitions, how you wish to be seen in the world, and the legacy you strive to build. It indicates your public persona, professional achievements, and the overall path you take to achieve your goals and make your mark on the world.

What the Midheaven Represents

- **Career and Public Life:** The MC is closely associated with your career, professional ambitions, and public reputation. It describes the type of work you are drawn to and the qualities you wish to express in your professional life. The sign and planets associated with the MC reveal your career path, the role you aspire to fulfill in society, and the nature of your public image.

- **Life Direction:** The MC represents your life's direction and your pursuit of goals. It indicates the type of achievements you strive for and what you hope to accomplish on a broader scale. It's the point in your chart that guides you toward personal development, outlining the purpose and mission that shape your journey.

- **Social Status and Reputation:** The Midheaven describes how you wish to be recognized by the world and the legacy you seek to create. It points to your reputation, social standing, and how others perceive you in a professional or public context. Your MC can give insight into the types of responsibilities you are willing to take on and the standards you set for yourself in society.

- **Authority Figures:** The MC is also linked to authority figures and your relationship with them, such as parents, mentors, bosses, or societal structures. It can reflect your attitudes toward authority, discipline, and the structures you navigate as you work toward your goals. Additionally, the MC is often associated with the "father" or the dominant parent figure in your life, shaping your views on success and ambition.

Qualities of the Midheaven

- **Ambitious and Goal-Oriented:** The Midheaven is ambitious, focusing on your drive to achieve and make a name for yourself in the world. It represents the qualities you cultivate to reach your highest potential and how you navigate the public sphere to attain your goals.
- **Outward-Focused:** Unlike the IC (Imum Coeli), which deals with your private, inner world, the MC is outward-focused, relating to how you interact with society and pursue success. It is about expressing your talents, skills, and ambitions in a way that contributes to your public image and sense of accomplishment.
- **Directive:** The MC serves as a directional point in your chart, guiding you toward your aspirations. It provides clarity on the path you need to take to fulfill your professional and societal roles. By understanding your MC, you gain insight into the qualities you should develop and the steps you can take to align with your life's purpose.

The Midheaven in the Natal Chart

- **Sign Placement:** The sign on the MC indicates the qualities you exhibit in your career, the type of work that suits you, and how you present yourself in public roles. For example, a Midheaven in Virgo suggests a detail-oriented, practical, and service-driven approach to your career. You may excel in roles that require precision, organization, or analytical skills, such as healthcare, education, or research. A Midheaven in Sagittarius, on the other hand, points to an adventurous, philosophical, and optimistic approach. You may thrive in careers involving travel, teaching, publishing, or fields that allow you to explore and share ideas on a broad scale.
- **Ruling Planet:** Each sign is associated with a ruling planet, which plays a significant role in your chart. The position and aspects of this ruling planet provide deeper insights into how your

Midheaven (MC) energy is expressed, particularly in your career, public image, and life direction. For example, if you have a Virgo Midheaven, Mercury is the ruling planet of your MC. The placement of Mercury in your chart will further influence how you approach your professional life and public roles. If Mercury is in the 12th house, for instance, you may excel in behind-the-scenes work or careers involving research, healing, or spirituality. Your professional path might reflect a focus on introspection, service, and the ability to uncover hidden truths or provide support to others in subtle but meaningful ways.

- **Aspects to the Midheaven:** The aspects that the MC forms with other planets in your chart influence your career path, public image, and how you pursue your ambitions. For example, a conjunction between the MC and Saturn can indicate a career characterized by discipline, hard work, and the need to overcome obstacles. This aspect may suggest that you achieve success through perseverance and a strong sense of responsibility. A square between the MC and Pluto might indicate power struggles, transformations, or deep personal changes related to your public life and career direction.

The Movement of the Midheaven (MC)

The Midheaven (MC) is the highest point in the natal chart and is directly opposite the Imum Coeli (IC). It changes signs approximately every 2 hours, moving in tandem with the Ascendant as the Earth rotates. This movement allows the MC to complete a full cycle through all 12 zodiac signs in 24 hours.

The Midheaven's "Home" – The Realm of Ambition and Achievement

- **Connection to the Tenth House:** The MC is inherently linked to the tenth house, the house of career, public roles, and reputation. This connection makes the MC the "home" of your ambitions and societal contributions. It reflects the type of legacy you want to create and the impact you wish to make in your professional life.

- Public Persona: The MC represents the qualities you present to the world and the persona you cultivate in your professional and public interactions. It is "at home" when you express the strengths of its sign placement in your career and public endeavors, allowing you to align with your true aspirations and purpose.

The Midheaven in Challenging Placements

The MC does not have traditional exaltations, detriments, or falls like planets, but its placement and aspects can present challenges in your career path, public life, and pursuit of ambitions.

- Challenging Aspects: When the MC forms difficult aspects (e.g., squares or oppositions) with planets like Saturn, Pluto, or Uranus, it may indicate struggles in achieving your career goals or building your public reputation. For example, a square with Saturn suggests that you may face obstacles, delays, or a sense of heavy responsibility in your professional life. This aspect can indicate that success requires patience, hard work, and learning from setbacks. A square with Uranus may point to sudden changes or disruptions in your career path, requiring adaptability and a willingness to embrace unconventional approaches.

- Balancing Public and Private Life: One of the primary challenges of the MC is balancing your public ambitions with your private life, represented by the IC. You may feel a tension between the demands of your career and the need for personal security and emotional fulfillment. Finding harmony between these areas involves cultivating a professional life that aligns with your values and provides a sense of personal satisfaction.

Summary

The Midheaven (MC) in astrology represents your public image, career aspirations, and life direction. It influences how you approach your ambitions, the qualities you project in your professional life, and the legacy you wish to build. Understanding the MC's sign, house influence, and aspects in your natal chart provides insights into your career path, social standing, and the strategies you use to achieve your goals. While the MC does not have traditional exaltations or detriments, its aspects can indicate challenges in your pursuit of success and the dynamics of your public life. By embracing the energy of the Midheaven, you can align with your true ambitions, develop your professional identity, and create a fulfilling life that reflects your highest aspirations.

6. Core Foundations of Birth Chart Interpretation

"Millionaires don't use astrology, billionaires do."
- J.P. Morgan

In this section, we're going to dive deeper into some of the more complex concepts of birth chart interpretation, such as modalities, elements, ruling planets, critical degrees, aspects, and orbs of influence. These ideas build upon the foundations we've already covered and will help you gain a more complete understanding of how your chart works as a whole.

As we explore these topics, you'll start to see how they interact to create the unique map of your life, revealing more layers of meaning in your chart. Modalities show how you approach action and change, while elements help understand the balance of energies like fire, earth, air, and water in your chart. Ruling planets illustrate how certain areas of your life are connected and influenced by planetary energy, and critical and anaretic degrees offer important insights into the intensity of certain placements. We'll also cover aspects and how the planets communicate with each other, rounding out your understanding of the chart's dynamics.

Some of these topics, like critical degrees and aspects, may seem a bit more challenging at first, but remember to take your time. Astrology is a lifelong journey, and it's not something that can be mastered overnight. Each new concept will add depth to your understanding, and even if it feels overwhelming, don't worry—you'll get there with patience and practice. As you move through this section, don't be afraid to re-read, highlight, and reflect on what you've learned. Every step you take is bringing you closer to interpreting your chart with confidence and clarity.

Remember, there is no rush. Be patient with yourself and enjoy the process—learning astrology is as much about self-discovery as it is about understanding the stars. You've come this far, and I'm here to guide you through the rest. Trust the process, and soon you'll find that the pieces start falling into place as you connect the dots between planets, signs, and houses.

Modalities

In astrology, the modalities—also known as the qualities or quadruplicities—describe the ways in which the zodiac signs express their energy and respond to the world. There are three modalities: Cardinal, Fixed, and Mutable, and each one represents a distinct mode of action or behavior. These modalities give insight into how a sign approaches change, initiates projects, and adapts to situations, adding an important layer to understanding the signs in a birth chart.

The twelve zodiac signs are divided evenly among the three modalities, with each modality influencing four signs. Cardinal signs are initiators and leaders, known for their dynamic energy and ability to set things into motion. Fixed signs, on the other hand, are stabilizers, known for their determination and consistency in maintaining focus once a direction is set. Mutable signs are adaptable and flexible, known for their ability to adjust and flow with changing circumstances.

Understanding the modalities helps to clarify not only the energy of a zodiac sign but also how that sign interacts with the world around it. Each modality brings a unique strength, but also potential challenges, and recognizing these qualities provides deeper insight into how each sign contributes to the overall cosmic balance. Throughout this section, we will explore each of the three modalities in detail, examining how they influence the zodiac signs they govern and how they shape behavior, relationships, and life approaches.

Cardinal Modality: Initiators of the Zodiac

The Cardinal modality represents the energy of initiation, leadership, and dynamic movement. Cardinal signs are known as the initiators of the zodiac, bringing fresh ideas, new projects, and bold actions into the world. These signs are associated with taking charge, starting new cycles, and being the first to take action. In astrology, the Cardinal modality governs four signs—Aries, Cancer, Libra, and Capricorn—and each one expresses this leadership energy in a distinct way.

Cardinal signs naturally embody qualities of action, motivation, and vision. They are the trailblazers who are not content to sit back and wait for things to happen; instead, they actively seek out new opportunities and are often the ones who set things in motion. Whether it's launching a new project, starting a relationship, or spearheading a change, Cardinal signs thrive on being at the forefront of any endeavor.

Qualities of Cardinal Signs:

- **Leadership and Initiative:** Cardinal signs excel in leadership roles because they are motivated by the desire to take charge and make things happen. They are naturally inclined to lead the way, providing direction and taking decisive action. This leadership can manifest in personal or professional settings, as Cardinal signs are often the ones who inspire others to take action.

- **Pioneering Spirit:** Cardinal signs are bold and forward-thinking. They are driven by the need to initiate new ideas, concepts, and paths. This pioneering spirit means they are often the first to try something new, embrace a challenge, or set out on a fresh adventure. Cardinal energy is all about breaking new ground and moving forward, often before others are ready to follow.

- **Dynamic and Active:** There is a restless energy associated with the Cardinal modality. These signs are constantly on the move, always looking for the next project, the next challenge, or the next opportunity. They are not ones to sit still, as they are motivated by the need to achieve and accomplish their goals. Cardinal signs are

driven by progress and action, rarely content with the status quo.
- **Goal-Oriented:** Cardinal signs are focused on achieving results. Once they set their sights on a goal, they are determined to reach it, often taking direct and decisive steps to make it happen. This focus on goals gives them a strong sense of purpose and direction, allowing them to move forward with clarity and confidence.

Cardinal Signs and Their Expression:
- **Aries (Fire Cardinal):** Aries embodies the most dynamic expression of the Cardinal modality. As a Fire sign, Aries is bold, assertive, and always ready to take the lead. Aries thrives on challenge and competition, and their cardinal energy is expressed through their courage, pioneering actions, and strong desire to be first.
- **Cancer (Water Cardinal):** Cancer's Cardinal energy is expressed through emotional leadership and nurturing. As a Water sign, Cancer takes initiative in caring for others, creating safe environments, and leading with empathy. Their focus is often on family, home, and emotional security, and they lead by building strong emotional connections.
- **Libra (Air Cardinal):** Libra's Cardinal energy is expressed through social leadership and relationship dynamics. As an Air sign, Libra takes initiative in forming partnerships, creating balance, and leading with diplomacy. Libra thrives on creating harmony and fairness in relationships, often acting as the mediator or peacemaker.
- **Capricorn (Earth Cardinal):** Capricorn embodies the most disciplined and strategic expression of the Cardinal modality. As an Earth sign, Capricorn's leadership is grounded in practicality and long-term planning. They take initiative in their careers, are goal-oriented, and excel in building lasting structures, whether in business or personal life.

Strengths of Cardinal Energy:
- **Proactive:** Cardinal signs are action-oriented, always ready to take the first step. They are proactive in addressing problems and

finding solutions, making them effective leaders and initiators.

- **Visionary:** With their progressive spirit, Cardinal signs often have a clear vision of what they want to achieve. They can inspire others with their ideas and are often ahead of the curve in terms of innovation.

- **Motivating:** Cardinal signs are natural motivators. Their dynamic energy and enthusiasm can ignite passion in others, encouraging those around them to take action and embrace new challenges.

Challenges of Cardinal Energy:

- **Impatience:** Cardinal signs can sometimes struggle with patience, particularly when others are not moving at the same pace. Their desire for action and results may lead them to become frustrated when things do not progress quickly.

- **Overbearing:** The leadership qualities of Cardinal signs can sometimes come across as domineering or overbearing. They may push too hard for things to go their way, which can lead to conflict in relationships or teams.

- **Restlessness:** Cardinal signs are always looking for the next thing to initiate, which can make them restless or dissatisfied if they feel stuck in routine or stagnation. They thrive on change and movement, and without it, they may feel frustrated or unfulfilled.

Excess of Cardinal Energy in Your Chart

When you have an excess of cardinal energy in your chart, it means that a significant number of planets are in cardinal signs (Aries, Cancer, Libra, or Capricorn). Cardinal energy is associated with leadership, initiation, and action. People with an abundance of this energy tend to be highly motivated, goal-oriented, and constantly driven to start new projects and ventures.

They thrive in situations that require initiative and are often seen as the ones who take charge, whether in work, social situations, or personal relationships. Their proactive nature means they rarely wait for opportunities—they create them. This energy is forward-moving and can make individuals with a lot of cardinal influence highly dynamic, assertive, and ready to make decisions quickly.

However, having an excess of cardinal energy can also present challenges. The constant need for action and the drive to always be moving forward can lead to impatience or burnout. People with a lot of cardinal energy may struggle with finishing what they start because they are more focused on initiating than sustaining. They might also come across as overly assertive, pushing others aside in their need to take control or lead.

Lack of Cardinal Energy in Your Chart

On the other hand, a lack of cardinal energy in your chart indicates that few or no planets are placed in cardinal signs. People with little cardinal energy may find it more challenging to take the initiative or step into leadership roles. They might prefer to go with the flow rather than push for change or new beginnings.

Without much cardinal energy, these individuals may feel more comfortable waiting for opportunities to come to them rather than actively seeking them out. This lack can lead to a more passive approach to life, where they rely on others to take the lead. Decision-making might also be slower, as there isn't the same urgency to take action as seen in those with high cardinal energy.

However, the lack of cardinal energy can also be a strength in certain situations. Individuals without much cardinal influence might be more patient and willing to observe and reflect before making decisions. They tend to be less impulsive and may excel in environments that require careful consideration and a steady approach.

Both an excess and a lack of cardinal energy offer unique strengths and challenges, and finding balance is key. Understanding how this energy plays out in your chart can help you harness its power and mitigate its difficulties.

The Role of Cardinal Energy in Astrology:

Cardinal energy represents the spark that gets things going. In the context of a birth chart, the presence of strong Cardinal energy indicates a person who is likely to be proactive, ambitious, and eager to take the lead in various aspects of life. These individuals may excel in leadership roles, whether in personal relationships, careers, or social movements, and they are often the ones who inspire others to follow their example.

However, it's important for Cardinal signs to balance their need for action with patience and consideration of others' perspectives. By learning to temper their drive with understanding and cooperation, those with strong Cardinal energy can become effective leaders who not only initiate but also see projects through to completion with lasting success.

Fixed Modality: Stabilizers of the Zodiac

The Fixed modality represents stability, persistence, and determination. Fixed signs are the stabilizers of the zodiac, providing the endurance and focus needed to see things through to completion. These signs are associated with maintaining what has been started, grounding energy, and providing structure to ensure long-term success. In astrology, the Fixed modality governs four signs—Taurus, Leo, Scorpio, and Aquarius—and each of these signs expresses this steady, unyielding energy in a unique way.

Fixed signs bring a sense of reliability and consistency to the zodiac. Once they commit to a course of action, they stick to it with unwavering focus. Unlike the Cardinal signs, which are all about initiating action, Fixed signs excel at continuing and completing what has been started. Their energy is resolute, making them dependable and capable of enduring challenges to achieve their goals. They possess a deep inner strength and a strong will, which makes them the foundation upon which lasting progress is built.

Qualities of Fixed Signs:
- **Persistence and Endurance:** Fixed signs are known for their ability to persevere through difficulties. Once they set their minds on something, they are relentless in their pursuit. They are not easily swayed by external circumstances or distractions, as they have a clear focus on their goals. This persistence makes Fixed signs incredibly resilient and able to weather life's challenges with determination and patience.
- **Stability and Reliability:** Fixed signs provide a grounding force in the zodiac. They are consistent, dependable, and loyal, making them the ones others can rely on in times of need. Whether in relationships, work, or personal endeavors, Fixed signs offer a sense of security because they stick to their commitments and are not prone to sudden changes. Their steady approach helps to build a solid foundation in both personal and professional areas.
- **Focus and Determination:** Fixed signs possess a laser-like focus when it comes to their goals. Once they commit to a task or

project, they pour all their energy into seeing it through to completion. This focus can sometimes make them resistant to change, but it also ensures that they achieve lasting results. Their determination is a defining characteristic, as they are not easily discouraged by setbacks or obstacles.

- **Strong Will and Conviction:** Fixed signs have a firm sense of what they believe in and are not easily swayed by outside opinions or trends. They are rooted in their convictions and are willing to stand their ground, even in the face of opposition. This strong will gives them the courage to defend their values and fight for what they believe is right, making them formidable forces when it comes to protecting what they care about.

Fixed Signs and Their Expression:

- **Taurus (Earth Fixed):** Taurus represents the most grounded expression of the Fixed modality. As an Earth sign, Taurus is focused on building security and stability, particularly in the material world. Taurus is known for its persistence in creating long-term success, whether through financial security, relationships, or personal comfort. Their Fixed energy manifests as an unshakable commitment to their goals and a steady, practical approach to life.

- **Leo (Fire Fixed):** Leo expresses the Fixed modality through loyalty, pride, and creative endurance. As a Fire sign, Leo is passionate and driven to maintain their vision of success. Leo's Fixed energy shows up as an unwavering commitment to their personal identity and creative expression, making them fiercely loyal to their values, loved ones, and goals. They take pride in their achievements and are determined to leave a lasting legacy.

- **Scorpio (Water Fixed):** Scorpio's Fixed energy is expressed through emotional depth and transformational power. As a Water sign, Scorpio is intensely focused on understanding the deeper aspects of life, often exploring hidden truths and navigating emotional complexity. Scorpio's Fixed nature allows them to maintain deep emotional connections and pursue transformative change with relentless focus, whether in relationships or personal

growth.
- **Aquarius (Air Fixed):** Aquarius embodies the Fixed modality through intellectual determination and social ideals. As an Air sign, Aquarius is focused on ideas, innovation, and humanitarian goals. Aquarius's Fixed energy shows up as a strong commitment to their vision of progress and a desire to challenge the status quo. They are resolute in their beliefs and dedicated to creating lasting social change, often pioneering unconventional approaches to achieve their goals.

Strengths of Fixed Energy:
- **Dependable:** Fixed signs can be relied on to see things through to the end. Their consistency and loyalty make them dependable in their connections, as they follow through on their commitments with dedication.
- **Resilient:** Fixed signs possess a deep inner strength that allows them to persevere through challenges. They are not easily discouraged by setbacks and have the ability to recover and continue pursuing their goals, no matter how difficult the circumstances.
- **Focused:** Fixed signs have an unparalleled ability to focus on a single task or objective. Their unwavering determination ensures that they remain committed to their goals, often achieving success through sheer persistence and hard work.
- **Loyal:** Fixed signs are known for their loyalty. Once they form bonds, whether in friendships, relationships, or work partnerships, they are deeply committed and protective. Their loyalty makes them trusted allies and long-term companions.

Challenges of Fixed Energy:
- **Stubbornness:** One of the challenges of the Fixed modality is the tendency to be inflexible. Fixed signs can become so focused on their goals that they resist change or new ideas, leading to stubbornness or an unwillingness to adapt to evolving circumstances.
- **Resistance to Change:** Fixed signs can struggle with change,

especially if it threatens their sense of stability or disrupts their carefully laid plans. They may cling to the familiar and resist new approaches, even when change is necessary for growth.

- **Overattachment:** Fixed signs can sometimes become overly attached to people, ideas, or situations. This attachment can make it difficult for them to let go, even when holding on is no longer beneficial. Their loyalty, while admirable, can lead them to stay in unhealthy situations out of a sense of duty or commitment.

- **Rigidity:** Fixed signs' commitment to their beliefs and goals can sometimes make them rigid in their thinking. They may struggle to compromise or see alternative perspectives, especially if they feel their position is being challenged.

Excess of Fixed Energy in Your Chart

When you have an excess of fixed energy in your chart, it means a significant number of planets are in fixed signs (Taurus, Leo, Scorpio, or Aquarius). Fixed energy is associated with stability, determination, and persistence. People with an abundance of fixed energy are often reliable, consistent, and incredibly focused on their goals. Once they set their mind on something, they are determined to see it through, often working tirelessly to achieve their objectives.

Individuals with a lot of fixed energy are known for their strong will and ability to stay the course, even in challenging situations. They are often seen as pillars of strength, able to withstand pressures that might cause others to waver. This quality can make them dependable friends, partners, and colleagues, as they are not easily swayed by external influences.

However, an excess of fixed energy can also present challenges. People with too much fixed energy may become rigid or resistant to change, holding onto habits, beliefs, or situations long after they've stopped serving them. Their strong attachment to stability and consistency can lead to stubbornness, where they refuse to adapt or consider alternative perspectives. This resistance to change can limit growth and create conflict in relationships, especially if flexibility or compromise is needed.

Lack of Fixed Energy in Your Chart

On the other hand, a lack of fixed energy in your chart indicates that few or no planets are placed in fixed signs. Individuals with little fixed energy may find it more challenging to maintain consistency or stay committed to long-term goals. They might struggle with follow-through, often losing interest in projects once the initial excitement fades. Without much fixed energy, they may find it difficult to ground themselves in routines or create lasting structures in their lives.

Those lacking fixed energy might be more adaptable and open to change, which can be a strength in situations that require flexibility. However, this can also lead to a tendency to drift or switch directions too easily, without fully committing to one path. They might start many projects but finish few, or they may struggle to hold their ground in situations that require firmness and resilience.

While a lack of fixed energy can make individuals more open to new experiences and ideas, it can also create instability. Developing a sense of consistency and finding ways to stay focused on long-term goals can help balance the lack of grounding that fixed energy provides.

In both cases, understanding how fixed energy operates in your chart—whether in excess or scarcity—can help you better navigate life's challenges. Finding a balance between determination and flexibility is key to making the most of this powerful modality.

The Role of Fixed Energy in Astrology:

Fixed energy provides the zodiac with stability, endurance, and the power to bring things to completion. In a birth chart, strong Fixed energy suggests a person who is reliable, persistent, and dedicated to their goals. These individuals are often seen as the backbone of any group or organization, providing the consistency and determination needed to turn ideas into reality.

However, Fixed signs must also learn to balance their stability with flexibility. While their ability to stay the course is a strength, being too rigid or resistant to change can hinder growth and adaptation. By learning to embrace change while maintaining their core values, Fixed signs can achieve great success without becoming stagnant or stuck.

Mutable Modality: Adapters of the Zodiac

The Mutable modality represents adaptability, flexibility, and the ability to embrace change. Mutable signs are the chameleons of the zodiac, providing the energy needed to adapt to shifting circumstances and go with the flow. These signs are associated with the end of seasons and symbolize transition, evolution, and the closing of one cycle to prepare for the next. In astrology, the Mutable modality governs four signs—Gemini, Virgo, Sagittarius, and Pisces— each expressing this fluid, changeable energy in its own unique way.

Mutable signs are known for their ability to be versatile and responsive. They are often the ones who adjust, revise, and refine the work that the Cardinal and Fixed signs have begun. While Cardinal signs initiate and Fixed signs solidify, Mutable signs complete the process by adapting to new information and guiding transitions. Their openness to change, coupled with their fluid nature, allows them to facilitate endings and pave the way for new beginnings, ensuring that nothing remains stagnant and evolution continues.

Qualities of Mutable Signs:

- **Adaptable and Flexible:** Mutable signs are incredibly adaptable. They thrive in dynamic environments where they can adjust to new circumstances and ideas. Unlike the Fixed signs, who prefer stability, or the Cardinal signs, who push forward with new initiatives, Mutable signs are comfortable with ambiguity and change. Their flexibility allows them to respond to whatever comes their way, making them resourceful problem-solvers.

- **Open-Minded and Curious:** Mutable signs are open to new ideas, perspectives, and experiences. They are not confined by rigid beliefs or methods, which allows them to explore various possibilities and experiment with different approaches. This curiosity drives their desire for continuous growth and learning, helping them evolve throughout life. Mutable signs often play the role of mediators, as they can see all sides of an issue and adapt their thinking to the changing needs of any given situation.

- **Communicative and Multifaceted:** Mutable signs are natural communicators and multitaskers. They are often skilled at juggling multiple interests, ideas, or tasks at once, which makes them versatile and resourceful in social and professional settings. Their ability to connect with others and convey their ideas effectively adds to their adaptability, as they can bridge gaps between people or concepts. Mutable signs are the connectors of the zodiac, bringing diverse viewpoints together and finding common ground.

- **Restless and Changeable:** Mutable signs can be restless, constantly seeking new experiences or shifting their focus from one thing to another. They are not ones to stay in one place for too long, whether mentally, emotionally, or physically. This restlessness allows them to remain open to change, but it can also lead to a lack of consistency or difficulty in sticking to long-term goals. Mutable signs are constantly evolving, and they welcome the fluidity of life as part of their natural state of being.

Mutable Signs and Their Expression:

- **Gemini (Air Mutable):** Gemini embodies the Mutable modality through its intellectual curiosity and versatility. As an Air sign, Gemini is driven by ideas and communication, constantly seeking new information and experiences. Gemini's Mutable energy manifests in its ability to adapt to changing social environments and its skill in seeing multiple sides of an issue. Geminis are excellent communicators who can quickly shift their perspective to accommodate different viewpoints, making them the social butterflies of the zodiac.

- **Virgo (Earth Mutable):** Virgo expresses the Mutable modality through practical adaptability and analytical refinement. As an Earth sign, Virgo is focused on tangible outcomes and the refinement of processes. Virgo's Mutable energy shows up in its ability to adjust to changing circumstances in a practical, detail-oriented way. Virgos are constantly seeking to improve systems and find more efficient methods, and their adaptability allows them to adjust their plans to ensure everything is working smoothly.

- **Sagittarius (Fire Mutable):** Sagittarius represents the Mutable modality through its adventurous spirit and open-mindedness. As a Fire sign, Sagittarius is driven by passion, enthusiasm, and the pursuit of knowledge. Sagittarius' Mutable energy allows them to adapt to new experiences, cultures, and philosophies, making them the explorers of the zodiac. Their love for freedom and adventure drives them to embrace the unknown, always seeking to expand their horizons and grow through new experiences.

- **Pisces (Water Mutable):** Pisces embodies the Mutable modality through its emotional fluidity and intuitive adaptability. As a Water sign, Pisces is deeply in tune with the emotional and spiritual currents of life. Pisces' Mutable energy is expressed through its ability to adapt to the emotional needs of others, often acting as a compassionate, empathetic presence in any environment. Their open, fluid nature allows them to navigate life's uncertainties with grace, relying on their intuition to guide them through ever-changing circumstances.

Strengths of Mutable Energy:

- **Adaptability:** Mutable signs excel in situations where flexibility and openness to change are required. Their ability to adjust to new circumstances and evolve with the flow of life makes them highly resourceful in both personal and professional contexts.

- **Versatility:** Mutable signs are often multifaceted, capable of juggling different tasks or roles with ease. Their openness to new experiences and ideas allows them to take on a wide range of interests and responsibilities, making them versatile and capable in a variety of areas.

- **Open-Mindedness:** Mutable signs are open to different perspectives and ways of thinking. They are not rigid in their beliefs or methods, which makes them excellent at adapting to new information and finding creative solutions to challenges.

- **Communicative:** Mutable signs are skilled communicators who can convey their ideas effectively and connect with others on a meaningful level. Their ability to see multiple sides of an issue allows them to act as mediators, bridging gaps between people or ideas.

- **Embracing Change:** Mutable signs are comfortable with change and often welcome it as an opportunity for growth. Their fluid nature allows them to navigate life's transitions with ease, making them resilient in the face of uncertainty or unpredictability.

Challenges of Mutable Energy:

- **Inconsistency:** Mutable signs' adaptability can sometimes make them inconsistent. They may shift their focus too frequently, making it difficult for them to stick with long-term projects or commitments. Their restless nature can lead to unfinished tasks or a lack of follow-through.

- **Restlessness:** Mutable signs are constantly seeking new experiences, which can make them restless or dissatisfied with routine. They may struggle with staying in one place or sticking to a steady path, as they are always looking for the next adventure or idea.

- **Overwhelmed by Choices:** Mutable signs' openness to possibilities can sometimes lead to decision fatigue. With so many options available, they may become overwhelmed by the choices in front of them, making it difficult to make firm decisions or commit to a particular course of action.

- **Lack of Boundaries:** Mutable signs are often so flexible and accommodating that they may have difficulty setting clear boundaries. Their desire to adapt to others' needs can lead to overextending themselves or losing sight of their own goals and priorities.

- **Difficulty with Closure:** Although Mutable signs help facilitate transitions, they may struggle with finality. Their tendency to keep options open or continuously adapt can make it challenging for them to fully let go of certain situations or projects.

Excess of Mutable Energy in Your Chart

When you have an excess of mutable energy in your chart, it means a significant number of planets are located in mutable signs (Gemini, Virgo, Sagittarius, or Pisces). Mutable energy is all about adaptability, flexibility, and the ability to adjust to changing circumstances. People with a lot of mutable energy are typically versatile, open-minded, and willing to go with the flow. They are skilled at navigating transitions and can easily shift gears when necessary, making them resourceful in unpredictable or fluid situations.

Individuals with an abundance of mutable energy are usually curious, eager to learn, and excellent at gathering and sharing information. They thrive in environments where they can explore different perspectives, and their ability to see multiple sides of an issue makes them strong communicators and problem-solvers. This quality can also make them empathetic and compassionate, as they can understand and adapt to the emotional needs of others.

However, having too much mutable energy can lead to certain challenges. People with an excess of this energy may struggle with indecision or lack of direction. Because they're so open to change, they may find it difficult to commit to one path or project, often switching focus before seeing something through to completion. This tendency to be overly flexible can also result in a lack of boundaries or consistency, as they may feel pulled in too many directions at once. Their desire to please or accommodate others can sometimes lead to them neglecting their own needs or losing sight of their long-term goals.

Lack of Mutable Energy in Your Chart

A lack of mutable energy in your chart indicates that few or no planets are placed in mutable signs. Individuals with little mutable energy may find it challenging to adjust to change or adapt to new situations. They may prefer stability and structure, sticking to routines and established ways of doing things rather than embracing flexibility. This lack of adaptability can make them more resistant to shifts in their environment, leading to a tendency to become set in their ways.

People with low mutable energy often have a clear sense of direction and are likely to stay committed to their goals once they've made a decision. However, they may struggle when faced with unexpected changes or when flexibility is required. They might have difficulty thinking outside the box or shifting their perspective, which can hinder their ability to grow or innovate.

While a lack of mutable energy can provide focus and consistency, it may also lead to rigidity or an inability to go with the flow. Learning to embrace change, be more open to new ideas, and develop adaptability can help balance this lack of flexibility, allowing them to better navigate life's inevitable transitions.

In both cases, whether there's an excess or lack of mutable energy, the key is finding balance. Too much adaptability can lead to scattered energy, while too little can result in resistance to change. Understanding where you fall on this spectrum can help you make the most of mutable energy in your chart.

The Role of Mutable Energy in Astrology:

Mutable energy represents the power of flexibility, evolution, and adaptability. In a birth chart, strong Mutable energy suggests a person who is open-minded, versatile, and capable of adjusting to life's changes with ease. These individuals are often quick to adapt to new environments, ideas, or social dynamics, making them highly resourceful and capable of thriving in a variety of settings.

However, Mutable signs must also learn to balance their adaptability with consistency. While their ability to embrace change is a strength, they may need to work on sticking to long-term goals or establishing clear boundaries. By learning to channel their versatility in a focused direction, Mutable signs can achieve great success without becoming overwhelmed by endless possibilities.

Elements

In astrology, each of the 12 zodiac signs is associated with one of the four classical elements: Fire, Earth, Air, and Water. These elements represent different types of energy that influence how the signs express themselves, interact with others, and approach life. Understanding the elements is like unlocking the core personality traits of each sign, making it easier to grasp the essence of your astrological chart.

In your natal chart, the elements can show you which energies are most prominent in your personality and which areas might need more balance. For example, if you have a lot of Fire and little Water, you might be full of passion and drive but could benefit from tuning into your emotions and the feelings of those around you. Conversely, if you're heavy on Earth but light on Air, you might be practical and reliable but could work on being more flexible and open-minded.

A well-balanced chart typically has a healthy mix of all four elements, though this isn't always the case. Recognizing where you might have an excess or a lack of an element can help you understand where to focus your growth. For instance, if your chart is low in Fire, you might need to actively cultivate enthusiasm and spontaneity. If you have an abundance of Air, you might want to focus on grounding your ideas into practical actions.

The elements provide a fundamental framework for understanding how the signs interact with each other and with the world. By grasping the qualities of each element, you gain insight into the motivations, strengths, and challenges of each zodiac sign and how these play out in your own life. The elements offer a straightforward yet profound way to connect with the core energies of the zodiac.

Fire: The Energy of Passion, Action, and Inspiration

The Fire signs—Aries, Leo, and Sagittarius—are associated with qualities of passion, action, inspiration, and dynamic energy. Fire is a force of life, creativity, and enthusiasm, driving individuals to pursue their desires, take risks, and embrace challenges. This element is all about forward momentum, confidence, and the urge to live life fully and authentically.

What the Fire Element Represents:
- **Passion and Enthusiasm:** Fire is synonymous with passion, representing a burning desire to pursue what excites and motivates you. Individuals with a strong Fire influence are often enthusiastic, driven by their inner fire to achieve their goals and express themselves fully. This passion can be contagious, inspiring others to take action and follow their own dreams.
- **Action and Initiative:** The Fire element is action-oriented, emphasizing the importance of taking initiative and moving forward with confidence. Fire signs are known for their ability to act decisively, often leading the way with their bold and adventurous spirit. This element encourages you to embrace challenges, take risks, and push beyond limitations.
- **Inspiration and Creativity:** Fire is a source of inspiration and creativity, fueling the imagination and sparking new ideas. Fire signs are often visionary, driven by a desire to create and innovate. This element is associated with the creative force that brings ideas to life, whether through art, leadership, or personal expression.
- **Courage and Confidence:** Fire is linked to courage and confidence, giving individuals the strength to face challenges head-on. Fire signs are typically brave and fearless, willing to stand up for their beliefs and take risks to achieve their goals. This element fosters self-assurance and a belief in one's ability to succeed.
- **Spontaneity and Excitement:** Fire is spontaneous and unpredictable, bringing a sense of excitement and adventure to life.

Fire signs often thrive on new experiences and the thrill of the unknown. This element encourages you to embrace the moment, seek out excitement, and live life with a sense of urgency and vitality.

- **Leadership and Influence:** The Fire element is often associated with leadership and influence, as those with strong Fire energy are naturally inclined to take charge and inspire others. Fire signs are often charismatic, drawing others to them with their dynamic energy and strong presence. This element fosters the qualities of leadership, motivation, and the ability to inspire change.

- **Transformation and Renewal:** Fire is a transformative force, symbolizing the ability to burn away the old and make way for the new. This element is linked to cycles of renewal, where challenges and obstacles are overcome through the power of transformation. Fire signs often have the ability to reinvent themselves and emerge stronger from adversity.

Fire Signs in Astrology:

- **Aries:** Represents the pioneering, courageous, and assertive qualities of Fire. Aries is the initiator, driven by a desire to take action and lead with confidence.

- **Leo:** Embodies the creative, expressive, and charismatic aspects of Fire. Leo is the performer, seeking to shine brightly and inspire others with their presence.

- **Sagittarius:** Reflects the adventurous, philosophical, and expansive nature of Fire. Sagittarius is the seeker, always pursuing new horizons and exploring the world with enthusiasm.

Excess Fire in Your Chart

Having an excess of Fire in your chart means you have a strong concentration of planets in the Fire signs—Aries, Leo, and Sagittarius. This abundance of Fire energy makes you energetic, enthusiastic, and full of life. You're likely confident, assertive, and naturally drawn to leadership roles. However, this can also lead to impulsiveness, restlessness, and a tendency to take risks without fully considering the consequences.

While your passion and boldness are strengths, it's important to balance this fiery nature to avoid burnout and overconfidence. Cultivating qualities of the other elements—like grounding yourself with Earth, nurturing your emotions with Water, and engaging your intellect with Air—can help you harness your Fire energy more effectively. This balance allows you to channel your drive and enthusiasm in ways that are both fulfilling and sustainable.

Lack of Fire in Your Chart

Having a lack of Fire in your chart means you may have few or no planets in the Fire signs. This can lead to a more calm, reflective, and cautious approach to life. You might find it harder to take initiative, feel less spontaneous, and may struggle with assertiveness or self-motivation.

Without strong Fire energy, you might rely more on others for motivation and prefer routine or predictable paths. To balance this, try engaging in activities that spark enthusiasm, practice assertiveness, and surround yourself with people who have strong Fire energy. By actively cultivating these qualities, you can bring more passion, confidence, and boldness into your life.

In summary, the Fire element in astrology represents the qualities of passion, action, inspiration, and dynamic energy. It drives individuals to pursue their goals with enthusiasm, take risks, and embrace challenges with courage and confidence. Fire is a force of creativity and transformation, bringing excitement, spontaneity, and a sense of adventure to life. Understanding the influence of the Fire element in your natal chart provides insight into where you are most likely to express your passions, where you find inspiration, and how you can harness your energy to lead, create, and transform. This element symbolizes the vitality and boldness needed to live life fully and authentically, with a burning desire to achieve and inspire

Earth: The Energy of Stability, Practicality, and Material Manifestation

The Earth signs—Taurus, Virgo, and Capricorn—are associated with qualities of stability, practicality, responsibility, and material manifestation. Earth is the grounding force that brings structure, reliability, and a focus on the tangible aspects of life. This element emphasizes the importance of building solid foundations, working steadily toward goals, and achieving results through patience, discipline, and hard work.

What the Earth Element Represents:
- **Stability and Grounding:** Earth is the element of stability and grounding, providing a solid foundation upon which to build a secure life. Individuals with a strong Earth influence are often dependable and focused on creating stability in their lives, whether through their career, relationships, or personal habits. This element fosters a sense of security and reliability.
- **Practicality and Realism:** The Earth element is associated with practicality and realism, emphasizing a down-to-earth approach to life. Earth signs are known for their ability to assess situations realistically, make practical decisions, and focus on what is achievable. This element encourages you to take a sensible, methodical approach to achieving your goals.
- **Material Manifestation:** Earth governs the material world, including wealth, resources, and physical well-being. It represents the ability to manifest ideas and dreams into tangible reality, whether through building a career, managing finances, or creating a comfortable home. Earth signs are often concerned with material success and the effective management of resources.
- **Responsibility and Discipline:** Earth is linked to responsibility and discipline, highlighting the importance of commitment, hard work, and perseverance. Earth signs are typically diligent and conscientious, taking their duties and obligations seriously. This element encourages you to be disciplined in your efforts, stay committed to your goals, and build

237

a life based on strong values.

- Patience and Endurance: The Earth element embodies patience and endurance, recognizing that true success often requires time and sustained effort. Earth signs understand the value of slow and steady progress, and they are willing to invest time and energy in long-term projects. This element teaches the importance of patience in achieving lasting results.

- Structure and Order: Earth is associated with structure and order, bringing a sense of organization and methodical planning to life. Earth signs often excel at creating systems, routines, and structures that bring order and efficiency to their environment. This element values consistency and the ability to bring order out of chaos.

- Connection to Nature and the Physical World: The Earth element has a deep connection to nature and the physical world. It represents an appreciation for the beauty of the natural environment, a love of the outdoors, and a focus on physical health and well-being. Earth signs often feel a strong bond with nature and may be drawn to activities that connect them with the earth, such as gardening, hiking, or conservation efforts.

Earth Signs in Astrology:

- Taurus: Represents the sensual, grounded, and resourceful qualities of Earth. Taurus is focused on security, comfort, and the enjoyment of the material world.

- Virgo: Embodies the analytical, detail-oriented, and service-oriented aspects of Earth. Virgo is the perfectionist, dedicated to organization, health, and the efficient management of resources.

- Capricorn: Reflects the ambitious, disciplined, and determined nature of Earth. Capricorn is the builder, focused on long-term goals, career success, and the creation of lasting achievements.

Excess Earth in Your Chart

Having an excess of Earth in your chart means you have a strong concentration of planets in Taurus, Virgo, or Capricorn. This gives you a grounded, practical, and reliable nature, with a strong focus on material success and stability. You're likely cautious, methodical, and have a solid work ethic, but you might also be resistant to change and overly focused on the material aspects of life.

While your Earth energy makes you dependable and productive, it can also lead to rigidity, perfectionism, and a lack of spontaneity. To balance this, try incorporating more creativity and spontaneity (Fire), connecting with your emotions (Water), and staying open to new ideas (Air). This will help you blend your practical strengths with a more flexible and well-rounded approach to life.

Lack of Earth in Your Chart

Having a lack of Earth in your chart means you may have few or no planets in Taurus, Virgo, or Capricorn. This can make it challenging for you to stay grounded, focused on practical matters, and establish routines. You might be more inclined toward abstract thinking and creativity, with less emphasis on material success or stability.

Without strong Earth energy, you may struggle with turning ideas into action, maintaining consistency, or managing day-to-day responsibilities. To balance this, focus on developing practical skills, establishing routines, and connecting with nature. These actions can help you bring more stability and grounding into your life, complementing your visionary and imaginative qualities.

In summary, the Earth element in astrology represents the qualities of stability, practicality, and material manifestation. It grounds individuals in the physical world, emphasizing the importance of building secure foundations, working steadily toward goals, and achieving tangible results through patience and discipline. Earth is the element of structure, order, and responsibility, bringing a methodical, realistic approach to life. Understanding the influence of the Earth element in your natal chart provides insight into where you are most likely to focus on material success, how you manage resources, and the importance of stability and grounding in your life. This element symbolizes the strength and endurance needed to create a secure and prosperous life, rooted in practicality and a deep connection to the physical world.

Air: The Energy of Intellect, Communication, and Social Connection

The Air signs—Gemini, Libra, and Aquarius—are associated with qualities of intellect, communication, social connection, and the exchange of ideas. Air is the element of the mind, governing thought processes, intellectual pursuits, and the ways in which we connect with others. This element emphasizes the importance of communication, learning, and the ability to see things from different perspectives.

What the Air Element Represents:
- **Intellect and Thought:** Air is the element of intellect, representing the power of the mind and the importance of ideas, knowledge, and understanding. Individuals with a strong Air influence are often curious, analytical, and focused on learning and mental exploration. This element encourages critical thinking, problem-solving, and the pursuit of wisdom.
- **Communication and Expression:** The Air element is closely linked to communication, emphasizing the importance of sharing ideas, exchanging information, and expressing oneself clearly and effectively. Air signs are known for their ability to articulate thoughts, engage in meaningful dialogue, and connect with others through language and expression. This element fosters open communication and the ability to convey complex ideas.
- **Social Connection and Relationships:** Air governs social interaction and the ability to connect with others on an intellectual and emotional level. Air signs are often sociable, friendly, and adept at building relationships based on mutual understanding and shared interests. This element highlights the value of social networks, collaboration, and the exchange of ideas within communities.
- **Curiosity and Open-Mindedness:** The Air element is associated with curiosity and a desire to explore new ideas, perspectives, and experiences. Air signs are typically open-minded

and adaptable, willing to consider different viewpoints and embrace new ways of thinking. This element encourages intellectual flexibility and the pursuit of knowledge in diverse fields.

- **Objectivity and Detachment:** Air is linked to objectivity and the ability to view situations from a detached, rational perspective. Air signs often excel at analyzing situations without letting emotions cloud their judgment, allowing them to make fair and balanced decisions. This element emphasizes the importance of logic, reason, and impartiality.

- **Innovation and Creativity:** The Air element fosters innovation and creative thinking, encouraging individuals to think outside the box and develop new ideas or solutions. Air signs are often visionary, driven by a desire to innovate and improve the world through intellectual and creative endeavors. This element supports experimentation and the pursuit of original concepts.

- **Movement and Change:** Air is a dynamic element, associated with movement, change, and the flow of ideas and information. Air signs are often restless, seeking variety and new experiences to keep their minds engaged. This element represents the ability to adapt to change and to keep up with the fast-paced flow of modern life.

Air Signs in Astrology:

- **Gemini:** Represents the adaptable, communicative, and inquisitive qualities of Air. Gemini is the messenger, focused on learning, exchanging ideas, and connecting with others through dialogue and curiosity.

- **Libra:** Embodies the harmonious, diplomatic, and relationship-oriented aspects of Air. Libra is the mediator, dedicated to balancing relationships, fostering cooperation, and finding fairness and justice in social interactions.

- **Aquarius:** Reflects the innovative, independent, and humanitarian nature of Air. Aquarius is the visionary, driven by a desire to bring about social change, embrace new ideas, and connect with the collective through intellectual and creative pursuits.

Excess Air in Your Chart

Having an excess of Air in your chart means you have a strong concentration of planets in Gemini, Libra, or Aquarius. This gives you a highly intellectual, curious, and communicative nature. You're likely an excellent communicator, enjoy learning, and thrive in social settings. However, this abundance of Air energy can also lead to restlessness, overthinking, and emotional detachment.

While your strengths lie in your ability to think critically and connect with others, you may struggle with staying grounded, taking decisive action, or connecting emotionally. To balance this, focus on grounding activities (Earth), connecting with your emotions (Water), and turning ideas into action (Fire). This will help you blend your intellectual strengths with practical and emotional depth.

Lack of Air in Your Chart

Having a lack of Air in your chart means you have few or no planets in Gemini, Libra, or Aquarius. This can lead to challenges with communication, intellectual pursuits, and social interactions. You might be more focused on practical tasks and less inclined toward abstract thinking or socializing.

Without strong Air energy, you may struggle with expressing your thoughts clearly, adapting to new ideas, or building a broad social network. To balance this, focus on improving communication skills, engaging in learning, and being open to new experiences. This will help you bring more flexibility, intellectual growth, and social connection into your life.

In summary, the Air element in astrology represents the qualities of intellect, communication, and social connection. It governs the realm of the mind, emphasizing the importance of learning, exchanging ideas, and building relationships based on mutual understanding. Air is the element of curiosity, open-mindedness, and adaptability, encouraging individuals to think critically, communicate effectively, and embrace change.

Understanding the influence of the Air element in your natal chart provides insight into where you are most likely to focus on intellectual pursuits, how you interact with others, and the importance of communication and social connection in your life. This element symbolizes the power of the mind to innovate, create, and connect with the world in meaningful ways.

Water: The Energy of Emotion, Intuition, and Deep Connection

The Water signs—Cancer, Scorpio, and Pisces—are associated with qualities of emotion, intuition, sensitivity, and deep connection. Water is the element of the soul, governing the realm of feelings, the subconscious, and the unseen. This element emphasizes the importance of emotional depth, empathy, and the ability to connect with others on a profound, often spiritual level.

What the Water Element Represents:
- **Emotion and Sensitivity:** Water is the element of emotion, representing the depths of feeling and sensitivity. Individuals with a strong Water influence are often highly empathetic, compassionate, and in tune with their own emotions as well as those of others. This element encourages the exploration of feelings, the expression of emotions, and the ability to connect with others on an emotional level.
- **Intuition and Psychic Awareness:** The Water element is closely linked to intuition and psychic awareness, emphasizing the ability to sense and understand things beyond the logical mind. Water signs are often intuitive, possessing a deep inner knowing and a strong connection to the subconscious. This element fosters a heightened awareness of the unseen, encouraging you to trust your instincts and listen to your inner voice.
- **Empathy and Compassion:** Water governs empathy and compassion, highlighting the importance of understanding and caring for others. Water signs are often nurturing, protective, and devoted to helping those in need. This element emphasizes the ability to feel deeply for others, to offer support and healing, and to create emotional bonds that foster a sense of belonging.
- **Depth and Complexity:** The Water element is associated with depth and complexity, representing the layers of the psyche and the mysteries of the human experience. Water signs are often drawn to exploring the hidden aspects of life, delving into the depths of their

245

own and others' emotions, and seeking to understand the complexities of the soul. This element encourages a deep, reflective approach to life.

- **Creativity and Imagination:** Water is linked to creativity and imagination, often inspiring artistic expression and the ability to create beauty from emotion. Water signs are often creatively gifted, using their emotional sensitivity and intuitive insights to produce art, music, writing, and other forms of creative expression that resonate on a deep emotional level.

- **Healing and Transformation:** The Water element is associated with healing and transformation, particularly on an emotional or spiritual level. Water signs often have a natural ability to heal, whether through offering comfort, providing emotional support, or guiding others through transformative experiences. This element fosters the process of emotional release, renewal, and growth.

- **Connection and Bonding:** Water is the element of deep connection, emphasizing the importance of forming meaningful bonds with others. Water signs often seek out relationships that are emotionally fulfilling and spiritually resonant, valuing intimacy, trust, and emotional security. This element highlights the power of connection to create lasting, transformative relationships.

Water Signs in Astrology:

- **Cancer:** Represents the nurturing, protective, and emotionally connected qualities of Water. Cancer is the caregiver, focused on home, family, and creating a safe, supportive environment for loved ones.

- **Scorpio:** Embodies the intense, transformative, and deeply passionate aspects of Water. Scorpio is the seeker, drawn to exploring the mysteries of life, embracing change, and forging powerful emotional connections.

- **Pisces:** Reflects the compassionate, imaginative, and spiritually attuned nature of Water. Pisces is the dreamer, connected to the realms of fantasy, creativity, and the collective unconscious, often seeking to heal and inspire others through their deep emotional insights.

Excess Water in Your Chart

Having an excess of Water in your chart means you have a strong concentration of planets in Cancer, Scorpio, or Pisces. This gives you a deeply emotional, intuitive, and sensitive nature. You're likely very empathetic, creative, and nurturing, with a strong ability to connect with others on an emotional level.

However, this abundance of Water energy can also lead to emotional overwhelm, moodiness, and difficulty setting boundaries. You might struggle with taking on others' emotions or escaping into fantasy when feelings become too intense.

To balance this, focus on grounding yourself (Earth), practicing clear communication (Air), and taking decisive action (Fire). This will help you channel your emotional depth and intuition in a way that's both fulfilling and stable.

Lack of Water in Your Chart

Having a lack of Water in your chart means you have few or no planets in Cancer, Scorpio, or Pisces. This can lead to challenges with emotional sensitivity, intuition, and forming deep emotional connections. You might be more focused on logic and practicality, finding it harder to express emotions or empathize with others.

Without strong Water energy, you may struggle with understanding emotions, both your own and those of others, and might rely more on reason than intuition. To balance this, work on developing emotional awareness, practicing empathy, and trusting your intuition. This will help you connect more deeply with your feelings and improve your relationships.

In summary, the Water element in astrology represents the qualities of emotion, intuition, and deep connection. It governs the realm of feelings, the subconscious, and the unseen, emphasizing the importance of empathy, compassion, and the ability to connect with others on a profound level. Water is the element of creativity, healing, and transformation, encouraging individuals to explore the depths of their emotions, trust their intuition, and form meaningful bonds with others. Understanding the influence of the Water element in your natal chart provides insight into where you are most likely to express your emotions, how you connect with others, and the importance of intuition and empathy in your life. This element symbolizes the power of the soul to heal, transform, and create deep, lasting connections that resonate on an emotional and spiritual level.

Modality and Element: How They Differ and Work Together

In astrology, modality and element are both fundamental components that describe the nature of the zodiac signs, but they refer to different layers of expression in a birth chart.

Modality: How the Sign Expresses Energy

The modality of a zodiac sign describes how it approaches action, change, and interaction with the world. It reflects the sign's fundamental approach to life, and it gives us insight into how a person operates or responds to different situations. The three modalities—Cardinal, Fixed, and Mutable—focus on the sign's role in initiating, sustaining, or adapting energy.

- **Cardinal Signs** (Aries, Cancer, Libra, Capricorn): Initiate action and are natural leaders. They are proactive, dynamic, and driven to start new projects.
- **Fixed Signs** (Taurus, Leo, Scorpio, Aquarius): Sustain and stabilize energy. They are persistent, reliable, and focused on maintaining consistency.
- **Mutable Signs** (Gemini, Virgo, Sagittarius, Pisces): Adapt and transform energy. They are flexible, versatile, and open to change.

In short, modality describes *how* the sign expresses its energy: whether it's initiating, maintaining, or changing it.

Element: The Nature of the Sign's Energy

The element of a zodiac sign reflects the core nature or essence of the energy associated with that sign. Each sign belongs to one of the four classical elements—Fire, Earth, Air, or Water—and this element defines the basic temperament and behavior of the sign. The element describes *what* the sign focuses on or how it interacts with the world on a deeper, more intrinsic level.

- **Fire Signs** (Aries, Leo, Sagittarius): Associated with passion, enthusiasm, and energy. Fire signs are dynamic, confident, and action-oriented.
- **Earth Signs** (Taurus, Virgo, Capricorn): Grounded, practical,

and focused on material reality. Earth signs value stability, consistency, and tangible results.
- **Air Signs** (Gemini, Libra, Aquarius): Intellectually driven, communicative, and social. Air signs are focused on ideas, relationships, and the exchange of knowledge.
- **Water Signs** (Cancer, Scorpio, Pisces): Emotional, intuitive, and sensitive. Water signs are deeply connected to feelings, instincts, and the subconscious.

In short, the element describes the *nature* of the sign's energy —whether it's passionate (Fire), grounded (Earth), intellectual (Air), or emotional (Water).

The Relationship Between Modality and Element

The combination of a sign's modality and element gives each sign its unique personality and approach to life. For example:
- Aries is a Cardinal Fire sign, meaning it initiates with passion, drive, and action.
- Taurus is a Fixed Earth sign, meaning it sustains energy in a practical, stable, and grounded way.
- Gemini is a Mutable Air sign, meaning it adapts and changes through communication, intellect, and flexibility.
- Cancer is a Cardinal Water sign, meaning it initiates through emotions, care, and nurturing.

By combining modality and element, you get a fuller picture of how each sign interacts with the world—modality tells us *how* the sign operates, while element describes the *nature* of the sign's energy.

Ruling Planets and Their Influence on the Rest of Your Chart

Reminder of the Sign's Ruling Planets:
- Aries is Ruled by Mars
- Taurus is Ruled by Venus
- Gemini is Ruled by Mercury
- Cancer is Ruled by the Moon
- Leo is Ruled by the Sun
- Virgo is Ruled by Mercury
- Libra is Ruled by Venus
- Scorpio is Ruled by Pluto and Mars
- Sagittarius is Ruled by Jupiter
- Capricorn is Ruled by Saturn
- Aquarius is Ruled by Uranus and Saturn
- Pisces is Ruled by Neptune and Jupiter

What Are Ruling Planets?
A ruling planet is the celestial body that governs a zodiac sign, embodying its core traits and guiding how that energy is expressed in your life. For example:
- Venus rules Taurus and Libra, infusing these signs with harmony, beauty, and connection.
- Mercury rules Gemini and Virgo, emphasizing communication, intellect, and adaptability.

How the Placidus System Works
In the Placidus system, houses can be unequal in size, meaning that zodiac signs may not always start on the house cusps. Multiple signs can fall within a single house, and both signs can still hold significance. However, the sign on the house cusp—the boundary at the beginning of the house—is generally considered the dominant sign. The ruling planet of the sign on the cusp has the most influence, directing the main energy of that house, but the sign that occupies the majority of the house can add additional traits or nuances to that area of life.

For example, if your Seventh House starts in Gemini but most of the house is in Cancer, Gemini (ruled by Mercury) would be the primary influence, while Cancer (ruled by the Moon) would also contribute to the interpretation. In short, the sign on the cusp takes precedence, but the sign that takes up the majority of the house adds layers of meaning, with both signs playing important roles.

How Ruling Planets Influence Your Chart

- **Identify the Sign(s) in Each House:** Each house in your chart may contain one or more zodiac signs. The ruling planet of the cusp sign in a house is the key influencer of that house's themes, determining how the energy is expressed.
- **Example:** If Gemini is on the cusp of your 7th house (relationships), Mercury—Gemini's ruling planet—shapes your approach to partnerships. This suggests a communicative, curious, and adaptable energy in relationships, reflecting Gemini's qualities.

Find the Ruling Planet's Placement

Once you identify the sign that influences a house, locate its ruling planet in your chart. There is a dynamic link between the house the ruling planet governs and the house it occupies.

- **Example:** If Mercury (ruling planet of Gemini) is located in your 12th house (spirituality, subconscious), it suggests that your relationships (7th house) are influenced by your inner world or subconscious thoughts. You may seek deeper, more meaningful connections or tend to keep parts of your relationships private or hidden.

Connecting Areas of Life

Ruling planets create bridges between the house they govern and the house they occupy. This connection shows how different aspects of your life are intertwined. The energy of the ruling planet manifests in different parts of your life depending on the houses involved.

Ruling Planet Connections

Ruling planet connections show how different houses in your chart are linked. These connections are based on which planet governs a sign and where that ruling planet is located in your chart.

- **Why they are important:** Ruling planet connections help you understand how different areas of your life are interconnected. They reveal how a zodiac sign's energy flows through different houses, explaining how one area of life impacts another.

How Ruling Planets Interact
- Blended House Themes

The ruling planets of each sign in a house create a layered effect. For instance, if your 2nd house (money, values) contains both Taurus and Gemini, Venus (Taurus's ruler) and Mercury (Gemini's ruler) both influence how you handle finances and self-worth. You might seek stability and beauty in material possessions (Venus), while also being flexible and communicative (Mercury) about managing resources.

- Where the Ruling Planet Directs Energy

The house where the ruling planet is located shows where the sign's energy is also expressed in your life.

- **Example:** If Venus (ruling planet of Taurus) is located in your 5th house (creativity, romance), your approach to finances (2nd house) will be expressed through creativity or romantic relationships. You may make financial decisions based on beauty, art, or creative expression.

- Interconnected Life Areas

Ruling planets form powerful connections between different areas of life. For example, if Aries rules your 10th house (career) and Mars (Aries's ruling planet) is in your 3rd house (communication), your career is influenced by how you communicate. You might excel in careers requiring assertive communication and taking initiative. This illustrates how ruling planets create a holistic view of how different parts of your life are connected.

Examples of Ruling Planets in Action:
- Mars (Ruling Aries and Scorpio):

- **Example:** If Aries rules your 1st house (self and identity) and Mars is located in your 7th house (relationships), it suggests that your sense of self is deeply shaped by your relationships. You might be assertive in partnerships, taking the lead and needing independence in one-on-one interactions.

- **Example:** If Scorpio rules your 4th house (home) and Mars is in your 10th house (career), your home life strongly influences your career ambitions. You may be driven to succeed professionally, with a desire for control at home fueling your public image. Family dynamics and privacy issues could impact your career choices, motivating you to assert yourself in the public sphere.

- Venus (Ruling Taurus and Libra):

- **Example:** If Taurus rules your 2nd house (money and values) and Venus is in your 5th house (creativity, romance), it shows that your approach to money and self-worth is strongly tied to creative pursuits or how you experience love and pleasure. You might find fulfillment through artistic expression or romantic connections.

- **Example:** If Libra rules your 7th house (relationships) and Venus is in your 10th house (career), you might seek balance and harmony in your professional partnerships, or your career may involve work in beauty, art, or diplomacy.

- Mercury (Ruling Gemini and Virgo):

- **Example:** If Gemini rules your 3rd house (communication) and Mercury is in your 12th house (spirituality, subconscious), your communication style might be influenced by hidden thoughts, dreams, or spiritual matters. You may keep your thoughts private or be drawn to writing and communicating about deeper, unseen topics.

- **Example:** If Virgo rules your 6th house (work and health) and Mercury is in your 1st house (self), you likely take a detail-oriented and analytical approach to work and health, and your identity may be closely tied to how you serve others or maintain daily routines.

- Jupiter (Ruling Sagittarius & Pisces):

- **Example:** If Sagittarius rules your 9th house (philosophy, travel) and Jupiter is in your 4th house (home and family), you might feel a strong need for expansion and growth in your home life. You may have a love for travel, philosophy, or spiritual growth that influences your family dynamics, or you may seek to create a home environment filled with learning and exploration.
- **Example:** If Pisces rules your 6th house (health, daily routines, service) and Jupiter is in your 12th house (spirituality, isolation, the subconscious), you might feel a deep calling to connect your daily work or routines with something greater than yourself, such as spiritual practices or serving others in a compassionate way. Your desire to expand and grow may come through introspection, meditation, or working behind the scenes. You could also feel drawn to careers in healing or serving vulnerable populations, as you naturally bring a sense of empathy and faith into your daily life.

- Saturn (Ruling Capricorn & Aquarius):

- **Example:** If Capricorn rules your 10th house (career) and Saturn is in your 7th house (relationships), your career goals might be tied to partnerships, or you may take a serious, responsible approach to both your professional and personal relationships.
- **Example:** If Aquarius rules your 2nd house (money and values) and Saturn is in your 11th house (friendships), your financial approach is shaped by social groups and long-term goals. You may take a disciplined approach to wealth, valuing collaboration with friends or involvement in community projects that reflect your ideals.

- Uranus (Ruling Aquarius):
- **Example:** If Aquarius rules your 11th house (friendships,social groups) and Uranus is in your 5th house (creativity, romance), you may have an unconventional approach to romance and creativity, often seeking excitement and change in these areas. Your friendships may also inspire your creative expression.

- Neptune (Ruling Pisces):
- **Example:** If Pisces rules your 12th house (spirituality, subconscious) and Neptune is in your 6th house (work, health), your daily routines may involve a spiritual or healing aspect. You might feel drawn to work that involves helping others on a deep, emotional level, or you could have a unique connection between your health and your inner spiritual life.

- Pluto (Ruling Scorpio):
- **Example:** If Scorpio rules your 8th house (transformation, shared resources) and Pluto is in your 2nd house (money, values), you may experience intense transformations related to money and resources. Your self-worth might undergo deep changes through shared resources or financial partnerships.

A Quick Note About Aspects

As you explore how ruling planets connect different houses in your chart, it's also important to know that planets interact with each other through aspects—specific angles between them that influence how their energy combines. While ruling planets show which areas of life are linked through house rulership, aspects reveal the relationships between planets themselves, which in turn shape how different life themes interact. Some aspects create ease and flow, while others bring tension and challenges. We'll explore aspects in detail later, but for now, just keep in mind that they add another dimension to how planetary energy moves through your chart.

Summary

In the Placidus system:

- Each house contains one or more signs, and the ruling planet of the cusp sign influences that house's themes most prominently.
- The ruling planet connects the house it influences to the house it occupies, creating dynamic links between different areas of life.
- Understanding where ruling planets are located in your chart reveals how various parts of your life are interconnected and helps you gain deeper insights into the flow of energy in your chart.

By grasping the significance of ruling planets, you can better understand the hidden connections that shape your experiences, offering a rich, personalized interpretation of your astrological chart.

Degrees

Degrees in Astrology: A Deeper Look

Degrees in astrology might seem like a small detail, but they are incredibly significant in understanding the full picture of your natal chart. Each degree within a sign adds a unique nuance to a planet's energy, making your chart truly one-of-a-kind.

In astrology, the sky is divided into 360 degrees, with each of the 12 zodiac signs occupying 30 degrees. The positions of planets and celestial points (like your Ascendant and Midheaven) are measured in degrees, providing a precise map of the sky at your birth.

You might also notice that degree placements in your chart are accompanied by a second number followed by an apostrophe ('). This second number represents minutes, with 60 minutes in each degree. For example, if a planet is placed at 14° 27' Taurus, the planet is located at 14 degrees and 27 minutes into Taurus. Once the minutes reach 60, it advances to the next degree. So 14° 59' is nearly at 15°, while 14° 01' is just past the 14th degree. This level of precision helps astrologers calculate aspects and planetary placements with greater accuracy, offering deeper insights into your chart.

Critical Degrees and Their Significance

Certain degrees within each zodiac sign hold special importance. These are known as critical degrees, and when a planet or point in your chart is at one of these degrees, it can bring extra focus or intensity to that area of your life.

For example:

- A planet at 0° in a sign embodies the raw, unrefined essence of that sign, representing a new beginning or initiation.
- A planet at 15° represents a midpoint, symbolizing balance in that sign's qualities.
- A planet at 29° (known as the "anaretic degree") is linked to completion and transitions, marking the end of a cycle in that sign. Planets at this degree can signify powerful endings and the potential for transformation.

In addition, some degrees are considered critical for specific modalities:
- For cardinal signs (Aries, Cancer, Libra, Capricorn), the critical degrees are 0°, 13°, and 26°.
- For fixed signs (Taurus, Leo, Scorpio, Aquarius), the critical degrees are 8°, 9°, 21° and 22°.
- For mutable signs (Gemini, Virgo, Sagittarius, Pisces), the critical degrees are 4° and 17°.

If you have planets or points at these degrees, they may express more strongly in your life, bringing heightened intensity to the themes of those signs and planets.

Degrees and Being "On the Cusp"

One of the most fascinating aspects of degrees is their relationship to cusps—the point at which one zodiac sign ends and another begins. A planet or celestial point near the 0° or 29° mark of a sign can be considered "on the cusp," meaning it straddles the boundary between two signs. While this planet is technically in one sign, it can be influenced by the energy of the neighboring sign.
- A planet at 29° of a sign is in the anaretic degree, carrying the weight of that sign's lessons and themes. However, because it is so close to the next sign, it may also pick up on the qualities of the following sign, creating a blend of energies.
- A planet at 0° in a sign is just beginning to take on the traits of that sign, but it may still carry some residual influence from the previous sign. This can make the planet's expression more complex, as it navigates the cusp energy.

For example, if your Sun is at 29° Scorpio, you may resonate strongly with Scorpio's intense, transformative energy, but you could also exhibit traits of Sagittarius, like a love for adventure and optimism. Similarly, if your Moon is at 0° Capricorn, it would primarily express Capricorn's practicality and discipline, but with a lingering emotional depth from Sagittarius.

Degrees and Aspects

Degrees don't just pinpoint where a planet is located—they

also help determine how it interacts with other planets and points in your chart. For instance, knowing your Sun is at 23° Leo rather than just in Leo can reveal potential aspects (the angles formed between planets, see Aspects section) with other planets in your chart. Aspects between planets influence how they work together or challenge one another, adding layers of complexity to your astrological profile.

By paying attention to degrees, you uncover subtle yet powerful influences that shape your personality and life path. Whether it's through critical degrees, cusp dynamics, or aspects, learning to interpret degrees brings a new level of depth to your understanding of astrology. Every detail in your chart contributes to the unique tapestry of your cosmic journey.

Critical Degrees for Cardinal Signs: Points of Intensified Energy

For cardinal signs—Aries, Cancer, Libra, and Capricorn—certain degrees are considered critical, meaning that planets or points located at these degrees are thought to express their energies more powerfully, with greater focus or challenge. The critical degrees for cardinal signs are often associated with heightened sensitivity, important turning points, or moments of action and decision-making.

What Critical Degrees Represent in Cardinal Signs:
- **Heightened Sensitivity to Action and Initiation**: Critical degrees in cardinal signs are associated with heightened sensitivity to themes of leadership, initiation, and forward movement. Planets or points at these degrees may emphasize the need for bold actions, emotional connections, balanced relationships, or strategic goals, depending on the sign. The energy of the sign becomes more pronounced, pushing you to take charge and lead in the area of life represented by the house they occupy.
- **Key Turning Points for Starting or Redirecting Paths**: Cardinal signs are initiators, so critical degrees here often indicate pivotal moments when you're called to start something new or change direction. These degrees can correspond to major life decisions, fresh beginnings, or shifts in focus that have long-term significance. They may also represent times when you must overcome inertia and take decisive action to propel yourself forward.
- **Intensified Drive and Ambition**: The energy of a planet or point at a critical degree in a cardinal sign is often amplified, leading to a stronger expression of the qualities associated with that sign. For example:
  - In Aries, the energy manifests as heightened courage, initiative, and determination.
  - In Cancer, it intensifies emotional leadership, nurturing instincts, or the ability to create foundations.
  - In Libra, it brings a greater focus on harmony, diplomacy, and

relational balance.

- In Capricorn, it strengthens ambition, discipline, and the drive for achievement.

- Challenges and Opportunities to Lead: Critical degrees in cardinal signs often present challenges that test your leadership and initiative. These degrees may bring circumstances where you are required to act with decisiveness, confidence, or resilience. They also offer opportunities for growth by stepping into leadership roles, taking calculated risks, or asserting yourself in new ways. The key is to balance the assertiveness and ambition of cardinal energy with focus and strategy.

Critical Degrees for Cardinal Signs:

For cardinal signs, the critical degrees are generally considered to be the following:

- 0°, 13°, and 26° of Aries
- 0°, 13°, and 26° of Cancer
- 0°, 13°, and 26° of Libra
- 0°, 13°, and 26° of Capricorn

Descriptive Overview of Each Degree:

- 0° (Critical Degree): The 0° degree is often referred to as the "critical" degree of a sign, representing the purest expression of that sign's energy. For cardinal signs, planets or points at 0° are highly significant, often indicating a powerful new beginning, a fresh start, or a decisive moment. This degree is associated with taking initiative, making bold moves, and embracing leadership qualities. It can also signify a sense of urgency or the need to take action quickly.

- 13° (Mid-Degree): The 13° degree is considered another critical degree in cardinal signs, representing a point of transition and adjustment. Planets or points at 13° often indicate a moment of reflection or reevaluation, where you may need to make adjustments to your plans or approach. This degree can also signify the need to find balance or harmony between different aspects of your life, especially in areas related to the cardinal sign's themes (e.g., self-assertion in Aries, home and family in Cancer, relationships in Libra, career in Capricorn).

- 26° (Late Degree): The 26° degree is associated with the culmination or final expression of a sign's energy. In cardinal signs, this degree often represents the completion of a cycle or the realization of long-term goals. Planets or points at 26° may indicate a time of consolidation, where you gather the results of your efforts and prepare to move forward. This degree can also signify the need to wrap up loose ends, make final decisions, or take responsibility for past actions.

In summary, the critical degrees for cardinal signs—0°, 13°, and 26°—represent points of intensified energy and significance in your natal chart. Planets or points at these degrees are associated with heightened sensitivity, key turning points, and moments of decisive action. The energy at these degrees is often more pronounced, leading to important challenges or opportunities in the areas of life governed by the cardinal signs: self-assertion (Aries), home and family (Cancer), relationships (Libra), and career (Capricorn). Understanding the influence of these critical degrees provides insight into where you may experience significant events, where you are called to take action, and how you can harness the intensified energy to achieve your goals.

Critical Degrees for Fixed Signs: Points of Stability and Intensity

For fixed signs—Taurus, Leo, Scorpio, and Aquarius—certain degrees are considered critical, often bringing heightened intensity, stubbornness, or a need for stability. Fixed signs are known for their determination, persistence, and resistance to change, and these qualities are often magnified at critical degrees. Planets or points located at these degrees in fixed signs may indicate areas of life where you experience strong, unyielding energy, requiring focus and a balanced approach to manage effectively.

What Critical Degrees Represent in Fixed Signs:
- **Heightened Sensitivity to Stability and Endurance**: Critical degrees in fixed signs emphasize heightened sensitivity to themes of consistency, resilience, and persistence. Planets or points at these degrees may highlight areas where you are deeply rooted, where you exhibit unwavering focus, or where you feel the need to create long-term stability. These placements often bring a greater awareness of what anchors you and where you may feel a strong emotional or physical attachment.
- **Determination and Willpower**: Fixed signs are associated with determination and resolve, and critical degrees within these signs amplify these qualities. Planets at these degrees often indicate areas of life where you are exceptionally steadfast, where you refuse to give up, or where you have the ability to weather challenges with remarkable endurance. These degrees often push you to stand firm in your decisions and see projects or goals through to completion.
- **Resistance to Change and the Need for Growth**: The critical degrees in fixed signs can reveal areas where you may resist change or struggle to let go of outdated habits, relationships, or beliefs. While this resistance can provide stability, it may also create challenges when adaptability is required. These degrees call on you to find a balance between holding your ground and recognizing when growth and transformation are necessary.
- **Intensified Focus and Strength**: Planets or points at critical

degrees in fixed signs intensify the traits of the sign. For example:
- In Taurus, they highlight heightened focus on material security, comfort, and perseverance.
- In Leo, they amplify creativity, self-expression, and the need to take center stage or lead.
- In Scorpio, they deepen emotional intensity, transformative power, and resourcefulness.
- In Aquarius, they magnify innovation, individuality, and the ability to challenge the status quo.

- Challenges and Opportunities for Long-Term Success: Critical degrees in fixed signs often present challenges that require patience, commitment, and a long-term perspective. These placements may bring opportunities to solidify plans, build enduring structures, or develop mastery in a particular area of life. The key is to harness the fixed energy to create lasting results while remaining open to necessary adjustments along the way.

Critical Degrees for Fixed Signs:

For fixed signs, the critical degrees are generally considered to be the following:
- 8°, 9°, and 21°, 22° of Taurus
- 8°, 9°, and 21°, 22° of Leo
- 8°, 9°, and 21°, 22° of Scorpio
- 8°, 9°, and 21°, 22° of Aquarius

Descriptive Overview of Each Degree:

- 8° and 9° Degrees: These degrees are often associated with strong, concentrated energy within the fixed signs. Planets or points at 8° and 9° in Taurus, Leo, Scorpio, or Aquarius may show areas where you are particularly determined, where you exhibit intense focus, and where you are resistant to outside influence. These degrees can indicate where you may need to balance persistence with flexibility or where you are likely to encounter challenges related to stubbornness or rigidity.

- 21° and 22° Degrees: The 21° and 22° degrees in fixed signs often signify a culmination or solidification of energy. Planets or points at these degrees may represent areas where you achieve stability and long-term success, often after a period of sustained effort. These degrees can also indicate where you may be deeply entrenched in your ways, requiring careful consideration of when to hold firm and when to adapt. The energy at these degrees is powerful and can lead to significant achievements if managed well.

In summary, the critical degrees for fixed signs—8°, 9°, 21°, and 22°—represent points of heightened intensity, stability, and persistence in your natal chart. Planets or points at these degrees are associated with strong focus, determination, and resistance to change. These degrees highlight areas of life where you may experience challenges related to inflexibility or where you have the potential to achieve significant long-term goals through dedication and hard work. Understanding the influence of these critical degrees provides insight into where you may need to balance persistence with adaptability, where your strengths lie, and how you can harness the powerful energy of the fixed signs to achieve success and stability.

Critical Degrees for Mutable Signs: Points of Adaptability and Sensitivity

For mutable signs—Gemini, Virgo, Sagittarius, and Pisces—certain degrees are considered critical, often highlighting areas where flexibility, adaptability, and sensitivity are heightened. Mutable signs are known for their ability to change, adapt, and go with the flow, and these qualities are often amplified at critical degrees. Planets or points located at these degrees in mutable signs may indicate areas of life where you experience heightened responsiveness to change, increased sensitivity, or a need for adaptability.

- **Heightened Sensitivity to Change and Flow**: Critical degrees in mutable signs emphasize heightened sensitivity to transitions, movement, and adaptability. Planets or points at these degrees often highlight areas where you are exceptionally attuned to shifts in your environment, where your perspective may fluctuate, or where you experience significant mental, emotional, or spiritual awareness. These placements encourage a deep connection with the flow of change and the ability to respond intuitively to new situations.

- **Adaptability and Versatility**: Mutable signs are associated with flexibility and a capacity for adjustment, and critical degrees within these signs amplify these traits. Planets at these degrees indicate areas of life where you are highly adaptable, able to shift gears easily, or inclined to explore different approaches. These placements emphasize your ability to navigate complex or dynamic situations with resourcefulness and creativity.

- **Restlessness and a Need for Variety**: The critical degrees in mutable signs often highlight areas where you may feel restless or crave variety and exploration. These degrees signify parts of life where you may seek constant growth, learning, or new experiences. While this openness can be a strength, it also challenges you to balance your desire for change with the need for stability and consistency in key areas.

- Fluidity and Multitasking Skills: Planets or points at critical degrees in mutable signs intensify your capacity for fluidity and versatility. These are the areas of life where you are likely to excel at multitasking, handling transitions, or managing diverse responsibilities. For example:
- In Gemini, they amplify communication, curiosity, and the ability to process information quickly.
- In Virgo, they heighten analytical thinking, attention to detail, and a focus on practical problem-solving.
- In Sagittarius, they magnify your thirst for knowledge, philosophical exploration, and adventurous spirit.
- In Pisces, they deepen your intuition, emotional understanding, and capacity for creative expression.

- Opportunities for Growth Through Change: Critical degrees in mutable signs often present opportunities to grow by embracing change and fluidity. These placements challenge you to remain open to new possibilities, let go of rigid expectations, and evolve through your experiences. The energy of mutable signs at critical degrees encourages you to adapt and refine your skills while navigating life's transitions.

Critical Degrees for Mutable Signs:

For mutable signs, the critical degrees are generally considered to be the following:
- 4°, 17° of Gemini
- 4°, 17° of Virgo
- 4°, 17° of Sagittarius
- 4°, 17° of Pisces

Descriptive Overview of Each Degree:

- 4° Degree: The 4° degree in mutable signs is associated with heightened adaptability and sensitivity. Planets or points at 4° in Gemini, Virgo, Sagittarius, or Pisces may indicate areas where you are particularly responsive to change, where you have a keen sense of awareness, or where you may experience frequent shifts in perspective. This degree can highlight your ability to adjust to new situations quickly and with ease, but it may also suggest a need for grounding or stability.

- 17° Degree: The 17° degree in mutable signs represents a point of significant versatility and fluidity. Planets or points at 17° in these signs may show areas where you excel in multitasking, managing change, or navigating complex situations. This degree often indicates a strong ability to adapt to new circumstances, but it may also suggest a tendency toward restlessness or a desire for constant variety. The energy at this degree encourages you to embrace change while also finding ways to maintain a sense of consistency or focus.

In summary, the critical degrees for mutable signs—4° and 17° —represent points of heightened adaptability, sensitivity, and versatility in your natal chart. Planets or points at these degrees are associated with a fluid, flexible approach to life, where you are particularly attuned to change and open to new experiences. These degrees highlight areas of life where you may experience restlessness or a need for constant movement, but also where you have the ability to navigate complex situations with ease. Understanding the influence of these critical degrees provides insight into where you may need to balance adaptability with stability, where your strengths lie in managing change, and how you can use the heightened sensitivity of the mutable signs to your advantage.

Anaretic Degree 29°: The Degree of Crisis and Transition

The anaretic degree, also known as the "degree of fate," refers to the 29th degree of any zodiac sign in a natal chart. This degree is considered particularly significant and is often associated with themes of crisis, urgency, and transition. The 29th degree is the final degree of a sign, marking the end of a cycle and the cusp of a new beginning. Planets or points located at the anaretic degree are thought to carry an intensified energy, as they are at the culmination of their journey through a sign, preparing to transition into the next. The anaretic degree often brings a sense of urgency to resolve unfinished business or to make important decisions before moving forward.

What the Anaretic Degree Represents:

- **Crisis and Urgency:** The 29th degree often brings a sense of urgency or even crisis. Planets or points here may signal areas of life where you feel pressure to act, make decisions, or resolve conflicts. This sense of "time running out" can lead to an overwhelming need for closure or completion before moving on.

- **Transition and Endings:** The anaretic degree is a point of transition, marking the end of a cycle where the planet has reached the peak of the sign's energy. It signals the need to let go of what no longer serves you, highlighting themes of closure, endings, and preparing to enter the energy of the next sign.

- **Culmination of Energy:** As the final degree of any sign, 29° represents a climax of the sign's lessons and experiences. The planet at this degree has mastered the sign's qualities but may feel an urgency to finish something unresolved. The energy of this degree is heightened, emphasizing the importance of bringing things to completion.

- **Intensified Energy and Pressure:** Planets at the anaretic degree tend to express their energy in a more intense, exaggerated way. This can lead to heightened emotions, strong impulses, or extreme behaviors related to the planet's function. The pressure to resolve issues before the planet moves into the next sign can create tension and even crisis-like situations, pushing you to act decisively.

- **Critical Decisions and Turning Points:** The 29th degree is often associated with pivotal moments in life. It can symbolize a crossroads where significant decisions must be made, especially in the areas governed by the planet and house in question. These moments often feel critical, as if you are facing an important test before moving forward.

- **Unresolved Issues and Karmic Lessons:** The anaretic degree can bring unresolved issues or unfinished business to the surface, representing a final karmic lesson. It may signal the need to integrate the lessons of the sign before transitioning into the energy of the next. This degree often highlights past challenges or karma that must be addressed before new growth can occur.

- **Instability and Change:** Because the 29th degree is a threshold between two signs, it can create a sense of instability or unpredictability. There may be unfinished business or a lack of mastery over the sign's energy, leading to feelings of restlessness or insecurity. This transitional energy can drive you to make quick decisions, especially if you feel unsteady or out of balance.

- **Heightened Awareness and Clarity:** At 29°, there is often an increased awareness of the planet's themes and the lessons associated with the sign. This heightened clarity can push you toward deeper reflection, making you more conscious of the decisions that need to be made. It's a moment of realizing the culmination of your experiences and preparing for the next phase of growth.

- **Fate and Destiny:** The anaretic degree is sometimes called the "degree of fate" due to its association with significant life events or turning points. Planets at 29° may be linked to fated experiences that feel unavoidable or destined. These events often lead to major shifts, marking a critical juncture on your life's path.

In summary, the anaretic degree (29°) in astrology represents a point of crisis, urgency, and transition in your natal chart. Planets or points at this degree are associated with the culmination of a cycle, heightened energy, and the need to resolve unfinished business before moving forward. The anaretic degree often brings a sense of pressure to take action, make decisions, or address unresolved issues, as the energy is on the verge of transitioning to a new phase. Understanding the influence of the anaretic degree in your chart provides insight into where you may face critical turning points, where you need to confront challenges, and how you can navigate the intensity of this degree to achieve closure and prepare for new beginnings. This degree marks a significant moment of change and transformation in your life's journey.

The 0° Degree of Any Sign: The Degree of New Beginnings and Pure Potential

The 0 degree in astrology is the very first degree of any zodiac sign. It represents the point of inception, marking the beginning of a new cycle or phase of energy. Planets or points located at 0 degrees are thought to embody the purest essence of that sign's qualities, making this degree highly significant in a natal chart. The 0 degree carries the energy of fresh starts, new opportunities, and the unformed potential that can be shaped into something meaningful. This degree often indicates a moment of initiation, where the energy is raw, untested, and ready to be developed.

What the 0° Degree of Any Sign Represents:
- **New Beginnings and Fresh Starts:** The 0° degree represents the beginning of a new phase, where the energy of the sign is pure, unfiltered, and full of potential. It marks a clean slate and the chance to embark on a new journey related to the qualities of the sign. This degree carries a pioneering spirit, full of enthusiasm and optimism for what lies ahead.
- **Pure Potential:** At 0°, the energy is in its most unrefined and pure state. This degree holds the promise of new growth, but the qualities of the sign are still in their nascent form, waiting to be developed. The 0° degree represents pure potential, offering an opportunity to shape the planet's energy according to your intentions and goals.
- **Raw and Untamed Energy:** Planets or points at 0° express the raw essence of the sign's qualities. This energy is instinctual, dynamic, and often unrestrained, reflecting the unformed nature of the sign at this degree. While this gives a fresh and exciting momentum, it may lack the refinement and mastery that comes with later degrees.
- **Inexperience and Exploration:** The 0° degree is often associated with inexperience, as it represents the start of a journey. Planets at this degree may express their energy in a youthful,

exploratory way, as you begin learning how to harness and direct the planet's qualities in the new sign. Mistakes or missteps can occur, but they are part of the process of growth and discovery.

- Powerful Initiation and Inception: The 0° degree marks the initiation of the sign's energy, where new ideas, projects, or experiences are first brought into existence. It's a degree of action, signaling the start of something significant and the first step into new territory. Planets at 0° are infused with the pioneering energy of the sign, making this degree a time for bold actions, transitions, and new identities.

- Untested Energy: The energy of 0° is untested, and while it holds great promise, it requires time, experience, and effort to fully develop. Planets at this degree operate with instinct and enthusiasm but may need nurturing and refinement to reach their full potential. This degree invites growth and evolution, though it may initially feel uncertain or exploratory.

- Pioneering Spirit and Innovation: The 0° degree embodies the pioneering spirit, urging you to take risks and explore uncharted areas of life. This degree encourages bold moves, innovation, and experimentation. It's about being brave enough to step into the unknown and embrace the journey with curiosity and confidence.

- Key Moments of Decision: Planets or points at 0° often correspond with key moments of decision, where the choices you make set the course for the future. This degree challenges you to align your actions with your true purpose and take steps that move you forward on your life path.

- Initiation of the Sign's Qualities: At 0°, the qualities of the sign are at their most essential and direct. For example, 0° Aries represents pure leadership, independence, and initiative, while 0° Libra symbolizes harmony, relationships, and balance. This degree marks the introduction of the sign's core themes and sets the tone for how these qualities will unfold throughout the planet's journey through the sign.

Qualities of 0° Degree

- **Instinctual and Dynamic:** Planets at 0° often express their energy in a dynamic, instinctual way. As the planet enters the sign, it operates with fresh enthusiasm and drive, pushing you to initiate change or take bold action. This degree is about acting on instinct, sometimes without fully considering long-term consequences.

- **Unformed but Potent:** The 0° degree is rich with potential but unformed, meaning the planet's energy is in its earliest stages of development. This can lead to bold action and innovation, but also missteps as the planet adapts to the sign's characteristics. It's a powerful degree for initiating change, though refinement comes later.

- **Opportunities for Growth:** While 0° represents inexperience, it also offers the greatest opportunities for growth and learning. This degree encourages you to embrace the planet's qualities with a sense of adventure, experimentation, and creativity. It marks the start of a long journey through the sign's lessons, allowing you to grow into the full expression of the planet's energy in that sign.

- **Excitement and Anticipation:** There's a palpable sense of excitement and anticipation at 0°. The planet is entering new territory, bringing a feeling of boundless possibilities and uncharted potential. This degree is often infused with optimism and enthusiasm, as you prepare to explore the sign's qualities in fresh and innovative ways.

In summary, the 0 degree in astrology represents a powerful point of new beginnings, pure potential, and the initiation of a new cycle. Planets or points at this degree embody the unrefined, raw energy of the sign they occupy, offering a fresh start and the opportunity to shape this energy in meaningful ways. The 0 degree marks moments of inception and decision-making, where you are called to take bold actions and set the course for the future. The 0 degree provides insight into where you are embarking on new journeys, where you possess untapped potential, and how you can harness this energy to create something original and impactful.

The 15° Degree of Any Sign: The Degree of Manifestation and Balance

The 15 degree in astrology represents a point of equilibrium within any zodiac sign. Positioned halfway through each sign's journey, the 15 degree embodies the maturation of the sign's qualities and the balance between the initial burst of energy and the consolidation of its expression. Planets or points located at 15 degrees are seen as possessing a steady, reliable, and highly manifesting energy, marking this degree as especially important in a natal chart. The 15 degree carries the energy of crystallization, where the sign's essence is neither in its raw, untested state nor in its final form, but rather at its most balanced and dynamic.

What the 15° Degree Represents:

- **Manifestation:** The 15 degree symbolizes the process of manifestation, representing the point where the energy of the sign is at its most concentrated and capable of taking form. Planets or points at this degree indicate areas of life where there is a strong potential for concrete realization and the ability to bring ideas into tangible existence. This degree highlights the power to shape intentions into reality and solidify what was initiated at the 0 degree.

- **Balance and Equilibrium:** At 15 degrees, the energy of the sign finds its equilibrium. This degree represents the balance between the early enthusiasm of the sign's beginning and the wisdom that comes from experience. The 15 degree offers the opportunity to harness the sign's qualities in a harmonious way, creating a sense of stability and evenness that allows for steady growth and expression.

- **Maturation of Energy:** The 15 degree is associated with the maturation of the sign's energy. By this point, the qualities of the sign have developed beyond their initial, untested state and are now in a phase of full expression. Planets or points at this degree may express themselves in a confident and steady manner, reflecting the sign's established traits and strengths. This degree indicates the point of maturity, where the sign's energy has ripened and become more defined.

- **Dynamic and Stable Force:** The energy at 15 degrees is dynamic yet stable, combining the vibrancy of the sign's potential with the solidity of its manifestation. This degree often brings a sense of groundedness and focus, supporting efforts to build, sustain, and enhance what has already been started. The 15 degree emphasizes the power of steady progress and the importance of maintaining balance amid change and activity.

- **Crystallization:** At the 15 degree, the sign's energy crystallizes, forming a clear and distinct expression of its qualities. This degree represents a moment where ideas, emotions, and projects solidify into their true form. The 15 degree highlights the power to crystallize intentions into reality, capturing the essence of the sign in a way that is both vibrant and enduring.

- **Peak Expression:** The 15 degree is often associated with the peak expression of the sign's qualities. Planets or points at this degree exhibit the full vibrancy and strength of the sign they occupy. This degree indicates the culmination of the sign's journey toward maturity, where the energy has reached its highest level of expression and influence.

- **Key Moments of Manifestation:** Planets or points at 15 degrees often coincide with key moments of manifestation, where efforts come to fruition and outcomes are realized. This degree challenges you to harness your resources, maintain balance, and focus on bringing your vision into reality. It encourages the use of patience, determination, and consistent effort to manifest your desires.

In summary, the 15 degree in astrology represents a powerful point of manifestation, balance, and the peak expression of a sign's qualities. Planets or points at this degree embody a dynamic yet stable energy, reflecting the maturity and crystallization of the sign they occupy. The 15 degree marks moments of manifestation and realization, where ideas and efforts take solid form. Understanding the influence of the 15 degree in your natal chart provides insight into areas where you possess a dynamic force, where balance can be achieved, and how you can harness this fixed energy to manifest your goals. This degree highlights the importance of maintaining equilibrium and perseverance, inviting you to explore and fully express the potential that lies within.

Aspects

Learning to Read Aspects in Your Natal Chart

Learning to read aspects in a natal chart might seem daunting at first, but it's much easier than it appears. Aspects are simply the angles formed by degrees, describing the relationships between planets, objects, and points in your natal chart. These angles show how the energies of different planets interact, influencing various areas of your life.

Think of your natal chart as a map of the sky at the moment you were born. The planets, objects, and points are like actors in a play, each with its own role. Aspects are the conversations happening between these actors, adding depth and richness to your chart's story. Depending on the angle between them, these conversations can be harmonious, challenging, or neutral. With a little patience and practice, you'll soon find that these connections are not only manageable but also incredibly rewarding to explore. Remember, you're more than capable of mastering this fascinating part of astrology!

Understanding Aspects Through Degrees

In astrology, degrees are essential for calculating aspects. Each zodiac sign spans 30 degrees, and the distance between planets is measured to determine whether an aspect forms between them. These planetary angles reveal how their energies interact, shaping different areas of life and influencing your personal experiences.

Astrologers use degree measurements to identify aspects and their effects. A conjunction (0-10 degrees) merges planetary energies for a powerful influence, while a square (90 degrees) creates tension and challenges. An opposition (180 degrees) represents a push-pull dynamic between two life areas. Meanwhile, trines (120 degrees) and sextiles (60 degrees) indicate harmony and ease, allowing energy to flow more smoothly.

Example Chart Towards the End of the Book

Towards the end of this book, I've included Lana Del Rey's

birth chart as an example to help you visually spot and interpret all the different aspects in her chart. You'll also find real-life examples from her chart, showcasing one example of each aspect along with its corresponding degrees. These examples illustrate how planets interact and provide practical guidance on interpreting aspects in a birth chart.

Additionally, in this section I've included very in-depth details on how to find and locate aspects in a birth chart, with a drawn diagram to explain the process. After exploring Lana's chart, you'll have the opportunity to apply these techniques to your own birth chart, gaining a clear understanding of how aspects shape your unique astrological blueprint and influence your life's experiences.

Exploring Major Aspects

As you become more comfortable with the basics, you'll discover that each aspect has its own unique energy and influence, shaping different areas of your life.

In the following sections, we'll dive into the major aspects—conjunctions, sextiles, trines, oppositions, and squares—breaking them down so you can easily understand their significance and how they play out in your chart. By the end, you'll be able to interpret these aspects with confidence and see how they bring your astrological story to life.

Orb of Influence: Understanding Degrees and Aspects

In astrology, the "orb of influence" refers to the range in degrees within which two planets, points, or celestial bodies can form an aspect. Aspects are the angles between these planets, influencing how their energies interact. However, aspects don't have to be exact to be felt; they can still exert an influence even if the planets are a few degrees off from the exact angle. This range is known as the "orb of influence."

What is the Orb of Influence?

The orb is a buffer zone around the exact degree of an aspect. For example, a conjunction is typically considered an exact aspect at 0 degrees, meaning two planets are right next to each other in the zodiac. However, an orb of influence allows this conjunction to still have an effect if the planets are, say, 5 degrees apart. Essentially, the orb sets the boundaries within which an aspect's influence is active, even if it is not precisely at the expected degree.

Why Are Orbs Important?

Orbs are crucial in astrology because they determine whether an aspect is close enough to be relevant in a chart. The tighter the orb, the more intense and immediate the aspect's influence. Conversely, a wider orb suggests a subtler or less direct effect. Understanding orbs helps refine readings, giving more weight to aspects that fall within a close range while considering those at wider orbs as background influences.

Standard Orbs for Major Aspects

The orb of influence varies depending on the type of aspect and the planets involved. Major aspects—such as conjunctions, oppositions, squares, trines, and sextiles—typically allow for a larger orb. Luminaries (the Sun and Moon) generally have the widest orbs, while outer planets tend to have tighter orbs. Here are the generally accepted orbs for major aspects:

- **Conjunction (0 degrees):** 8-10 degrees. A conjunction is considered the most powerful aspect, and its orb can be quite wide. Some astrologers use up to 10 degrees for personal planets (Sun, Moon, Mercury, Venus, Mars) and slightly less for outer planets.
- **Opposition (180 degrees):** 8-10 degrees. Like conjunctions, oppositions carry a strong influence, so a similar orb range applies.
- **Square (90 degrees):** 7-8 degrees. Squares are known for creating tension and challenges, so they are given a relatively wide orb.
- **Trine (120 degrees):** 6-8 degrees. Trines represent ease and harmony, and while their orb is slightly smaller than that of conjunctions and oppositions, they are still quite influential.
- **Sextile (60 degrees):** 4-6 degrees. Sextiles are gentler aspects that indicate opportunities and talents, so they have a somewhat narrower orb than the more dynamic aspects.

Variations in Orbs: Planets, Points, and Personal Influence
Different celestial bodies can affect the orb size:
- **The Luminaries (Sun and Moon):** The Sun and Moon are given the widest orbs due to their powerful influence in a chart. The Sun typically has an orb of up to 10-12 degrees, while the Moon can influence up to 8-10 degrees. This means aspects involving the Sun and Moon are often felt more strongly, even when they are not exact.
- **Personal Planets (Mercury, Venus, Mars):** These planets are closer to Earth and represent more personal aspects of life, so they usually have a moderate orb range of about 6-8 degrees for major aspects.
- **Outer Planets (Jupiter, Saturn, Uranus, Neptune, Pluto):** Outer planets have a slower movement and broader influence over generational trends. Therefore, they typically have a narrower orb range of about 5-7 degrees, although some astrologers allow wider orbs for conjunctions and oppositions.
- **Points and Angles (Ascendant, Midheaven, Nodes):** Points and angles in a chart, such as the Ascendant (rising sign) or Midheaven (MC), also have orbs of influence. The orb for these

points is generally tighter, usually around 2-3 degrees, given their specific roles in defining personal and contextual aspects of the chart.

Applying Orbs in Chart Interpretation

In a natal chart, the orb of influence helps astrologers prioritize aspects. When two planets form an aspect within a tight orb (close to the exact degree), the influence is strong and noticeable in the person's life. For example, if someone's Sun is at 10° Aries and their Mars is at 12° Aries, the conjunction between these two planets is very powerful, being only 2 degrees apart.

Wider orbs (e.g., 8-10 degrees for major aspects) still have an impact but are often experienced as less immediate or pronounced. These aspects can act as background themes that shape underlying patterns or longer-term challenges and strengths.

- **Example:** If a person's Venus at 16° Leo squares their Moon at 21° Taurus, this Venus-Moon square with a 5-degree orb indicates a moderately strong influence, suggesting tension in balancing emotional needs with desires for pleasure and harmony in relationships. However, if the orb were wider—such as Venus at 15° Leo and the Moon at 23° Taurus (an 8-degree orb)—this square would still create friction, but its impact might be less prominent in daily interactions.

Summary

The orb of influence in astrology is a critical concept that defines the range in which an aspect between two planets or points can still exert its power. Tight orbs indicate strong and immediate influences, while wider orbs suggest more subtle, background effects. By understanding and applying the orb of influence, astrologers can accurately assess how planetary interactions shape personality, behaviors, and life experiences, providing a nuanced and personalized interpretation of the natal chart.

Conjunction: The Union of Energies

In astrology, a conjunction occurs when two or more planets are positioned very close to each other in the natal chart, typically within a range of 0 to 10 degrees apart. This aspect is considered one of the most powerful and influential because it represents the merging or blending of planetary energies. When planets are in conjunction, their influences are fused together, often amplifying their effects and creating a powerful focal point in the chart. The nature of a conjunction can vary depending on the planets involved— some combinations create harmony and synergy, while others may generate tension or intensify certain traits. A conjunction reflects unity, focus, and the integration of planetary qualities.

What a Conjunction Represents:
- **Merging of Energies:** A conjunction brings together the energies of the planets involved, resulting in a potent and unified expression. The qualities of the planets are combined, often making this aspect one of the strongest influences in the chart. It can lead to a significant focus on the traits and themes associated with the planets involved in the conjunction.
- **Amplification:** When planets are in conjunction, their effects are amplified, making their influence more pronounced and visible. This can intensify the characteristics and behaviors associated with the planets, leading to a heightened expression of those qualities. A conjunction can make certain aspects of your personality or life experience stand out more prominently, adding intensity to the area of life governed by the planets and the house they occupy.
- **Unity and Integration:** Conjunctions symbolize unity and integration, as the planets work together to create a cohesive expression. This aspect encourages the blending of different energies, talents, or interests into a single, focused manifestation. It can create a sense of wholeness or completeness in the areas governed by the planets in conjunction, helping you integrate seemingly different parts of your personality or life into a unified approach.

- **Concentration of Power:** A conjunction represents a concentration of power, where the combined energies of the planets create a strong and focused influence. This can lead to increased drive, determination, or passion in pursuing goals related to the planets involved. The conjunction often brings a sense of purpose and direction, pushing you to channel this energy into achieving something significant in the areas of life highlighted by the conjunction.

- **Potential for Conflict or Harmony:** The nature of a conjunction depends on the planets involved and their inherent qualities. Some conjunctions can be harmonious, creating a smooth and supportive energy, while others may bring about conflict or tension as the planets' energies struggle to coexist. For example, a conjunction between Venus and Jupiter can be positive and expansive, enhancing love and abundance, whereas a conjunction between Mars and Saturn might create frustration or blocked energy, requiring patience and discipline to balance these opposing forces.

- **Key Area of Focus:** Conjunctions highlight a key area of focus in the natal chart, where the combined energies of the planets play a central role in your life. This aspect can indicate an area where you are particularly strong, where you experience significant challenges, or where you are likely to achieve success. The house where the conjunction occurs often shows the life area where this energy will be concentrated and most influential.

- **Beginning of a New Cycle:** Conjunctions in a natal chart represent the blending of two planetary energies, creating a unified force that marks the beginning of a new cycle in the areas of life they influence. These planets act as seeds, setting the stage for personal development and growth. For instance, a Sun-Moon conjunction can reflect an individual with a strong inner drive to initiate and create, while a natal Jupiter-Saturn conjunction might suggest a person attuned to larger social and structural themes.

How to Recognize a Conjunction in a Chart
- **Degrees of Separation:** In a natal chart, a conjunction occurs

when two or more planets are within 0 to 10 degrees of each other. Some astrologers use a tighter orb for conjunctions, especially with faster-moving planets, while allowing a broader orb for slower-moving planets or luminaries (Sun and Moon). The closer the planets are in degrees, the stronger the conjunction's influence. If the planets are within 1 or 2 degrees, the conjunction is considered especially powerful and can have a dominating force.

- **Same Sign and House:** A conjunction generally occurs between planets that are in the same zodiac sign and the same house. If you see two or more planets clustered together in one sign or house, this indicates a conjunction. However, conjunctions can also occur across house cusps or between planets in neighboring signs (known as an "out-of-sign" conjunction), although their expression may be more complex in such cases.

- **Aspects List or Grid:** Many astrology software programs or chart calculators will list conjunctions in an aspects table or display them in an aspects grid. Conjunctions are usually marked with the symbol (☌) or the word "Conjunction." These tools help you quickly identify where conjunctions are occurring in your chart, often highlighting them in bold or with special colors.

Example Conjunction Between Venus and the North Node

In the chart on the next page, there is a conjunction between Venus, the North Node, and the Descendant, showing a profound blending of energies related to love, partnerships, and personal growth. Venus is in the 6th house (health, work, and daily routines) at 14° Taurus, while the North Node is in the 7th house (relationships and partnerships) at 16° Taurus, and the Descendant (the cusp of the 7th house) is at 15° Taurus. Despite Venus and the North Node being in different houses, their close orb (within 2 degrees) unites them with the Descendant, creating a powerful point of focus in Lana's chart.

This conjunction suggests that themes of love, beauty, and harmony (Venus) are deeply tied to Lana's life purpose and soul growth (North Node) through partnerships and one-on-one connections (7th house). The inclusion of the Descendant emphasizes

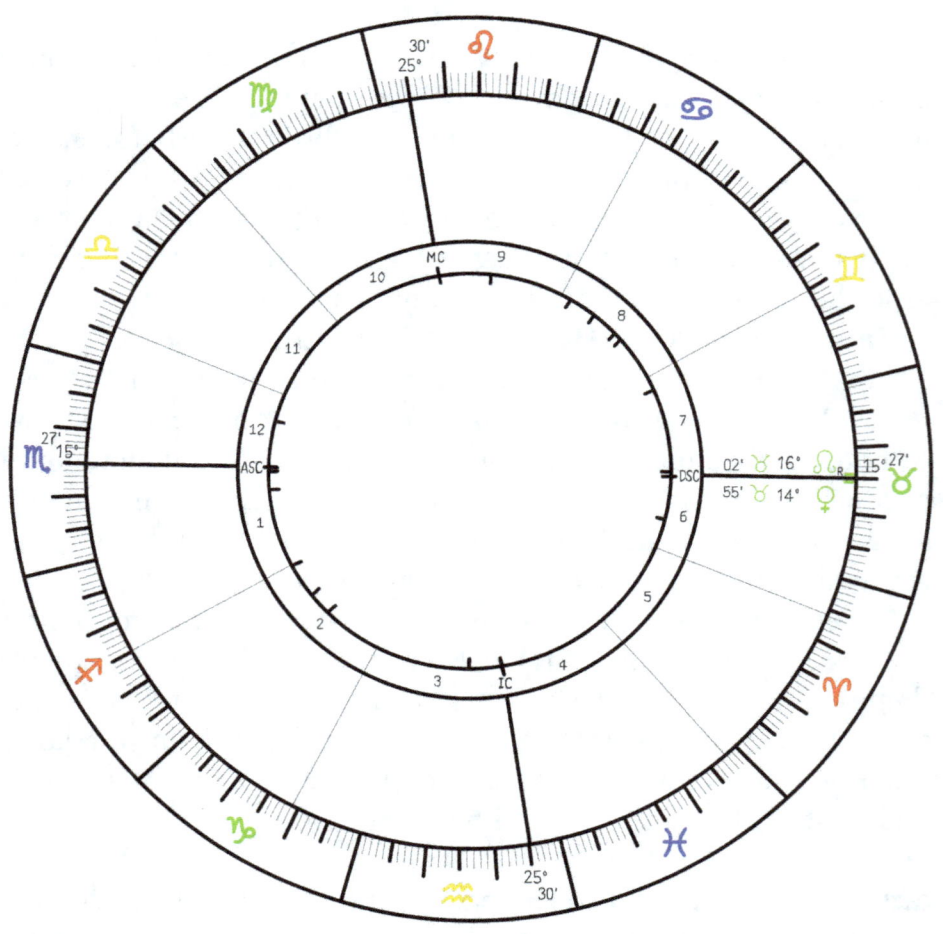

the importance of relationships as a mirror for her personal development. Since the 6th house represents daily work and routines, Venus here suggests that Lana seeks harmony, grace, and artistic expression in her everyday life. Her work—often tied to creative endeavors and music—becomes a vehicle for bringing balance and beauty into the world. However, the pull toward the North Node and the Descendant in the 7th house indicates that relationships and collaborations are central to her life's mission. Partnerships may inspire her, challenge her, or act as catalysts for her evolution.

The Descendant's involvement in this conjunction reinforces the idea that Lana's journey is not just about personal achievement but also about the lessons and growth she experiences through intimate connections. In her music, themes of love, longing, and vulnerability are prevalent, reflecting the deep integration of Venusian energy with her North Node's purpose. This aspect suggests that her art and her relationships are intertwined, as both are areas where she learns, grows, and fulfills her soul's mission.

Visually, this chart highlights how planets close in degrees, even across house boundaries, can work together powerfully. The conjunction between Venus, the North Node, and the Descendant bridges the 6th and 7th houses, demonstrating how energies from different areas of life—daily routines, partnerships, and personal growth—blend to create a larger narrative of purpose and connection in Lana's life.

Additional Considerations for Conjunctions

- **Planets Involved:** The meaning and impact of a conjunction depend heavily on the planets involved. Some planets blend more harmoniously than others, while others create tension. For example, a conjunction between the Sun and Mercury can enhance mental clarity and communication, while a conjunction between Mars and Pluto may intensify ambition, drive, and even aggressive tendencies.

- **Combustion (with the Sun):** When a planet is in conjunction with the Sun and within 8°30' of it, the planet is said to be combust. This weakens or overshadows the planet's influence because the Sun's powerful energy dominates. However, if the planet is exceptionally close to the Sun—within 17 minutes of a degree (a fraction of one degree)—this is called cazimi, or "in the heart of the Sun." In this case, the planet is thought to gain heightened strength and significance due to the Sun's concentrated energy.

- **Out-of-Sign Conjunctions:** In some cases, two planets may be in conjunction by degree but located in different zodiac signs. This is called an out-of-sign conjunction and can create a more complex dynamic. The planets are still blending their energies, but the differing signs add a layer of tension or conflict as the signs' qualities contrast.

- **Retrograde Planets:** If one or both planets involved in a conjunction are retrograde, this can alter the way the conjunction expresses itself. Retrograde planets often bring introspection or delays, so the conjunction's energy may manifest more inwardly, or its impact may be more subtle and require more time to unfold.

- House Influence: The house in which the conjunction occurs plays a crucial role in determining which area of life is most affected. For example, a conjunction in the 10th house may indicate a strong focus on career and public reputation, while a conjunction in the 7th house highlights relationships and partnerships.

In summary, a conjunction represents the merging or blending of planetary energies, creating a powerful and unified influence in the natal chart. This aspect amplifies the traits and characteristics of the planets involved, resulting in a concentrated focus in the areas of life associated with the conjunction. Conjunctions can bring harmony or tension, depending on the planets, but they always signify an important and potent aspect of your personality and life experience. Understanding conjunctions in your chart provides insight into where you may experience heightened energy, intense focus, and the integration of different aspects of yourself into a cohesive whole. Conjunctions reveal key areas where combined planetary influences shape your path, presenting both opportunities and challenges that play a central role in your journey.

Additionally, recognizing a conjunction in your chart involves noting the degrees of separation between planets (within 10 degrees), checking for planets in the same sign and house, and identifying their influence in your life based on the house and sign placement. Conjunctions often mark important areas where you will experience personal growth, transformation, and a powerful synergy of energies.

Sextile: The Aspect of Opportunity and Harmony

In astrology, a sextile occurs when two planets are approximately 60 degrees apart from each other in the natal chart. This aspect is considered one of the most favorable and harmonious, creating opportunities, ease, and natural talents. The sextile aspect represents an easy flow of energy between the planets involved, leading to cooperation and mutual support without the intensity or challenges that can arise with other aspects. When planets are in a sextile, they enhance each other's positive qualities, offering opportunities for growth and progress with relatively little resistance.

What a Sextile Represents:

- **Opportunities and Growth:** A sextile aspect indicates areas of life where opportunities naturally present themselves, offering potential for growth, learning, and development. These opportunities often arise in a way that feels organic, but they require awareness and effort to fully take advantage of the benefits they bring. Sextiles suggest that with a little intention, you can unlock significant progress.

- **Harmonious Cooperation:** Sextiles symbolize a balanced and cooperative flow of energy between the planets involved. The qualities of these planets work together in a way that encourages mutual support and creates a sense of alignment, helping you navigate situations with confidence and ease. This cooperation fosters growth, creativity, and problem-solving.

- **Ease of Expression:** The sextile aspect allows the qualities of the planets to manifest smoothly, making it easier to express your ideas, talents, and creativity. While this ease is not entirely effortless, it feels natural and productive. In areas influenced by a sextile, you may find it simpler to communicate effectively or channel your energy toward constructive outcomes.

- **Areas of Natural Potential:** Sextiles highlight areas where you have natural potential or emerging talents. These strengths may not feel fully developed but can flourish with attention and practice. The planets in a sextile often point to latent abilities that, once recognized, can be refined and used effectively in your personal or professional life.

- **Encouragement for Exploration:** Sextiles promote an openness to new ideas, perspectives, and experiences. This aspect encourages curiosity and adaptability, making it easier to embrace change and seek out opportunities for growth. The harmonious flow of energy in a sextile helps you feel confident as you step into uncharted territory.

- **Supportive Energy for Progress:** The energy of a sextile is supportive and uplifting, providing a stable foundation for pursuing goals and overcoming challenges. While it doesn't guarantee results on its own, this aspect offers the encouragement and resources needed to move forward. In areas influenced by a sextile, things tend to feel manageable and rewarding when you take action.

- **Balanced and Productive Interactions:** A sextile aspect fosters balanced interactions between the planets, leading to productive outcomes in the areas of life they influence. Whether it's relationships, work, or personal projects, the sextile creates an atmosphere of cooperation and mutual benefit, helping you achieve goals and maintain harmony.

How to Recognize a Sextile in a Chart

- **Degrees of Separation:** In a natal chart, a sextile occurs when two planets are approximately 60 degrees apart. Sextiles are considered "soft" or harmonious aspects, meaning that the planets involved are working together rather than in opposition or conflict. The closer the planets are to the exact 60-degree mark, the stronger the sextile's influence.

- **Compatible Elements:** Sextiles usually occur between planets that are in compatible elements. For example, planets in Fire signs (Aries, Leo, Sagittarius) often form sextiles with planets in Air signs (Gemini, Libra, Aquarius), and planets in Earth signs (Taurus, Virgo, Capricorn) typically sextile planets in Water signs (Cancer, Scorpio, Pisces). This elemental compatibility enhances the ease of expression and cooperation between the planets.

- **Aspect Grids and Tables:** In many astrology software programs or chart calculators, sextiles are displayed in the aspects table or grid. Sextiles are often marked with the symbol (✳) or indicated as "60°" in aspect listings. These tools can help you quickly identify where sextiles are occurring in your chart and how they influence different areas of your life.

Example Sextile Between the Moon and Chiron

In the chart below, we see a sextile between the Moon in Leo and Chiron in Gemini. A sextile is a harmonious aspect that occurs when two planets are approximately 60 degrees apart, creating a flow of supportive energy between them. In this case, the Moon is at 10°

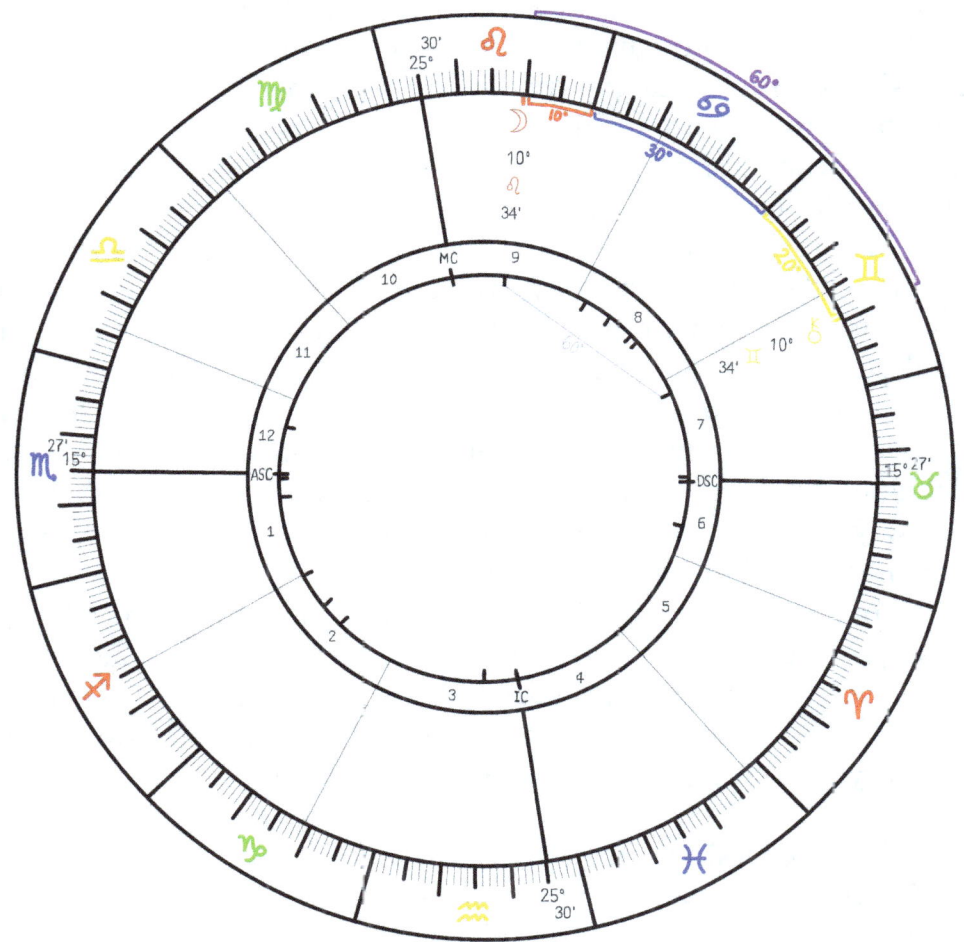

Leo in the 9th house, and Chiron is at 10° Gemini in the 7th house, forming a precise 60-degree angle.

This sextile reflects a harmonious exchange between the Moon's emotional nature and Chiron's themes of healing and vulnerability. The Moon in the 9th house suggests that emotions are processed through exploration, whether intellectual, philosophical, or creative, while Chiron in the 7th house ties emotional healing to relationships. This aspect indicates that these areas of life support each other, allowing emotional experiences to be transformed into growth and deeper understanding.

With this sextile, emotions (Moon) and the process of healing (Chiron) work together in a way that encourages self-awareness and personal evolution. Challenges in relationships (Chiron) may naturally inspire emotional reflection and expression (Moon), making it easier to find meaning in difficult experiences. Rather than emotional wounds remaining unresolved, this aspect suggests a natural inclination to integrate them into a broader perspective, whether through storytelling, learning, or personal philosophy.

The connection between the Moon in Leo and Chiron in Gemini further emphasizes expression, suggesting that emotions and past wounds may be processed through communication, creativity, or intellectual pursuits. There is an ease in translating personal experiences into something that can be shared with others, whether through art, writing, or meaningful conversations. This sextile highlights how emotional depth and healing work together, shaping the way personal experiences are understood, expressed, and ultimately transformed into wisdom.

In the visual chart, the sextile between the Moon and Chiron highlights the bridge between her emotional world (9th house) and her experiences in relationships (7th house). This flow of energy supports her ability to find healing through self-expression, creativity, and meaningful connections with others.

Additional Considerations for Sextiles
   - **Planets Involved:** The nature of the sextile is influenced by the planets involved. For example, a sextile between Mercury and

Venus would indicate ease in communication and relationships, promoting charm, diplomacy, and creative expression. On the other hand, a sextile between Mars and Saturn would suggest that your drive and ambition are well-supported by discipline and structure, helping you achieve long-term goals with steady progress.

- **Sextiles and Houses:** The house in which the sextile occurs is crucial in understanding the specific area of life it affects. For instance, a sextile between planets in the 12th house (subconscious, spirituality, and hidden matters) and the 2nd house (finances and values) might indicate that financial opportunities or material stability flow naturally through spiritual practices, inner work, or creative inspiration. Meanwhile, a sextile between the 3rd house (communication) and the 5th house (creativity) suggests that creative self-expression comes easily through communication, teaching, or writing.

- **Effort Required:** While sextiles are considered positive aspects, they may not be as forceful or intense as aspects like conjunctions or squares. Because sextiles create ease and potential, it's essential to take advantage of the opportunities they present. Without conscious effort or initiative, the energy of a sextile can pass by without being fully realized. Recognizing a sextile in your chart encourages you to actively engage with the supportive energies and make the most of them.

In summary, a sextile represents a harmonious and supportive aspect that brings opportunities, ease of expression, and highlights natural talents. It fosters cooperation and balance between the planets involved, creating an environment where energies work together smoothly. Sextiles encourage growth, learning, and progress, making it easier to achieve success and positive outcomes in the areas influenced by the sextile. A sextile in your natal chart reveals where you can take advantage of favorable circumstances and develop your strengths with less resistance. Sextiles are recognized in charts by looking for planets that are 60 degrees apart, often in compatible elements. While sextiles create ease and flow, it's important to take initiative to fully benefit from the opportunities they present. By harnessing the supportive energy of a sextile, you can build on your strengths, achieve personal and professional growth, and experience a greater sense of harmony and balance in your life.

Trine: The Aspect of Flow and Natural Harmony

In astrology, a trine occurs when two planets are approximately 120 degrees apart in the natal chart. This aspect is considered one of the most favorable, harmonious, and supportive, symbolizing a natural flow of energy between the planets involved. A trine reflects ease, balance, and cooperation, where things come naturally and effortlessly. This aspect often highlights areas where you experience success, inherent talents, emotional balance, and creative potential without needing to struggle. Trines bring a sense of grace and positivity, making the expression of the planetary energies smooth and productive.

What a Trine Represents:

- **Natural Harmony and Flow:** A trine indicates a natural harmony between the planets, allowing their energies to flow together effortlessly. This aspect creates an easy and balanced interaction, supporting growth and success without requiring force or conflict. In the areas of life governed by the planets involved, there's a sense of alignment and ease, where things naturally fall into place.

- **Ease and Grace:** The energy of a trine is characterized by ease and grace, making it one of the most favorable aspects in astrology. This aspect suggests that the qualities represented by the planets involved are expressed fluidly, without obstacles or difficulties. Trines create a graceful approach to actions, decisions, and relationships, allowing you to handle situations with poise and confidence.

- **Inherent Talents and Strengths:** Trines often highlight areas of life where you possess natural talents and strengths. The harmonious relationship between the planets suggests that you have a natural ability to excel in the areas they influence. Whether it's intellectual, creative, or interpersonal skills, trines reveal where you can succeed with minimal effort because of your innate abilities.

- **Support and Cooperation:** This aspect reflects a strong sense of support and cooperation between the planets. The trine fosters collaboration and mutual understanding, leading to productive and positive outcomes in the areas of life it touches. You may find that you naturally attract helpful circumstances and people, making it easier to navigate relationships, projects, and endeavors with mutual benefit.

- **Creative Expression:** Trines are often associated with creativity and artistic expression. The smooth flow of energy between the planets fosters inspiration, imagination, and the ability to create beauty in the world. This aspect can help you tap into your creative potential effortlessly, allowing your artistic or innovative ideas to take shape with minimal resistance. Whether in art, writing, design, or other forms of creativity, trines create the conditions for easy and successful self-expression.

- **Emotional and Psychological Balance:** Trines contribute to emotional and psychological balance, helping you maintain a sense of inner harmony and well-being. The planets involved in a trine support each other, leading to stability in your mental and emotional health. This aspect can provide emotional resilience, helping you navigate challenges with calmness and a positive outlook. You're likely to feel at ease with yourself, balanced, and at peace in the areas affected by the trine.

- **Favorable Conditions:** Trines bring favorable conditions and opportunities into your life, often without requiring significant effort. These aspects are associated with good fortune, where the universe seems to align in your favor. The energy of a trine helps you attract lucky breaks and positive circumstances, offering a smoother path to achieving your goals. This aspect represents areas where you can move forward with confidence, knowing that the planets are working together to support your success.

How to Recognize a Trine in a Chart

- **Degrees of Separation:** In a natal chart, a trine occurs when two planets are approximately 120 degrees apart. Trines are considered "soft" or harmonious aspects, where the energies flow naturally between the planets. The closer the planets are to the exact 120-degree mark, the stronger the trine's influence.

- Same Element: Trines typically occur between planets in the same element, such as Fire (Aries, Leo, Sagittarius), Earth (Taurus, Virgo, Capricorn), Air (Gemini, Libra, Aquarius), or Water (Cancer, Scorpio, Pisces). The elemental connection between the planets enhances the ease of interaction and flow, making it simpler for the planets to cooperate.

- Aspect Tables and Grids: Astrology software programs or chart calculators often display trines in aspect tables or grids. Trines are typically marked with the symbol (△) or indicated as "120°" in aspect listings. These tools allow you to quickly identify where trines are occurring in your chart and the areas of life where you can expect ease and harmony.

Example Trine Between the South Node and Mercury

In the chart on the next page, there is a trine between the South Node in Scorpio and Mercury in Cancer, creating a harmonious connection between karmic lessons and emotional communication. The South Node is located at 16° Scorpio in the 1st house (representing self-identity, personal expression, and past-life traits), while Mercury is positioned at 16° Cancer in the 8th house (governing communication, thought processes, transformation, intimacy, and shared resources). This alignment reflects a smooth flow of energy between Lana's innate, deeply ingrained qualities (South Node) and her intuitive, emotionally charged way of thinking and communicating (Mercury).

The South Node in Scorpio in the 1st house suggests that Lana enters this life with an intense, magnetic presence and a deep connection to personal transformation. Scorpio's influence gives her a natural depth and emotional intensity, making her someone who feels things profoundly. She may instinctively reflect on the past, process emotions inwardly, and then communicate them in a way that resonates deeply with others. This placement indicates a familiarity with themes of resilience, rebirth, and self-reinvention, traits that may have been developed through past experiences or even carried over from previous lifetimes. There is a strong self-awareness

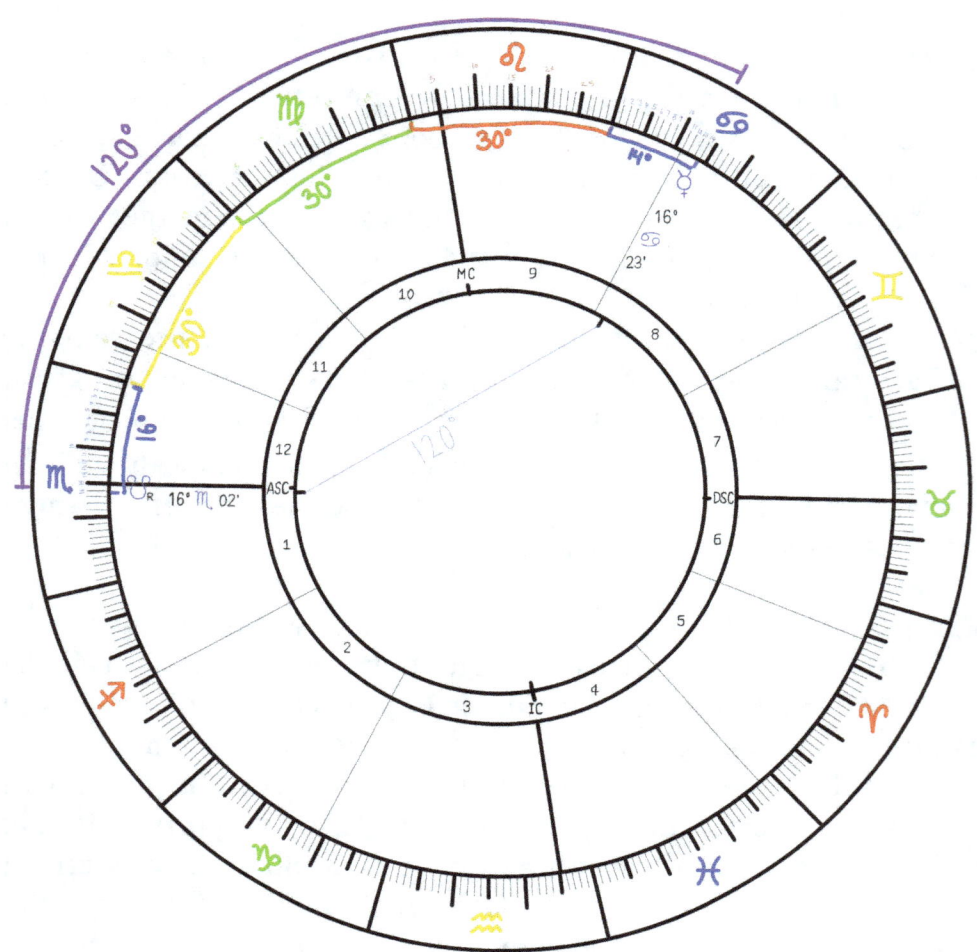

and emotional depth in this placement, but it can also bring a tendency toward solitude, secrecy, or an over-identification with personal struggles.

Meanwhile, Mercury in Cancer in the 8th house highlights a deeply intuitive and emotionally perceptive way of thinking and communicating. This placement suggests a mind attuned to themes of vulnerability, intimacy, and transformation, with a tendency to process thoughts through an emotional and symbolic lens rather than a purely logical one. Mercury in Cancer speaks softly but powerfully, evoking nostalgia and sentimentality, while the 8th house influence adds an almost mystical, hypnotic depth to her words and ideas.

The trine between the South Node and Mercury suggests that Lana's deeply ingrained emotional intensity (South Node) flows naturally into her way of expressing herself (Mercury), creating an effortless connection between self-perception and communication. She may instinctively know how to put feelings into words in a way that leaves a lasting impact on others, drawing from personal experiences of transformation and emotional depth. This aspect also suggests a poetic, almost hypnotic quality to her speech and writing, as her words likely carry the emotional weight of past experiences and a subconscious understanding of life's deeper, hidden layers.

This alignment also reflects Lana's ability to channel her own emotional evolution into her communication style, whether through intimate conversations, lyrical storytelling, or the way she expresses herself in everyday life. With Mercury in the 8th house, she is drawn to profound discussions, uncovering hidden truths, and exploring the psychological and emotional undercurrents that shape human relationships. The ease of this trine allows for a natural blending of her deeply ingrained emotional awareness (South Node) with her ability to articulate and express these insights (Mercury).

Visually, the chart displays the 120-degree angle between the South Node and Mercury, highlighting how these energies work together seamlessly. This trine supports Lana's ability to integrate emotional depth, subconscious awareness, and intuitive thinking, shaping both her self-perception and the way she shares her thoughts with the world.

Additional Considerations for Trines

- **Planets Involved:** The nature of the trine depends on the planets involved. For example, a trine between Venus and Jupiter can bring luck, abundance, and ease in love and finances, while a trine between Mercury and Uranus can highlight intellectual brilliance, innovative thinking, and creative problem-solving. Different planetary combinations in a trine will express their harmonious energies uniquely.
- **Trines and Houses:** The house placement of the planets in a trine provides insight into which areas of life will experience ease and flow. For instance, a trine between planets in the 5th house (creativity) and the 9th house (higher learning) suggests that you

will experience creative inspiration through learning and philosophical exploration. A trine in the 1st house (self) and the 10th house (career) can indicate natural leadership abilities and ease in public roles.

- Maximizing the Gift of a Trine: Trines represent ease, grace, and natural flow, often highlighting areas where talents or opportunities come effortlessly. However, because things feel so natural in these areas, it's easy to overlook or underutilize the gifts they provide. To fully maximize the potential of a trine, it's important to recognize and consciously engage with these blessings. By nurturing and developing the opportunities a trine offers, you can transform its effortless flow into meaningful achievements.

In summary, a trine represents a harmonious and favorable aspect that brings ease, flow, and natural alignment between the planets involved. It highlights areas of life where you possess inherent talents and strengths, experience emotional and psychological balance, and benefit from favorable conditions. Trines indicate where you can express your creativity, achieve positive outcomes, and enjoy support and cooperation from others. This aspect brings a sense of grace and confidence, making it easier to navigate life and achieve success.

Trines are typically recognized by planets that are 120 degrees apart, often in the same element. While trines create effortless energy, it's essential to actively engage with the opportunities they present to avoid complacency. By understanding the trine's influence in your natal chart, you gain insight into the areas where you are most likely to experience harmony, ease, and success. Trines reveal the smooth, supportive energy that helps you navigate life's challenges and opportunities with grace and confidence.

Opposition: The Aspect of Tension and Balance

In astrology, an opposition occurs when two planets are directly opposite each other, typically about 180 degrees apart in the natal chart. This aspect is characterized by dynamic tension between the planets, reflecting a push-and-pull energy that requires balance and integration. Oppositions often bring to light areas of life where there may be conflict, indecision, or polarization, but they also offer powerful opportunities for growth by challenging you to find harmony between seemingly contradictory forces. The tension created by an opposition can lead to significant personal insight, helping you develop a deeper understanding of your own needs and desires.

What an Opposition Represents:

- **Tension and Conflict:** Oppositions represent a tension between two opposing forces or energies. The planets involved may seem to be at odds, creating inner or outer conflict. This aspect often brings to light areas of your life where you experience struggle, indecision, or competing desires. Oppositions highlight where you feel pulled in different directions, making it necessary to find a way to reconcile these opposing forces.

- **Polarization:** An opposition reflects polarization, where two parts of your personality or life are pulling you in opposite directions. This can lead to feelings of being torn between conflicting goals, needs, or values. The opposition creates a clear division between the planets, forcing you to confront and integrate these opposing perspectives. Finding balance between the two energies is the key to resolving the tension created by this aspect.

- **Need for Balance:** The primary challenge of an opposition is to achieve balance between the two planets involved. Oppositions require you to find a middle ground where both energies can be expressed in a healthy and constructive way. Without balance, oppositions can lead to inner conflict or external struggles in relationships and decision-making. However, when you learn to harmonize these opposing forces, you can experience significant growth and personal integration.

- **Complementary Forces:** Although oppositions often represent conflict, they also signify complementary forces. Each planet in an opposition holds something the other lacks, and together they can create a more complete and well-rounded expression of their energies. The opposition encourages you to integrate the strengths of both planets, resulting in a more balanced and nuanced approach to life. Learning to see the opposing planets as complementary rather than contradictory is essential to working with this aspect.

- **Projection and Relationships:** Oppositions are closely linked to relationships and interactions with others, particularly one-on-one dynamics. Often, the qualities of one planet in the opposition are projected onto others, leading to challenges in relationships that require negotiation and compromise. This aspect can reveal how you relate to others, where you may unconsciously project your inner conflicts, and where you need to work on understanding and integrating different perspectives. Oppositions in the chart can mirror the dynamics of partnerships and relationships, showing you what you seek in others and what you need to learn about yourself through these interactions.

- **Awareness and Insight:** An opposition can bring awareness and insight into the areas of life where you experience tension or conflict. By highlighting opposing forces, this aspect encourages you to become more conscious of the underlying issues and develop strategies for dealing with them. Oppositions can lead to greater self-awareness, helping you understand your inner contradictions and how they play out in your life. This awareness allows you to make more conscious decisions and resolve conflicts with greater clarity.

- **Opportunities for Growth:** Despite the tension it creates, an opposition offers significant opportunities for growth and development. By learning to navigate the challenges of an opposition, you can achieve greater balance, maturity, and self-mastery. This aspect encourages you to grow by embracing both sides of the spectrum—the push and pull of the planets involved—

and integrating their opposing forces into a cohesive whole. The opposition ultimately teaches you how to work with tension and turn conflict into a source of personal empowerment and understanding.

How to Recognize an Opposition in a Chart
- **Degrees of Separation:** In a natal chart, an opposition occurs when two planets are approximately 180 degrees apart. The planets are located on opposite sides of the zodiac in opposing signs. The closer the planets are to being exactly 180 degrees apart, the stronger the tension and influence of the opposition. This aspect is considered a "hard" aspect due to the inherent conflict between the planets.
- **Opposing Signs:** Oppositions occur between planets in opposing zodiac signs. These signs are on opposite sides of the zodiac wheel and represent opposite qualities. For example, an opposition between Aries (self-assertion) and Libra (relationships) reflects a conflict between independence and cooperation, while an opposition between Taurus (stability) and Scorpio (transformation) highlights a tension between security and change.
- **Aspect Tables and Grids:** Astrology software programs or chart calculators often display oppositions in an aspect table or grid. Oppositions are usually marked with the symbol (σ°) or indicated as "180°" in aspect listings. These tools help you quickly identify where oppositions are occurring in your chart and which areas of life are likely to be influenced by this dynamic tension.

Example Opposition Between Pluto and Lilith
In the chart on the next page, there is an opposition between Pluto in Scorpio and Lilith in Taurus, reflecting a powerful push-pull dynamic between transformation and rebellion. Pluto is located at 2° Scorpio in the 12th house (the house of the subconscious, hidden matters, and spiritual transformation), while Lilith is at 2° Taurus in the 6th house (the house of daily routines, health, and service). This opposition highlights tension between Lana's inner depths and her outward need for autonomy and defiance in her everyday life.

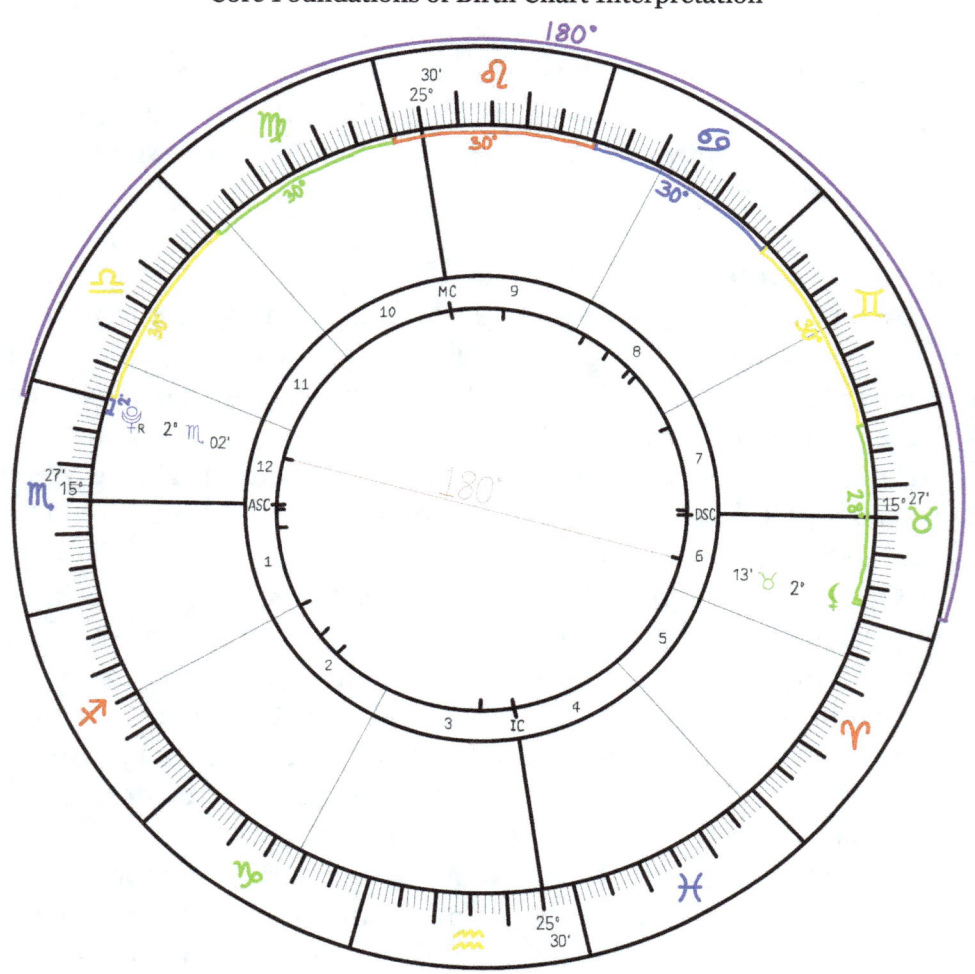

Pluto in the 12th house suggests that Lana possesses immense subconscious power and an affinity for exploring hidden or taboo aspects of life. This placement often speaks to a deep connection with transformation, spiritual growth, and emotional intensity—all themes that resonate deeply with her music and persona. On the other hand, Lilith in the 6th house represents a desire to rebel against societal norms and expectations in her daily routines, health, and work. Lilith's energy in Taurus may push her to prioritize personal values and sensual pleasures while rejecting rigid structures or imposed limitations in her day-to-day life.

This opposition suggests a conflict between Lana's drive for spiritual and emotional rebirth (Pluto) and her instinct to assert independence and resist conformity (Lilith). On one side, Pluto's influence calls her to surrender, transform, and explore the depths of her psyche. On the other side, Lilith challenges her to hold on to her autonomy and resist losing herself in the demands of routine or service. This dynamic tension may mirror the contrast often present in her music—between themes of surrendering to love, desire, or transformation and the need to reclaim power, independence, and individuality.

The opposition also reflects the way Lana's creative process may be fueled by this inner conflict. Her ability to channel deep, hidden emotions into her work (Pluto) while maintaining an unapologetic sense of self-expression (Lilith) creates a unique blend of vulnerability and defiance that resonates with her audience. The tension between these energies ultimately drives growth, as it forces her to confront and integrate the polarities of transformation and independence.

Visually, the chart illustrates this 180-degree angle between Pluto and Lilith, symbolizing how these opposing forces create a dynamic interplay that shapes Lana's life and artistry. This aspect highlights her ability to navigate themes of power, transformation, and rebellion, both in her inner world and her external expression.

Additional Considerations for Oppositions

- **Planets Involved:** The nature of an opposition depends heavily on the planets involved. For example, an opposition between Mars and Venus might reflect a conflict between assertiveness and cooperation, creating tension in relationships or expressing desires. An opposition between Saturn and Jupiter can represent a tension between expansion and restriction, requiring a balance between optimism and caution in achieving goals.

- **Oppositions and Houses:** The houses in which the opposition occurs are key to understanding the areas of life most affected by this tension. For instance, an opposition between planets in the 1st house (self) and 7th house (partnerships) might highlight conflicts between personal needs and relationship dynamics. An opposition between the 4th house (home) and 10th house (career) could indicate a struggle to balance home life with career ambitions.

- **Challenges and Growth:** While oppositions are often viewed as challenging aspects, they offer tremendous potential for growth. The tension created by an opposition can push you to evolve by confronting your inner contradictions and external conflicts head-on. Learning to balance opposing forces in your life can lead to greater self-awareness, emotional maturity, and resilience.

In summary, an opposition represents a dynamic aspect of tension and balance between two opposing forces. It highlights areas of life where you may experience conflict, polarization, or the need to reconcile competing energies. The key to working with an opposition is to find balance and harmony between the planets involved, integrating their energies in a way that allows for personal growth and development. Oppositions offer opportunities for greater self-awareness, growth, and maturity by helping you confront inner contradictions and external conflicts.

Oppositions are recognized in charts by looking for planets that are 180 degrees apart, often in opposing zodiac signs. While oppositions create tension, they also offer the potential for profound personal insight and growth. Understanding the opposition's influence in your natal chart provides insight into where you may face challenges, how you can achieve balance, and how you can use this tension as a catalyst for greater self-mastery. The opposition reveals the push-and-pull dynamic that shapes your journey, helping you embrace and harmonize opposing forces in your life.

Square: The Aspect of Challenge and Tension

In astrology, a square occurs when two planets are approximately 90 degrees apart in the natal chart. This aspect is known for creating tension, friction, and challenges between the planets involved. Unlike the harmonious flow of a trine or sextile, a square indicates conflict and obstacles that need to be overcome. However, the pressure generated by a square can be a powerful motivator for personal growth and transformation, pushing you to take action and make necessary changes. Squares highlight areas where you need to develop resilience, confront inner and outer struggles, and work through difficulties in order to achieve success and integration.

What a Square Represents:

- **Conflict and Tension:** A square represents conflict between the energies of the planets involved, leading to tension and internal or external struggles. The energies of the planets in a square don't blend easily, creating friction that must be confronted and resolved. This aspect often brings feelings of frustration, as things don't flow smoothly, and challenges arise in the areas of life influenced by the planets. The square forces you to deal with conflict head-on and find constructive solutions to manage the tension.

- **Challenges and Obstacles:** Squares are often associated with challenges, obstacles, and delays that require determination and effort to overcome. The planets involved in a square create situations where you must work hard to achieve your goals, often presenting difficulties that need to be addressed before progress can be made. However, these challenges are not purely negative— they present opportunities for growth and personal development as you learn to navigate through the difficulties and overcome the obstacles in your path.

- **Motivation and Drive:** While squares can be challenging, they are also energizing and motivating. The tension created by a square generates a sense of urgency and drive, pushing you to take action, confront issues, and make necessary changes. Squares are catalysts for movement, forcing you out of complacency and motivating you to tackle problems head-on. They provide the energy needed to push through adversity and achieve your goals, even when the process is difficult.

- **Inner Conflict:** Squares often reflect inner conflict, where different parts of your personality or life are at odds with one another. This can lead to feelings of being pulled in opposing directions, with competing desires, goals, or needs that must be reconciled. The square aspect challenges you to integrate these conflicting aspects of yourself and find a way to work through the internal struggles it creates. This process of self-integration can lead to significant personal growth and understanding.

- **Dynamic and Active Energy:** The energy of a square is dynamic and active, demanding engagement and effort. Unlike more harmonious aspects, such as trines, which allow things to flow naturally, a square forces you to take action and confront the issues it presents. Squares don't allow for passivity—they require you to engage with the conflict, make decisions, and work through obstacles in order to create balance and resolution. This aspect is about taking charge and actively working through challenges, rather than waiting for things to resolve on their own.

- **Growth Through Struggle:** Squares are often seen as catalysts for growth through struggle. The conflict and tension they create can lead to personal development, as you learn to navigate difficulties and build resilience. Squares teach you how to face adversity and develop problem-solving skills, leading to greater strength and wisdom. The process of working through the challenges of a square can be difficult, but it ultimately leads to growth, self-mastery, and a greater understanding of yourself and the world around you.

- **Creative Tension:** While squares can be frustrating, they also generate creative tension. The friction between the planets involved can spark innovation and push you to find new solutions. This aspect forces you to think outside the box and explore possibilities you may not have considered otherwise. Squares can drive creativity and originality, as the pressure they create requires you to break through limitations and come up with fresh approaches to the challenges you face.

How to Recognize a Square in a Chart

- **Degrees of Separation:** In a natal chart, a square occurs when two planets are approximately 90 degrees apart. Squares are considered "hard" aspects because of the tension and conflict they create between the planets. The closer the planets are to an exact 90-degree separation, the stronger the influence of the square.
- **Different Modalities (Qualities):** Squares often occur between planets in different signs of the same modality (Cardinal, Fixed, Mutable). For example, a square between Aries and Cancer represents a clash between two Cardinal signs with strong, initiating energy, while a square between Taurus and Leo reflects a struggle between two Fixed signs with stubborn and unyielding qualities.
- **Aspect Tables and Grids:** Astrology software or chart calculators often display squares in aspect tables or grids. Squares are usually marked with the symbol (□) or indicated as "90°" in aspect listings. These tools help you quickly identify where squares are occurring in your chart and the areas of life most likely to be influenced by conflict and tension.

Example Square Between Jupiter and the North Node

In the chart on the next page, there is a square between Jupiter in Aquarius and the North Node in Taurus, reflecting a tension between expansion and intellectual freedom (Jupiter) and Lana's soul's growth through stability and commitment in relationships (North Node). Jupiter is located at 16° Aquarius in the 3rd house (the house of communication, learning, and thought processes), while the North Node is at 16° Taurus in the 7th house (the house of partnerships and one-on-one connections). This square suggests that Lana may feel pulled between her natural curiosity, independence in thinking, and desire for freedom of expression versus the lessons she is meant to learn through trust, commitment, and stability in

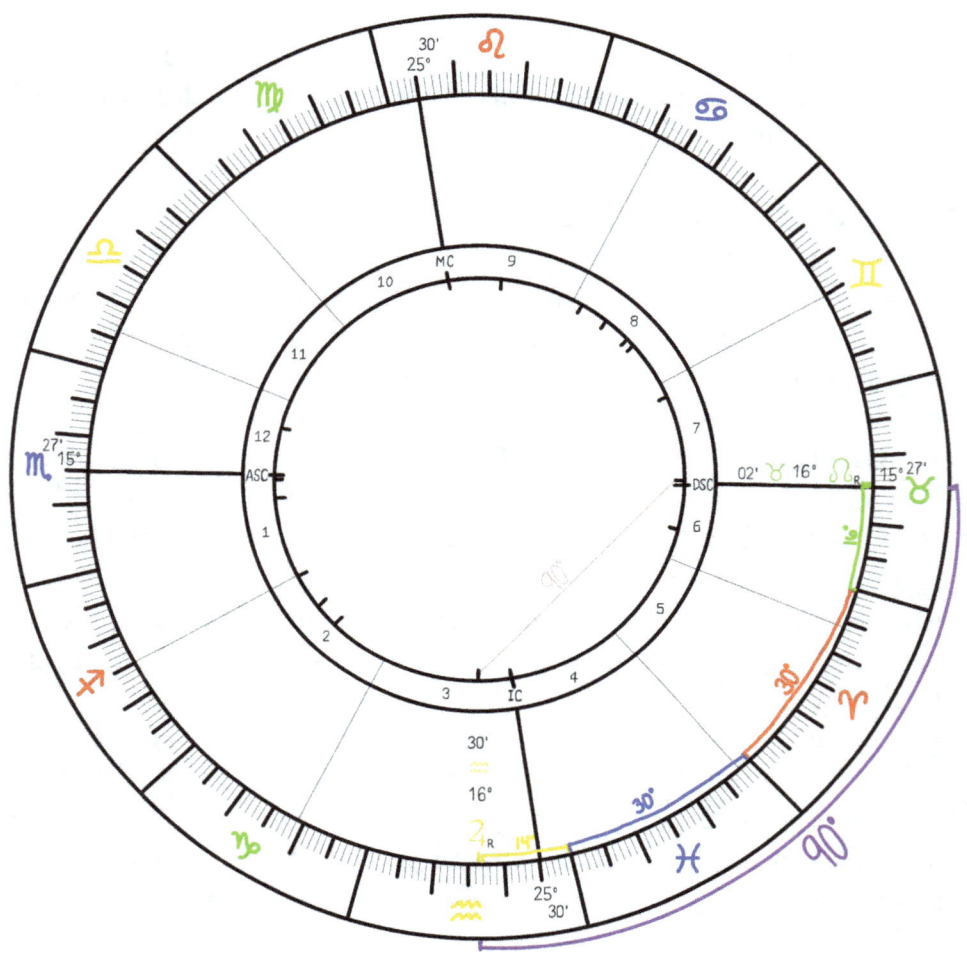

relationships.

Jupiter in Aquarius in the 3rd house points to Lana's expansive and unconventional way of thinking. She likely has a deep intellectual curiosity, a strong desire for mental stimulation, and a tendency to challenge traditional ideas. This placement suggests that she thrives on new experiences, diverse perspectives, and the freedom to express herself without limitations. However, with the North Node in Taurus in the 7th house, her growth comes from learning how to create steady, reliable connections with others, rather than remaining detached or overly focused on personal freedom.

The square between Jupiter and the North Node creates a push-pull dynamic in Lana's life, where she may struggle to balance her love for exploration and intellectual independence (Jupiter) with the need to develop meaningful, grounded relationships (North Node). There could be a tendency to resist deep commitments or feel restless in partnerships, as she is naturally drawn to openness and fluidity in communication and interactions. However, the North Node's lessons encourage her to embrace stability, patience, and trust in close relationships, even when they challenge her sense of independence.

This tension also suggests that Lana may find it difficult to fully commit to one perspective or relationship, often seeking variety and spontaneity. At times, she might feel that relationships restrict her freedom, but the North Node in Taurus teaches her that true stability does not limit growth—it provides a foundation for deeper, more meaningful experiences. Over time, learning to integrate her intellectual expansion with relational stability will allow her to find balance between these opposing forces.

Visually, the chart shows the 90-degree angle between Jupiter and the North Node, emphasizing the dynamic tension between Lana's pursuit of knowledge and personal freedom (Jupiter in the 3rd house) and her soul's growth through trust, commitment, and partnership (North Node in the 7th house). This square pushes her toward finding harmony between these two life areas, ultimately helping her evolve into a more balanced version of herself.

Additional Considerations for Squares

- **Planets Involved:** The nature of the square depends on the planets involved. For example, a square between Mars and Saturn may reflect a conflict between action and restriction, creating frustration or a feeling of being blocked in your efforts. A square between Venus and Pluto may indicate struggles in relationships, power dynamics, or deep emotional conflicts that need to be addressed. Understanding the planets involved in the square can help you navigate the specific challenges they present.
- **Squares and Houses:** The houses where the square occurs are essential in understanding the areas of life affected by the tension. For instance, a square between planets in the 4th house (home) and 7th house (relationships) might reflect challenges between

your home life and partnerships, while a square between the 2nd house (finances) and 5th house (creativity) might indicate financial struggles that impact your ability to pursue creative passions.

- **Challenges and Growth:** While squares are often seen as challenging aspects, they are also powerful drivers of growth. The tension and friction they create push you to develop resilience, confront obstacles, and find ways to integrate conflicting energies. Squares are aspects of action, requiring you to take charge of the challenges they present and transform tension into personal growth.

In summary, a square represents a challenging aspect that creates tension, conflict, and obstacles between the planets involved. It highlights areas of life where you may face struggles, where energies are at odds, and where you need to take action to overcome difficulties. While squares create friction, they also generate motivation and drive, pushing you to confront issues, make necessary changes, and grow through adversity.

Squares are recognized in charts by looking for planets that are 90 degrees apart, often in different signs of the same modality (Cardinal, Fixed, Mutable). Understanding the square's influence in your natal chart provides insight into where you may experience challenges, how to navigate them, and how to use the tension to your advantage. Squares reveal the potential for personal growth through the process of engaging with and overcoming life's obstacles, helping you build resilience and develop strong problem-solving skills. By embracing the challenges presented by a square, you can turn conflict into a powerful force for personal development and success.

How to Calculate Aspects Within A Birth Chart

There are three different ways you can calculate aspects within a birth chart:

1. You can use a computer generated software to calculate all of the aspects in your birth chart. On horoscopes.astro-seek.com, you can calculate your birth chart and then below, it will list out the aspects within your chart, you can also specify the orb of influence you would like to see, so you can choose a threshold of 0° or increase it as you would like

2. You can recognize aspects within your chart by looking at the lines in the center of your chart. Depending on what website you use, the lines may be different colors, on horoscopes.astro-seek.com the lines are red and blue.

- The **LONG** blue lines represent Trines (120° apart) △
- The **SHORT** blue lines represent Sextiles (60° apart) ✳
- The **LONG** red lines represent Oppositions (180° apart) ⚬
- The **SHORT** red lines represent Squares (90° apart) ☐
- Conjunctions are not represented by lines because the planets/objects are 0° to 10° (orb of influence) away from each other. So you can spot a conjunction in a chart by looking at what planets/objects are close together. ♂

3. You can also calculate aspects by individually counting the degrees between each planet on your birth chart. I used this method while calculating Lana Del Rey's chart. This may seem very tedious (and it is!) but this can ensure you are seeing all of the aspects in a chart that a computer generated software may not display.

- To use this method, look at two planets in your chart you would like to calculate the aspect between (not all planets have aspects to each other, this is why we calculate the degrees between them to see if they form an aspect)

- Using Lana's chart, let's calculate the aspect between Mercury and the South Node.

- Her Mercury is in 16° Cancer in the Eighth House
- Her South Node is in 16° Scorpio in the First House

- The first thing to notice here is that Mercury and the South Node are both at 16°. This suggests a potential aspect with a 0° orb of influence, but to confirm, we need to calculate how many degrees are actually between them.

Step 1: Count the Number of Signs Between the Two Points

- The easiest way to do this is to count how many signs are between Mercury and the South Node, as each sign contains 30°. We want to stay below 190° (since major aspects don't go above 190°) when counting the degrees between two objects/planets, so start from the side that has fewer signs between the two objects/planets.
- Looking at Lana's chart, the shortest distance between Mercury and the South Node is clockwise, moving from the South Node to Mercury.
- There are three signs (Leo, Virgo, and Libra) between Cancer and Scorpio.
- Since each sign = 30°, we calculate:
    - 30° (Leo) + 30° (Virgo) + 30° (Libra) = 90°

Step 2: Add the Specific Degrees of Each Point

- Now, we need to add the degrees of Mercury in Cancer and the South Node in Scorpio:
    - Mercury is at 16° Cancer, but since we are counting clockwise through Cancer (on the side of the cusp of Leo), we land at 14°
    - The South Node is at 16° Scorpio, so we count from the beginning of Scorpio (on the cusp side of Libra) up to 16°.
    - 14° (Mercury in Cancer) + 16° (South Node in Scorpio) = 30°

Final Calculation:

- Now, adding everything together:
- 30° (Leo) + 30° (Virgo) + 30° (Libra) + 14° (Mercury in Cancer) + 16° (South Node in Scorpio) = 120°
- Since 120° is the angle for a trine, this confirms a trine aspect with a 0° orb of influence.

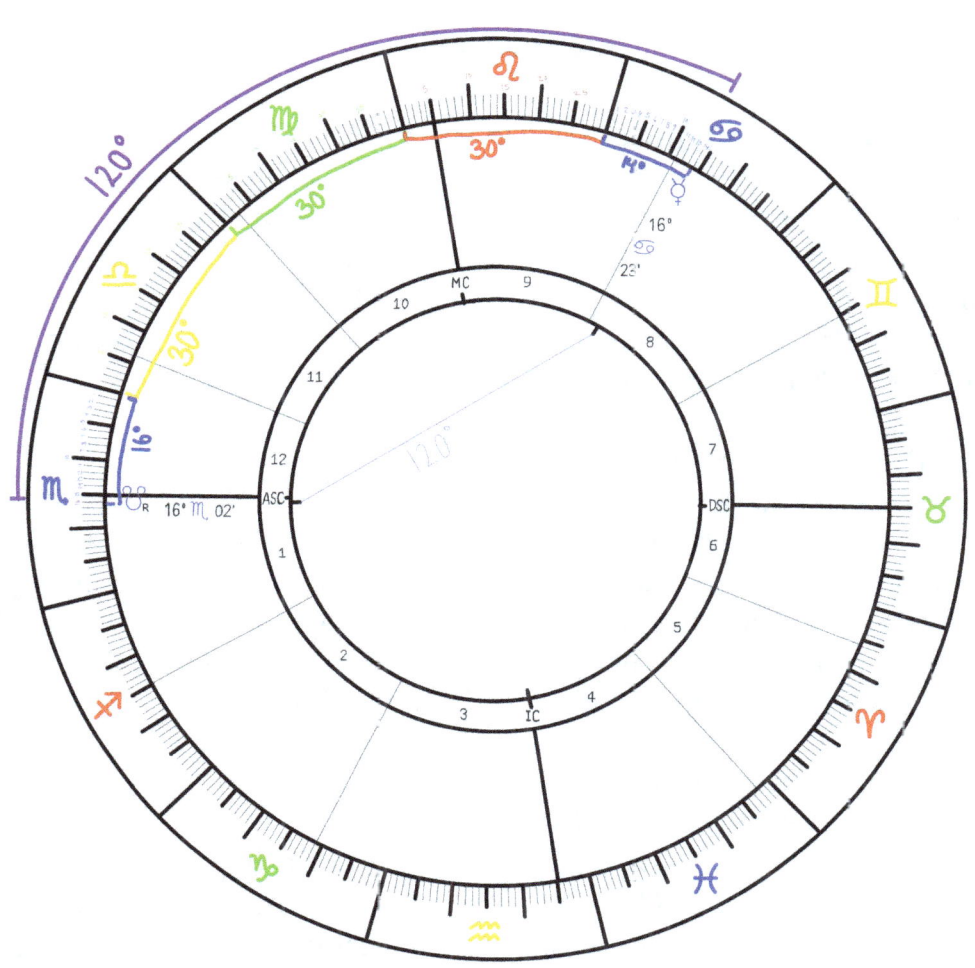

Reference Visual: The diagram above illustrates this process step by step.

Stelliums

What Defines a Stellium?

A stellium occurs when three or more planets are clustered together in the same sign or house in a birth chart. This creates an intense concentration of energy, making the themes of that sign and house highly dominant in a person's life. Stelliums often overshadow even the Sun sign, meaning someone with a Sun in Libra but a stellium in Scorpio may strongly embody Scorpio traits.

The Power of a Stellium

A stellium acts like a spotlight, amplifying the qualities of a sign or house and making them a central theme in a person's identity. It can heighten natural talents but also create imbalances, as energy is focused in one area rather than spread across the chart. This intensity can manifest as obsession, mastery, or deep emotional connections to the areas represented by the stellium.

Breaking Down Stelliums

To interpret a stellium, consider:

- **The Planets Involved:** Each planet brings a different expression. A Venus-Mars-Mercury stellium in Aries, for example, intensifies passion (Mars), communication (Mercury), and attraction (Venus) in an impulsive, direct way.

- **The Sign:** The sign shapes how the stellium expresses itself. A Pisces stellium may create highly intuitive, emotional, or artistic energy, while a Capricorn stellium may manifest as ambition and structure.

- **The House:** The house tells us *where* this energy plays out. A 10th house stellium emphasizes career and public image, while a 4th house stellium highlights family and home life.

Types of Stelliums

- **Sign Stellium:** Three or more planets in the same zodiac sign, intensifying that sign's traits in the person's personality.

- **House Stellium:** Three or more planets in the same house, creating a strong life focus in that house's themes, regardless of the signs involved.
- **Mixed Stellium:** A blend where planets are in different signs but in the same house, or vice versa, adding complexity to the interpretation.

The Challenges of Stelliums
While stelliums can be a source of great power, they also bring challenges:
- **Imbalance:** A stellium creates an overwhelming focus in one area, sometimes at the expense of others.
- **Difficulty Seeing Other Perspectives:** Someone with a 7th house stellium may be overly focused on relationships, struggling to prioritize themselves.
- **Internal Conflicts:** If a stellium includes conflicting planets (e.g., Mars and Saturn), the person may feel torn between drive (Mars) and restriction (Saturn).

Harnessing Stellium Energy
To work with a stellium's energy effectively:
- **Develop Awareness:** Recognize where the stellium's energy dominates and work to create balance.
- **Use Supporting Placements:** Look at opposing signs/houses to find areas that can help bring harmony.
- **Lean Into Its Strengths:** A 3rd house stellium (communication) benefits from writing, speaking, and learning, while a 12th house stellium (spirituality, solitude) thrives with introspection and creative expression.

Stelliums in Practice
Identifying a stellium in a chart helps explain why certain themes dominate a person's life. A 1st house stellium may naturally command attention, while a 6th house stellium can create a strong focus on work and routine. Stelliums reveal why some life areas feel more prominent and offer insight into managing their intensity.

7. Tying It All Together

"Astrology represents the summation of all the psychological knowledge of antiquity."
- Carl Jung

Tying It Together: Understanding the Bigger Picture

As you've learned throughout this book, astrology is a complex system made up of many different parts. Before we can see how all the pieces work together, it's essential to first understand the individual components: the houses, signs, planets, aspects, degrees, orb of influence, elements, modalities, and ruling planets. Each of these elements plays a distinct role in your birth chart, and only when you grasp their individual meanings can you begin to weave them together into a cohesive whole.

Why It's Important to Study the Pieces Individually

It can be tempting to jump right into the fun part—interpreting what your Sun in Aries means or how your Moon in Capricorn affects you—but without a solid foundation in the basics, these interpretations might feel shallow or confusing.
- **The Houses** represent the **where** of astrology. They show us which areas of life a planet's energy will manifest, whether it's your career, relationships, home life, or personal growth. Each house governs a specific domain, like the 1st house representing the self, or the 7th house representing partnerships.
- **The Signs** represent the **how**. They color how the planet expresses itself in a particular area of life. For example, Mars in Libra expresses action and drive (Mars) in a balanced, diplomatic way (Libra), while Mars in Aries expresses that same energy more boldly and directly.
- **The Planets** represent the **what**. They signify the actual energy or influence being expressed. The Sun, for instance, represents your core identity and ego, while Venus governs love, beauty, and relationships. These are the driving forces behind your chart.

By understanding these components on their own, you develop a much clearer picture of their roles before they are combined.

The Process of Tying It All Together

Once you have a solid grasp of what each house, sign, and planet represents, it becomes much easier to see how they interact with each other. This is the key to astrology—understanding how the energies blend, overlap, and influence each other in unique ways. Here's how to approach it:

1. Start with the Planet (the What): First, identify the planet in a particular placement. Each planet governs a specific energy or influence in your life. For example, Mars represents action and desire, while the Moon represents emotions and instincts.

2. Add the Sign (the How): Next, see which zodiac sign the planet is in. This sign determines how that planet's energy is expressed. For instance, if Mars is in Virgo, the action-oriented energy of Mars will be expressed in a meticulous, detail-oriented way, compared to Mars in Leo, which would express that energy boldly and with confidence.

3. Locate the House (the Where): Finally, look at the house where the planet is located. The house shows where in your life that planetary energy will play out. If your Mars is in the 7th house, for example, your action and drive will focus on partnerships and relationships, whereas Mars in the 10th house would direct that energy toward career and public image.

The Role of Ruling Planets and How They Connect the Houses

In addition to planets being placed in different houses, ruling planets play a significant role in tying your chart together. Every zodiac sign is ruled by a planet, and when a sign occupies a house, its ruling planet connects that house to the house that planet is in. Even if a house doesn't have any planets, the ruling planet of the sign on the house cusp shows where the energy of that house is being expressed.

For example, if Taurus rules your 7th house (relationships) and Venus is the ruling planet of Taurus, you would look to where Venus is located in your chart to understand how relationships will be influenced. If Venus is in your 11th house (friends, social groups), this could mean that friendships and group activities are central to your romantic life.

Ruling planets create a network of connections between the houses, revealing how different areas of your life are intertwined.

This concept is key to fully understanding how the energies in your chart manifest.

The Role of Aspects, Degrees, and Orb of Influence

To truly see the bigger picture, we must also consider the aspects between planets and other points in the chart. Aspects reveal the relationships between planets and how they influence each other's energies.

- **Aspects**: Aspects are the angles formed between planets, and they reveal how planets interact with one another. For example, a trine between two planets indicates harmonious energy, while a square suggests tension and challenges. These connections between planets add a dynamic layer to the interpretation, showing whether the energies flow easily or face obstacles.

- **Degrees and Orb of Influence**: Degrees represent the exact position of planets in a sign, and they are critical when determining aspects. Planets that are within a certain orb of influence—a specific number of degrees apart—form aspects. For example, two planets that are 90 degrees apart create a square aspect. Knowing the degree of a planet is essential because aspects are formed within specific degree ranges, and the closer the planets are to exact degree alignment, the stronger the aspect's influence.

Understanding the role of aspects and degrees adds depth to your chart interpretation, showing not just how individual planets function, but how they work together (or in opposition) to influence your life's patterns.

The Influence of Element and Modality

Additionally, elements and modalities help to describe how a planet's energy operates within a sign.

- **Elements** (Fire, Earth, Air, Water) describe the core nature of a sign. Fire signs are passionate and dynamic, Earth signs are practical and grounded, Air signs are intellectual and communicative, and Water signs are emotional and intuitive. The balance (or imbalance) of elements in your chart can reveal whether you lean more toward action, stability, thought, or emotion.

- **Modalities** (Cardinal, Fixed, Mutable) describe how a sign expresses its energy. Cardinal signs are initiators and leaders, Fixed signs are stabilizers and persistent, and Mutable signs are adaptable and flexible. The distribution of modalities in your chart can show whether you are more driven to start projects (Cardinal), maintain stability (Fixed), or adapt to change (Mutable).

By examining the element and modality of a planet, you gain a deeper understanding of how its energy will manifest. For example, Mars in a Fire sign like Leo will be bold and action-oriented, while Mars in a Fixed sign like Taurus will express itself more steadily and cautiously.

The Importance of Seeing the Bigger Picture

When you first look at a birth chart, it may seem like a complex jumble of symbols. But once you break it down, understanding the individual pieces allows you to see how everything comes together. Learning the basics first ensures that when you tie the planets, signs, and houses together, you aren't just memorizing interpretations—you're understanding how astrology works on a deeper level.

Here's an example of how to "tie it together":

Let's say you have Venus (the planet of love, relationships, and beauty) in Scorpio (a sign known for depth, passion, and intensity) in the 5th house (which rules creativity, self-expression, and romance).

First, understand that Venus is about how you express love and seek pleasure. With Venus in Scorpio, you approach relationships with intensity, desire deep emotional connections, and might have a tendency to be secretive or guarded in love. Now, add the fact that Venus is in the 5th house. This means that this intense approach to love is most apparent in your creative endeavors and romantic life. You might be drawn to passionate, transformative romances or find that your creative work is fueled by emotional intensity.

Now let's add an aspect: Suppose your Venus in Scorpio forms a trine (a harmonious aspect) to Mars in Pisces in your 9th house (which rules higher learning and exploration). This trine suggests that your emotional intensity (Venus in Scorpio) and your actions and desires (Mars in Pisces) work together smoothly. You likely channel your romantic passion and creative energy into spiritual or intellectual pursuits, perhaps finding love or inspiration while traveling, studying, or engaging in deep philosophical discussions. The trine aspect makes it easier for you to integrate your emotions with your actions, leading to a smooth flow of energy between these two areas of your life.

Another example:

If you have Mercury (the planet of communication and thought) in Gemini (a sign known for adaptability, curiosity, and quick thinking) in the 10th house (which rules career and public image), the meaning unfolds like this: Mercury represents how you communicate, Gemini colors that communication style with wit and versatility, and the 10th house shows that this will primarily manifest in your career or how you present yourself to the public. This combination would suggest someone who is adept at communicating in their professional life, perhaps excelling in roles where adaptability and mental sharpness are key.

Let's add an aspect: Now imagine Mercury in Gemini forms a square (a challenging aspect) to Saturn in Virgo in the 1st house (which rules your personal identity and how you appear to others). This square suggests tension between your communication style and your sense of discipline or personal presentation. While you may be witty and adaptable (Mercury in Gemini), you might feel restricted or overly self-critical (Saturn in Virgo) when expressing yourself, especially in professional settings. This aspect could manifest as a tendency to doubt your own words or struggle with perfectionism in how you communicate in your career, but the square also offers an opportunity for growth through learning to balance self-expression with structure and responsibility.

These examples show how you tie the "what" (planet), "how" (sign), and "where" (house) together to reveal the bigger picture. By understanding all these layers, you can see how the chart reflects not just isolated traits, but an interconnected web of influences that shape your life path.

Practice Tying It Together

Now that you know how to break down and tie the pieces together, practice is key. Take the time to look at different planets in your chart, consider their signs, locate their houses, and evaluate their aspects, degrees, and orb of influence. By doing this, you'll develop a much richer understanding of your chart. And remember, each chart is unique. No two people will have the same combination of signs, planets, houses, aspects, and degrees, which is why astrology is such a powerful tool for self-awareness and growth.

In the next section, we will completely dissect Lana Del Rey's chart, applying everything we've discussed in this book. This will give you a detailed example of how to tie it all together using real placements and aspects. After that, you'll have the chance to do the same for your own chart in the DIY Chart section, where you can analyze your own placements and draw meaningful connections.

8. An Example Birth Chart: Lana Del Rey

Born on 06/21/1985 in Manhattan, New York, United States at 4:47 PM ET.

"I always have a good astrologer to guide me."
- Eleanor Roosevelt

Example Birth Chart: Lana Del Rey

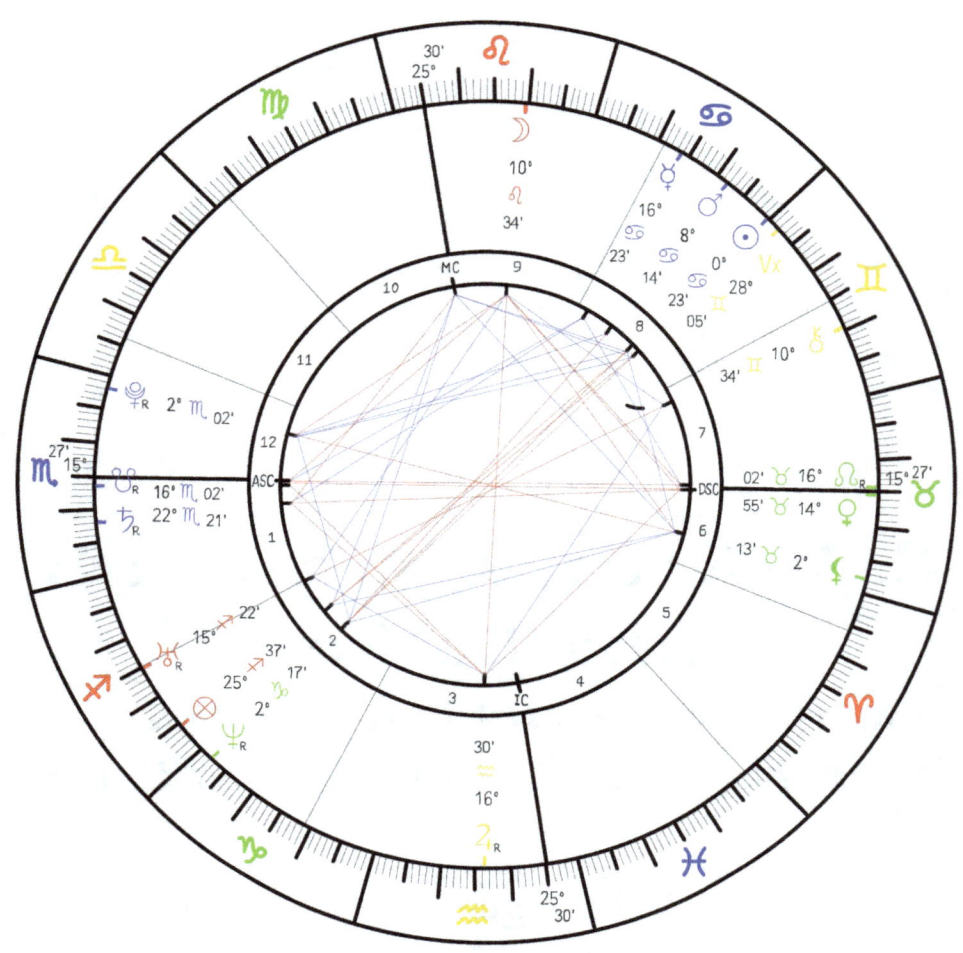

Signs:

- Aries ♈
- Taurus ♉
- Gemini ♊
- Cancer ♋
- Leo ♌
- Virgo ♍

- Libra ♎
- Scorpio ♏
- Sagittarius ♐
- Capricorn ♑
- Aquarius ♒
- Pisces ♓

Planets, Objects, & Angles:

- Sun ☉
- Moon ☾
- Mercury ☿
- Venus ♀
- Mars ♂
- Jupiter ♃
- Saturn ♄
- Uranus ♅ ♁
- Neptune ♆
- Pluto ♇

- Part of Fortune ⊗
- Vertex Vx
- North Node ☊
- South Node ☋
- Chiron ⚷
- Lilith ⚸
- Ascendant ASC
- Imum Coeli IC
- Descendant DSC
- Midheaven MC

Houses:

- First House
- Second House
- Third House
- Fourth House
- Fifth House
- Sixth House

- Seventh House
- Eighth House
- Ninth House
- Tenth House
- Eleventh House
- Twelfth House

Lana Del Rey has:

- Sun 0° in Cancer in the Eighth House
- Moon 10° in Leo in the Ninth House
- Mercury 16° in Cancer in the Eighth House
- Venus 14° in Taurus in the Sixth House
- Mars 8° in Cancer in the Eighth House
- Jupiter 16° in Aquarius in the Third House
- Saturn 22° in Scorpio in the First House
- Uranus 15° in Sagittarius in the Second House
- Neptune 2° in Capricorn in the Second House
- Pluto 2° in Scorpio in the Twelfth House
- Part of Fortune 25° in Sagittarius in the Second House
- Vertex 28° in Gemini in the Eighth House
- North Node 16° in Taurus in the Seventh House
- South Node 16° in Scorpio in the First House
- Chiron 10° in Gemini in the Seventh House
- Lilith 2° in Taurus in the Sixth House
- Ascendant 15° in Scorpio (always on the cusp of the First House)
- Imum Coeli 25° in Aquarius (always on the cusp of the Fourth House)
- Descendant 15° in Taurus (always on the cusp of the Seventh House)
- Midheaven 25° in Leo (always on the cusp of the Tenth House)

You can also see that Lana Del Rey does not have any planets or objects in her fourth, fifth, tenth, or eleventh houses, but this does not mean these houses are insignificant in her chart.

Each house has one or more signs within it, and as we reviewed earlier, each house represents an area in our life. The houses are the "where" of a birth chart. Each sign represents how the energy in that house will manifest. Additionally, this is where ruling planets play a big role. Even though a house may not have any planets within it, the ruling planet of the sign occupying that house can provide key insights into how that area of life will be expressed and how it connects to other areas of her life.

Personal Planets:

Sun in Cancer in the Eighth House

Lana's core identity is deeply tied to emotions, transformation, and intensity. The Sun in Cancer in the 8th House suggests profound emotional depth and a natural connection to themes of loss, rebirth, and personal evolution. This placement indicates that she experiences emotions on a deep, private level and is drawn to uncovering hidden truths—whether within herself or in the world around her. The 8th House, associated with psychology, intimacy, and personal transformation, may make her highly introspective, attuned to unspoken energies, and naturally inclined to seek deeper meaning in her experiences. There can also be a tendency toward emotional protectiveness, as this placement often creates a need for trust and security before opening up fully to others.

Moon in Leo in the Ninth House

Her emotional world thrives on passion, self-expression, and a desire for fulfillment. A Moon in Leo suggests that she craves recognition, warmth, and appreciation in her personal life, often feeling most emotionally secure when she is seen, valued, and able to express herself freely. This placement fosters a strong presence, a natural sense of confidence, and a deep need for joy and creativity in everyday life. With the Moon in the 9th House, emotional fulfillment is often found through exploration—whether through philosophy, travel, or expanding personal beliefs. She may have a strong connection to seeking higher meaning, broadening perspectives, and viewing life through a larger, more visionary lens. This placement also reflects an innate curiosity about different cultures, spiritual concepts, or storytelling as a way to process emotions and make sense of the world.

Mercury in Cancer in the Eighth House

Mercury in Cancer gives Lana a deeply intuitive and emotionally perceptive communication style. This placement suggests that her mind processes thoughts through feelings, relying on memory, intuition, and personal connections to understand the world. There is often a natural sensitivity in the way she expresses herself, with a tendency to communicate in a nurturing, reflective, and deeply personal manner. In the 8th House—associated with transformation, depth, and hidden matters—Mercury enhances an interest in uncovering emotional truths and exploring the complexities of human emotions and relationships. This placement indicates that she thinks deeply about life's more profound subjects, seeks meaningful conversations, and prefers to communicate in ways that feel intimate and emotionally resonant.

Venus in Taurus in the Sixth House

Venus in Taurus enhances Lana's appreciation for comfort, stability, and deep, lasting connections. This placement suggests a strong attachment to sensual pleasures, valuing physical affection, beauty, and emotional security in relationships. Venus in Taurus brings a patient, devoted approach to love, favoring loyalty and consistency over fleeting passions. In the 6th house, Venus influences not only daily routines and acts of service but also her relationship with work. She may have the desire to create a pleasant, aesthetically pleasing, or harmonious work environment, as well as an appreciation for careers that involve creativity, beauty, or caregiving. This placement can indicate she finds fulfillment in work that allows for stability and steady growth, preferring a role where dedication and consistency lead to long-term rewards. She may also have a natural ability to bring warmth and ease into practical matters, making love, beauty, and comfort an integrated part of both her daily life and professional pursuits.

Mars in Cancer in the Eighth House

Mars in Cancer expresses motivation and drive through emotional depth rather than direct aggression. This placement suggests Lana is protective, persistent, and deeply connected to her feelings when pursuing goals. Her actions are often guided by intuition, emotional security, and a desire to protect what is meaningful. In the 8th house—associated with transformation, power, and the subconscious—Mars intensifies emotional experiences, fueling a strong need for depth and meaning in personal pursuits. This placement can indicate she has a natural ability to navigate complex emotional dynamics, a powerful inner resilience, and a tendency to experience personal growth through deep emotional and psychological shifts.

Social & Generational Planets:

Jupiter in Aquarius in the Third House

Jupiter in Aquarius expands Lana's intellectual curiosity and broadens her perspective, making her naturally drawn to unconventional ideas, progressive thinking, and innovation. This placement suggests a strong interest in exploring unique philosophies, challenging societal norms, and seeking wisdom beyond traditional structures. In the 3rd house—governing communication, learning, and thought processes—Jupiter enhances her ability to think abstractly, express big ideas, and engage in meaningful discussions. This placement often indicates a mind that thrives on exploration, whether through education, diverse perspectives, or exchanging ideas that push boundaries. There may also be a talent for recognizing patterns, making unexpected connections, and introducing new perspectives that inspire or challenge others.

Saturn in Scorpio in the First House

Saturn in Scorpio in the 1st house gives Lana a composed, disciplined, and intense presence. This placement suggests a strong sense of self-control, emotional depth, and a reserved yet powerful demeanor. There may be an air of mystery, as well as a tendency to approach life with caution and seriousness. Saturn's influence in the 1st house often points to early life challenges or personal hardships that require resilience and self-mastery. Over time, this placement fosters a deep sense of wisdom, emotional endurance, and a capacity for profound introspection. The combination of Saturn's discipline and Scorpio's depth can indicate that Lana moves through life with a quiet strength, valuing transformation, privacy, and personal growth.

Uranus in Sagittarius in the Second House

Uranus in Sagittarius fosters an independent and unconventional mindset, often drawn to questioning beliefs, exploring new philosophies, and challenging societal norms. This placement suggests Lana has a natural inclination toward freedom in thought and an aversion to rigid structures or traditional expectations. In the 2nd house—governing values, material security, and self-worth—Uranus brings unpredictability and a nontraditional approach to stability. She may have a tendency to prioritize independence over financial security, preferring flexibility and personal freedom over conventional measures of success. This placement can also indicate shifting financial circumstances, innovative ways of earning income, or a unique perspective on what truly holds value in life.

Neptune in Capricorn in the Second House

Neptune in Capricorn blends imagination with ambition, creating a balance between visionary thinking and disciplined effort. This placement suggests that Lana dreams big but approaches long-term goals with patience and strategy. In the 2nd house—governing both material security and self-worth—Neptune adds a sense of fluidity and idealism to these areas of life. She may have a deep, almost intuitive connection to personal value and a tendency to seek fulfillment beyond traditional financial success. However, Neptune's influence can also bring uncertainty or shifting circumstances in income, requiring clarity and grounding to avoid disillusionment. This placement suggests that her self-worth may be shaped by intangible or creative pursuits, making it important to define her security on her own terms rather than through external validation or material achievements.

Pluto in Scorpio in the Twelfth House

Pluto in Scorpio intensifies the connection to themes of

transformation, power, and the subconscious. This placement suggests Lana has a deep, introspective nature and is drawn to uncovering hidden truths and embracing personal evolution. In the 12th house—associated with solitude, the unconscious mind, and spiritual transcendence—Pluto creates a powerful inner world, often marked by periods of isolation, deep psychological reflection, and a strong connection to unseen forces. This placement may indicate struggles with surrendering control, but it also grants a profound ability to navigate the depths of the psyche, facilitating personal and collective healing. She likely has a natural draw toward exploring life's mysteries, emotional intensity, and the unseen forces that shape human experience.

Points & Objects:

Part of Fortune in Sagittarius in the Second House

Lana's greatest fortune comes from embracing freedom, exploration, and self-expression. With the Part of Fortune in the 2nd house—governing both financial stability and self-worth—personal fulfillment is closely tied to cultivating independence and aligning with deeply held values. This placement suggests that prosperity and inner satisfaction come when she trusts in her own path rather than adhering to conventional definitions of success. She may have an intuitive understanding that material security flows most easily when rooted in authenticity, personal growth, and a sense of purpose rather than external validation.

Vertex in Gemini in the Eighth House

The Vertex represents fated encounters and life-altering experiences that shape personal growth. In Gemini, this placement suggests that Lana's destiny is closely linked to communication, learning, and exchanging ideas with others. With the Vertex in the 8th house—associated with transformation, deep emotional bonds, and hidden truths—significant relationships or experiences may bring profound shifts in her perspective. Encounters with others may feel destined to challenge existing beliefs, uncover deeper emotional truths, or facilitate personal renewal. This placement encourages her to embrace intellectual curiosity and openness to transformative connections that leave a lasting impact.

North Node in Taurus in the Seventh House

Lana's life path (North Node) is centered on developing stability, patience, and trust in relationships. With this placement, she is learning to shift from self-reliance toward building meaningful connections that provide emotional and material security. There is a strong pull toward finding balance in partnerships, where mutual support and reliability play a key role in her growth. However, embracing trust and stability may take time, as this path requires letting go of past tendencies toward control, emotional intensity, or self-isolation. Over time, she is encouraged to cultivate steady, grounded relationships that bring a sense of peace, teaching her that true security comes not just from independence but from shared commitment and trust.

South Node in Scorpio in the First House

Lana's past-life tendencies (South Node) suggest a deep-rooted intensity, emotional depth, and self-reliance. This placement indicates a natural inclination toward solitude, secrecy, and navigating life's challenges independently. She may feel comfortable in periods of personal transformation, preferring to process emotions privately rather than rely on others. However, in this lifetime, she is meant to shift toward stability, trust, and partnership, learning that true security comes not from isolation but from building lasting, dependable connections with others. Embracing patience and emotional openness will be key to balancing this transformation.

Chiron in Gemini in the Seventh House

Chiron, the wounded healer, in Gemini suggests challenges related to communication, self-expression, and feeling truly understood. This placement may indicate struggles with confidence in one's voice, difficulties in articulating thoughts, or wounds stemming from misunderstandings. In the 7th house—governing partnerships and one-on-one connections—these challenges often manifest in relationships, where there may be fears around trust, love, and mutual understanding. Experiences of miscommunication, emotional distance, or heartbreak may play a significant role in Lana's personal growth, ultimately teaching her the importance of open dialogue, vulnerability, and developing deeper, more secure connections with others.

Lilith in Taurus in the Sixth House

Lilith represents raw, untamed energy, and in Taurus, it manifests as a strong-willed, sensual, and independent nature. This placement suggests Lana has a deep connection to personal values, pleasure, and autonomy, often resisting external control or expectations. In the 6th house—governing work, routines, and daily responsibilities—Lilith challenges conventional structures, creating a tendency to reject rigid schedules, authority, or societal norms related to productivity. Lana may have an inner struggle with finding balance between personal freedom and the need for stability, as well as a desire to approach work and daily life on her own terms rather than conforming to external pressures.

Angles:

Ascendant in Scorpio

Lana's rising sign shapes how she presents herself to the world and the first impression she leaves on others. Scorpio rising gives her an intense, magnetic, and enigmatic presence, drawing people in with an air of mystery and depth. This placement suggests a naturally private and observant nature, with a strong sense of personal boundaries and emotional resilience. Scorpio's influence enhances themes of transformation and reinvention, making her someone who navigates life with a quiet but powerful intensity, often revealing only what she chooses to share.

Imum Coeli (IC) in Aquarius

The IC (Imum Coeli), the lowest point of the chart, represents her emotional foundation, inner world, and upbringing. With Aquarius here, her early environment may have been unconventional, unpredictable, or emotionally distant in some way. This placement suggests a strong need for personal freedom and individuality from a young age, shaping an independent approach to emotions and home life. Security may not have come from traditional nurturing but rather from intellectual exploration, unique experiences, or a sense of detachment from emotional intensity. Over time, she is encouraged to find a balance between independence and deeper emotional connections, creating a foundation that allows both personal freedom and a sense of belonging.

Descendant in Taurus

With Taurus ruling Lana's relationships and partnerships, she seeks stability, reliability, and emotional security in her connections. This placement suggests a deep appreciation for loyalty, physical affection, and shared values, as well as a preference for relationships that feel grounded and enduring. She may be drawn to partners who provide a sense of comfort and consistency, valuing trust and long-term commitment over fleeting connections. However, Taurus' strong attachment to familiarity can also make it difficult to accept change, leading to challenges in letting go when relationships evolve or no longer serve her growth. There may be a tendency to hold on tightly to what feels safe, even when change is necessary.

Midheaven (MC) in Leo

The MC (Midheaven) in Leo suggests Lana has a strong presence in the public sphere, a natural charisma, and an innate ability to stand out. This placement indicates a deep-seated drive to be recognized for her talents and personal expression, leading her to seek a path that allows for visibility, leadership, and creativity. There is a strong sense of purpose tied to confidence, individuality, and inspiring others, making it essential for her to pursue work that feels personally meaningful and fulfilling. With Leo's influence, success is often linked to embracing her authentic self, taking bold steps toward ambition, and maintaining a sense of pride in achievements.

This placement encourages developing a career that allows for self-expression, passion, and a lasting impact, whether through creative pursuits, leadership roles, or any avenue where her presence can shine.

Modalities:

- Cardinal Energy: **x4** (Sun, Mercury, Mars, Neptune)
- Fixed Energy: **x12** (Venus, North Node, Lilith, Descendant, Moon, Midheaven, Saturn, Pluto, South Node, Ascendant, Jupiter, Imum Coeli)
- Mutable Energy: **x4** (Vertex, Chiron, Uranus, Part of Fortune)

Lana Del Rey's chart reveals a strong dominance of fixed energy, with 12 planets and points falling under fixed signs. This suggests a deeply persistent, loyal, and unwavering nature. Fixed energy is known for its determination, resistance to change, and ability to stay the course, which likely manifests in her mindset, relationships, and personal endeavors. She may have a strong sense of identity and conviction, preferring stability and consistency over frequent change. This fixed influence also suggests an ability to remain focused on long-term goals, navigate challenges with resilience, and hold firm to her values and beliefs.

Though her chart is dominated by fixed signs, she also has notable cardinal energy (Sun, Mercury, Mars, Neptune) and mutable energy (Vertex, Chiron, Uranus, Part of Fortune), with four placements in each. The presence of cardinal energy indicates that she is capable of taking initiative and leading when necessary, particularly in her creative projects and communication. Her mutable energy adds a layer of adaptability, showing that despite her strong fixed nature, she can adjust and evolve when circumstances demand it, allowing for versatility in her work and personal growth.

The combination of these modalities suggests that while Lana is primarily focused and steadfast, she is also able to balance moments of leadership and change, blending stability with innovation.

Elements:

- Fire: **x4** (Uranus, Part of Fortune, Moon, Midheaven)
- Earth: **x5** (Neptune, Lilith, Venus, Descendant, North Node)
- Air: **x4** (Jupiter, Imum Coeli, Chiron, Vertex)
- Water: **x7** (Pluto, Ascendant, South Node, Saturn, Sun, Mars, Mercury)

This chart shows a strong emphasis on Water, indicating that she is deeply emotional, intuitive, and sensitive, with a strong focus on personal connections, inner experiences, and emotional depth. Water-dominant individuals often process life through feelings, relying on instinct and deep emotional awareness to navigate relationships and situations. This influence suggests she may be highly perceptive, attuned to subtle energies, and drawn to experiences that evoke strong emotions.

The next most prominent element is Earth, which balances this emotional depth with practicality, stability, and a grounded approach to life. Earth energy emphasizes a connection to the physical world, making material security, long-term goals, and tangible achievements important. This suggests a pragmatic side that values consistency and reliability, ensuring that emotions do not entirely override logic and structure.

While Fire and Air are less dominant, their presence still plays a significant role. Fire provides passion, creativity, and motivation, allowing her to act with enthusiasm and determination when inspired. Though not the most prominent force in her chart, it contributes bursts of energy and a drive to pursue what excites her. Air, on the other hand, brings intellectual curiosity, adaptability, and strong communication skills. It enhances her ability to think critically, exchange ideas, and see situations from multiple perspectives.

Overall, this mix of elements suggests she is emotionally deep yet grounded, able to merge sensitivity with practicality. While her Water and Earth influence may make her introspective and deliberate, Fire and Air ensure she remains capable of intellectual insight, dynamic action, and meaningful expression.

Lana Del Rey's Critical Degrees:

Sun at 0° in Cancer

0° of any sign represents a fresh beginning, the purest expression of that sign's energy, and a strong potential for new developments. With the Sun at 0° Cancer in the 8th House, this placement intensifies themes of emotional depth, transformation, and self-identity. Cancer's influence highlights strong instincts, heightened sensitivity, and a deep connection to personal roots, while the 8th House ties these qualities to themes of renewal and emotional evolution. This degree suggests an undiluted expression of Cancerian energy, making emotional awareness, security, and transformation central to her identity.

Saturn at 22° Scorpio

22° in fixed signs is often associated with intense karmic challenges, major turning points, and transformative life lessons. With Saturn at this degree in the 1st House, these themes are directly tied to self-discipline, identity, and resilience. In Scorpio, this placement emphasizes lessons surrounding power, control, and emotional depth, often requiring inner strength and mastery over personal struggles. Saturn in the 1st House suggests an approach to life marked by seriousness, caution, and a strong sense of responsibility. Challenges related to self-expression, trust, and transformation may necessitate embracing vulnerability while maintaining firm personal boundaries. Over time, this placement fosters endurance, wisdom, and emotional resilience, reinforcing a path of self-mastery.

Uranus at 15° Sagittarius

15° of any sign is a highly significant degree, often intensifying the planet's expression and bringing heightened focus or impact. With Uranus at this degree in the 2nd House, themes of innovation, disruption, and unpredictability strongly influence values, material security, and self-worth. In Sagittarius, this placement amplifies a desire for financial independence and unconventional approaches to stability, often leading to sudden shifts in priorities regarding resources. She may have a tendency to reject traditional financial structures, seek alternative income sources, or redefine personal security. This placement suggests a nonconformist approach to material stability, valuing freedom and exploration over rigid financial expectations, with unexpected changes shaping her relationship with money and self-sufficiency.

Ascendant at 15° Scorpio

With the Ascendant at 15°, the way she presents herself to the world is deeply infused with Scorpio's intensity, mystery, and transformative nature. This placement enhances her magnetic presence, strong personal boundaries, and an ability to project both power and depth. It suggests her persona is shaped by resilience, privacy, and an innate ability to reinvent herself through life's challenges.

Descendant at 15° Taurus

With the Descendant at 15°, Lana's relationships and partnerships are strongly influenced by Taurus' need for stability, loyalty, and security. This placement emphasizes a deep attachment to dependable connections, a preference for long-lasting commitments, and a desire for emotional and material consistency in close relationships. However, it may also highlight struggles with possessiveness, attachment, or resistance to change, making it important for her to find balance between security and growth in partnerships.

Lana Del Rey's Ruling Planets and Their Influence on the Rest of Her Chart:

First House (Identity, appearance, self-expression, personality):
- **Scorpio (Cusp sign, 15° of the first house): Ruled by Pluto & Mars**

- Pluto is located in Lana's twelfth house
- Pluto governs transformation, and its placement in Scorpio in the 12th House indicates that Lana's identity (First House) is deeply shaped by subconscious forces, hidden matters, and personal healing. With Pluto in its domicile sign, this influence is especially potent, suggesting she carries an aura of depth, mystery, and intensity. The connection between Scorpio in the First House and Pluto in the 12th suggests that much of her personal power comes from introspection, solitude, and confronting the unseen—whether in herself or in the world around her. This placement may indicate a private yet profound internal evolution, where she experiences identity shifts through deep psychological or spiritual awakenings.

- Mars is located in Lana's eighth house
- Mars governs drive and action, and with Mars in Cancer in the 8th House, her energy is directed toward emotional depth, transformation, and intimate connections. Unlike the direct, outward aggression typically associated with Mars, its placement in Cancer brings a more protective, emotionally driven approach to assertion. This suggests that Lana's identity is shaped by deeply personal and private emotional experiences, with a tendency to act based on instinct and emotional security. With the 8th House connection, her sense of self may be influenced by themes of power, shared resources, and psychological transformation, giving her a persistent yet indirect approach to asserting herself—one that operates through emotional depth rather than overt force.

- Sagittarius (15° of the first house): Ruled by Jupiter
  - Jupiter is located in Lana's third house
  - Jupiter governs expansion and wisdom, and with Jupiter in Aquarius in the 3rd House, her energy is directed toward intellectual exploration, innovation, and communication. Jupiter in Aquarius enhances her independent thinking and curiosity, emphasizing a natural inclination toward unconventional ideas and broadening perspectives. With the 3rd House connection (communication, learning, thought processes), her sense of self

342

is closely tied to exchanging ideas and seeking knowledge that challenges societal norms. This placement suggests that she navigates life with an open mind, approaching self-expression with a mix of optimism, originality, and a desire to push boundaries through thought and conversation.

Second House (Finances, possessions, self-worth, material security):
- **Sagittarius (Cusp sign, 15° of the second house): Ruled by Jupiter**
  - **Jupiter is located in Lana's third house**
    - With Sagittarius ruling the 2nd House and Jupiter in Aquarius in the 3rd, Lana's financial security and self-worth are closely tied to communication, learning, and intellectual exploration. Jupiter in Aquarius suggests an unconventional approach to material stability, where income or resources may come from innovative ideas, networking, or engaging with progressive industries. This placement highlights an expansive, forward-thinking mindset when it comes to finances, valuing freedom and adaptability over rigid structures. The connection between the 2nd House and the 3rd House suggests that self-expression, writing, or exchanging ideas may play a key role in her material success, with financial opportunities potentially arising from her ability to connect with others and challenge traditional ways of thinking.
- **Capricorn (19° of the second house): Ruled by Saturn**
  - **Saturn is located in Lana's first house**
    - With Capricorn also ruling part of the 2nd House and Saturn in Scorpio in the 1st, there is a more serious, disciplined approach to financial matters that contrasts with the expansive influence of Jupiter. Saturn in the 1st House suggests that her self-worth and approach to security are deeply tied to personal resilience and control, making her strategic and cautious about building long-term stability. The influence of Scorpio on Saturn adds emotional depth to her relationship with finances, indicating that power, transformation, and resourcefulness play a role in how

she manages wealth. The connection between the 2nd House and the 1st House suggests that financial stability and self-worth are directly linked to her sense of identity, where maintaining control over her resources may be essential to her personal confidence and security.

Third House (Communication, siblings, learning, local environment):
- **Capricorn (Cusp sign, 11° of the third house): Ruled by Saturn**
  - **Saturn is located in Lana's first house**
  - With Capricorn ruling the 3rd House and Saturn in Scorpio in the 1st, Lana's communication style is closely tied to her sense of identity, bringing a serious, deliberate, and structured approach to how she expresses herself. Saturn in Scorpio intensifies this influence, suggesting that she may choose her words carefully, valuing depth, control, and precision in her interactions. This placement implies a reserved or calculated communication style, where she speaks with authority and intention rather than impulsiveness. The connection between the 3rd House and the 1st House suggests that her self-image plays a strong role in how she communicates, possibly making her cautious about revealing too much while ensuring her words carry significance.
- **Aquarius (25° of the third house): Ruled by Uranus & Saturn**
  - **Uranus is located in Lana's second house**
  - With Aquarius also ruling part of the 3rd House and Uranus in Sagittarius in the 2nd, there is an unconventional, independent streak in how she learns and communicates. Uranus in the 2nd House ties financial security and self-worth to originality, suggesting that her ability to express new and innovative ideas may influence her material success. This placement can indicate a rebellious or forward-thinking communication style, one that seeks intellectual freedom and resists conformity. The connection between the 3rd and 2nd Houses suggests that her way of thinking and speaking may shape her financial

opportunities, with her unique perspectives or knowledge serving as a potential source of stability and value.

Fourth House (Family, home life, roots, emotional foundation):
- **Aquarius (Cusp sign, 5° of the fourth house): Ruled by Uranus & Saturn**
- **Uranus is located in Lana's second house**
> - With Aquarius on the cusp of the 4th House and Uranus in Sagittarius in the 2nd, Lana's emotional foundation and home life are influenced by unconventional values and shifting material circumstances. Uranus in Sagittarius suggests an independent or non-traditional approach to family, possibly indicating a home environment shaped by change, exploration, or an unconventional belief system. The connection between the 4th House (home, family) and the 2nd House (finances, values) suggests that her sense of security may be tied to financial independence or fluctuating material conditions, making stability something she seeks but may struggle to maintain.

 - **Saturn is located in Lana's first house**
> - With Saturn as Aquarius' co-ruler and placed in Scorpio in the 1st, there is a strong sense of responsibility tied to family and emotional roots. This placement suggests that her early experiences may have shaped her identity in a serious or intense way, possibly instilling a deep need for control, resilience, or emotional self-sufficiency. The connection between the 4th House and the 1st House implies that family expectations or early life experiences had a lasting impact on how she presents herself to the world, reinforcing a need for emotional discipline and self-mastery.

- **Pisces (27° of the fourth house): Ruled by Neptune & Jupiter**
 - **Neptune is located in Lana's second house**
> - With Pisces also ruling part of the 4th House and Neptune in Capricorn in the 2nd, there is an idealistic or dreamy quality attached to her perception of home and family. Neptune in Capricorn grounds this vision with a more pragmatic or

structured approach, suggesting that while she may long for a deeply meaningful or spiritually fulfilling home life, she also recognizes the need for financial stability and long-term security. The connection between the 4th and 2nd Houses suggests that her emotional foundation is tied to material concerns, and she may seek comfort in tangible achievements or structured environments, even if there is a tendency for financial uncertainty or disillusionment.

 - **Jupiter is located in Lana's third house**
- With Jupiter, Pisces' traditional ruler, in Aquarius in the 3rd house, learning, communication, and intellectual exploration play a key role in her emotional development. This placement suggests that she may have grown up in an environment where ideas, education, or broad perspectives were emphasized, shaping her emotional outlook. The connection between the 4th and 3rd Houses indicates that she may feel most at home in conversations, storytelling, or expanding her knowledge, finding emotional fulfillment through intellectual stimulation and open-minded exploration. Jupiter's influence here may also suggest that she carries a philosophical or optimistic approach to understanding her past and family experiences, using knowledge as a way to find meaning in her emotional journey.

Fifth House (Creativity, romance, children, self-expression):
- Pisces (Cusp sign, 2° of the fifth house): Ruled by Neptune & Jupiter
 - **Neptune is located in Lana's second house**
- With Pisces on the cusp of the 5th House and Neptune in Capricorn in the 2nd, Lana's creativity and approach to romance are influenced by imagination, idealism, and a strong connection to material security. Neptune in Capricorn brings a structured yet dreamy approach to artistic expression, suggesting that her creativity is shaped by both inspiration and discipline. The connection between the 5th House (creativity, romance) and the 2nd House (finances, self-worth) indicates that her artistic pursuits may be tied to her sense of value and financial stability.

She may seek to ground her creative vision in tangible success, using her work as a means to create long-term security while still maintaining an ethereal, poetic quality in her self-expression.

- Jupiter is located in Lana's third house
- With Jupiter as Pisces' traditional ruler and placed in Aquarius in the 3rd house, communication, learning, and intellectual exploration play a key role in her creativity and romantic experiences. Jupiter in Aquarius suggests that her self-expression thrives in unconventional, thought-provoking, and socially aware themes, allowing her to blend philosophy and innovation into her artistic pursuits. The connection between the 5th and 3rd Houses indicates that storytelling, writing, and exchanging ideas may be central to her creative expression. This placement suggests an expansive, curious approach to both love and art, where intellectual stimulation and originality are essential components of fulfillment.

- Aries (24° of the fifth house): Ruled by Mars
  - Mars is located in Lana's eighth house
  - With Aries also ruling part of the 5th House and Mars in Cancer in the 8th, there is an intense and emotionally driven approach to both romance and creativity. Mars in Cancer directs passion inward, creating a deeply personal, protective, and intuitive approach to self-expression. The connection between the 5th House (creativity, romance) and the 8th House (transformation, intimacy, shared resources) suggests that her creative work and romantic life are influenced by deep emotional experiences, power dynamics, and themes of transformation. This placement indicates that love and artistic expression are not taken lightly—both may involve emotional depth, vulnerability, and a strong desire for meaningful connection.

Sixth House (Work, daily routines, health, service):
- Aries (Cusp sign, 6° of the sixth house): Ruled by Mars
  - Mars is located in Lana's eighth house
  - With Aries ruling the 6th House and Mars in Cancer in the 8th, Lana's approach to work and daily routines is deeply tied to

emotional intensity, transformation, and personal connections. Mars in Cancer brings a protective, intuitive energy to her work, suggesting that she may prefer environments where she can nurture or emotionally invest in what she does. The connection between the 6th House (work, health, routines) and the 8th House (transformation, shared resources, emotional depth) suggests that her work may involve deep emotional exchanges, power dynamics, or themes of renewal and healing. She may thrive in roles that require resilience, emotional intelligence, and the ability to navigate complex or deeply personal matters.

- Taurus (15° of the sixth house): Ruled by Venus
  - Venus is located in Lana's sixth house
    - With Taurus also ruling part of the 6th House and Venus in Taurus in the 6th, there is a strong emphasis on bringing beauty, comfort, and harmony into her daily life. Venus in its domicile sign enhances her appreciation for stability and pleasure in her work environment, suggesting that she may be drawn to careers that allow for artistic expression, meaningful relationships, or a sense of balance. This placement indicates a preference for routines that are slow, steady, and enjoyable, valuing consistency over chaos. The connection between the 6th House and Venus in Taurus suggests that she may prioritize wellness practices that are soothing and restorative, favoring self-care, relaxation, and a holistic approach to health.

Seventh House (Relationships, marriage, partnerships, agreements):
- Taurus (Cusp sign, 15° of the seventh house): Ruled by Venus
  - Venus is located in Lana's sixth house
    - With Taurus ruling the 7th House and Venus in Taurus in the 6th, Lana's relationships and partnerships are closely tied to her daily work, routines, and sense of stability. Venus in its domicile sign emphasizes a strong appreciation for loyalty, comfort, and harmony in relationships, suggesting that she seeks dependable, grounded connections. The connection between the 7th House

(partnerships) and the 6th House (work, routines, service) indicates that she may meet partners through her work environment or that shared routines and responsibilities play a significant role in her relationships. She may prefer partnerships that bring a sense of ease and support into her daily life, valuing consistency and mutual care in her connections.

- **Gemini (15° of the seventh house): Ruled by Mercury**
  - **Mercury is located in Lana's eighth house**
    - With Gemini also ruling part of the 7th House and Mercury in Cancer in the 8th, communication, emotional depth, and transformation play a crucial role in her partnerships. Mercury in Cancer suggests an intuitive, emotionally driven communication style, where deep conversations and personal understanding are key to maintaining strong relationships. The connection between the 7th House (relationships) and the 8th House (shared resources, transformation, intimacy) indicates that her partnerships may involve significant emotional depth, financial or energetic exchanges, or profound personal change. She may be drawn to intellectually stimulating partners who can also provide emotional security, and her relationships may evolve through deep conversations, trust-building, and shared emotional or financial responsibilities.

Eighth House (Transformation, shared resources, death, rebirth):
- **Gemini (Cusp sign, 15° of the eighth house): Ruled by Mercury**
  - **Mercury is located in Lana's eighth house**
    - With Gemini on the cusp of the 8th House and Mercury in Cancer also in the 8th, Lana's approach to transformation, shared resources, and deep emotional matters is heavily influenced by intellect and emotional communication. Mercury in Cancer suggests that her thought processes and communication style are deeply intuitive and emotionally charged, making her highly perceptive when navigating complex emotional or financial situations. The connection between Mercury and the 8th House indicates that she may process

transformation through reflection, deep conversations, or emotional introspection. She may have a natural ability to articulate profound emotional experiences, and her personal evolution is likely shaped by the way she understands and communicates her feelings.

- Cancer (19° of the eighth house): Ruled by the Moon
- The Moon is located in Lana's ninth house

- With Cancer also ruling part of the 8th House and the Moon in Leo in the 9th, emotional depth and transformation are closely tied to her search for meaning, higher learning, and personal growth. The Moon in Leo suggests that she experiences emotional transformation in a way that is expressive, bold, and creatively fueled, possibly finding healing through storytelling, philosophy, or exploration of different perspectives. The connection between the 8th and 9th Houses indicates that deep emotional experiences and changes may push her toward greater self-discovery, shaping her worldview and spiritual beliefs. This placement suggests that she may feel a strong emotional drive to seek knowledge and understanding as a way to process intense emotional or financial changes.

Ninth House (Travel, higher education, philosophy, spirituality):
- Cancer (Cusp sign, 11° of the ninth house): Ruled by the Moon
- The Moon is located in Lana's ninth house

- With Cancer ruling the 9th House and the Moon in Leo also in the 9th, Lana's emotional well-being is closely connected to her search for meaning, wisdom, and personal growth. The Moon in Leo adds an expressive, creative, and deeply personal element to her beliefs, suggesting that she may process emotions through storytelling, artistic expression, or philosophical exploration. This placement indicates that travel, education, and spiritual pursuits may provide her with a sense of emotional security and purpose, as she seeks experiences that nurture both her heart and her understanding of the world. The connection between the Moon and the 9th House suggests that her intuition and emotions play a key role in shaping her worldview, and she may be drawn to learning environments or spiritual practices that allow her to express her inner self with confidence and authenticity.

- Leo (25° of the ninth house): Ruled by the Sun
- The Sun is located in Lana's eighth house
- With Leo also ruling part of the 9th House and the Sun in Cancer in the 8th, her pursuit of knowledge and personal growth is deeply tied to transformation, emotional depth, and uncovering hidden truths. The Sun in Cancer suggests that her core self is shaped by deep emotional connections, family history, and a desire for security, but its placement in the 8th House indicates that she seeks knowledge that fundamentally transforms her understanding of herself and the world. The connection between the 8th and 9th Houses suggests that her intellectual and spiritual exploration is not surface-level—it is a journey of emotional rebirth and empowerment. She may be drawn to subjects that explore psychology, mysticism, or the hidden aspects of human nature, using her insights to bring depth and meaning to her experiences.

Tenth House (Career, public image, reputation, ambitions):
- Leo (Cusp sign, 5° of the tenth house): Ruled by the Sun
- The Sun is located in Lana's eighth house
- With Leo ruling the 10th House and the Sun in Cancer in the 8th, Lana's career and public image are shaped by themes of transformation, emotional depth, and power dynamics. The Sun in Cancer suggests that her ambitions are influenced by personal and emotional connections, possibly drawing her toward careers where nurturing, protection, or emotional storytelling play a role. However, with the Sun positioned in the 8th House (shared resources, rebirth, the hidden), her career may also involve navigating complex emotional, financial, or psychological themes. The connection between the 10th and 8th Houses suggests that her public presence carries an air of mystery, intensity, or depth, and she may experience significant career

transformations throughout her life.
- Virgo (27° of the tenth house): Ruled by Mercury
- Mercury is located in Lana's eighth house
- With Virgo also ruling part of the 10th House and Mercury in Cancer in the 8th, communication and intellect play a key role in how she builds her career and manages her public image. Mercury in Cancer suggests that her voice and ideas are deeply influenced by emotions, memory, and intuition, giving her a reflective, thoughtful approach to her work. The connection between the 10th House (career, reputation) and the 8th House (depth, transformation, shared resources) reinforces the idea that her success may come from her ability to articulate complex emotional or psychological experiences, whether through writing, speaking, or artistic expression. This placement suggests that her career path is not just about external success but also about deep personal transformation and uncovering hidden truths.

Eleventh House (Friendships, groups, social networks, aspirations):
- Virgo (Cusp sign, 3° of the eleventh house): Ruled by Mercury
- Mercury is located in Lana's eighth house
- With Virgo ruling the 11th House and Mercury in Cancer in the 8th, Lana's friendships and social networks are deeply influenced by emotional depth, transformation, and intellectual intimacy. Mercury in Cancer suggests that she values close, emotionally intelligent conversations in her social circles, preferring friendships that offer trust, security, and meaningful exchanges. The connection between the 11th House (friendships, aspirations) and the 8th House (transformation, shared resources, power dynamics) suggests that she may form friendships that profoundly impact her, or that her social connections involve themes of emotional or financial exchange. Her aspirations may be shaped by deep emotional experiences, seeking out friendships and group associations that encourage

personal evolution and psychological insight.
- Libra (24° of the eleventh house): Ruled by Venus
  - Venus is located in Lana's sixth house
    - With Libra also ruling part of the 11th House and Venus in Taurus in the 6th, there is an emphasis on stability, beauty, and harmony in her friendships and social life. Venus in Taurus suggests she values friendships that are loyal, supportive, and bring a sense of comfort. The connection between the 11th House (social networks) and the 6th House (work, daily routines) indicates that she may build friendships through her work or daily habits, forming bonds with those she interacts with regularly. This placement suggests that she thrives in relationships that provide both aesthetic and emotional balance, and she may aspire to create harmony and beauty within her social groups or career.

Twelfth House (Subconscious, solitude, endings, hidden matters):
- Libra (Cusp sign, 6° of the twelfth house): Ruled by Venus
  - Venus is located in Lana's sixth house
    - With Libra ruling the 12th House and Venus in Taurus in the 6th, Lana's subconscious mind and hidden matters are closely tied to her work, routines, and sense of balance in daily life. Venus in Taurus emphasizes a need for stability and harmony, suggesting that she may find peace through structured routines, creative outlets, or cultivating beauty in her environment. The connection between the 12th House (solitude, the subconscious) and the 6th House (work, daily habits) implies that her emotional well-being is reflected in her daily life—when she feels centered in her routine, she may experience greater inner peace. This placement also suggests that acts of service, caregiving, or working in a peaceful, aesthetically pleasing environment could be a source of emotional healing for her.
- Scorpio (15° of the twelfth house): Ruled by Pluto & Mars
  - Pluto is located in Lana's twelfth house
    - With Scorpio also ruling part of the 12th House and Pluto in Scorpio in the 12th, there is a profound intensity in her

subconscious world. Pluto in its domicile sign here suggests deep psychological transformation, hidden emotional power, and a need to confront fears or past traumas in solitude. This placement indicates that much of her inner growth comes through introspection and personal healing, possibly drawn to exploring the mysteries of life, spirituality, or the subconscious mind. The connection between the 12th House and Pluto in the 12th reinforces that her internal world is complex and transformative, with a strong ability to regenerate and find strength through facing the unknown.

- Mars is located in Lana's eighth house
- With Mars in Cancer in the 8th, there is an emotional intensity to her subconscious motivations. Mars in the 8th House directs her inner drive toward deep emotional and psychological exploration, making themes of transformation, intimacy, and power dynamics key aspects of her hidden world. The connection between the 12th and 8th Houses suggests that her personal growth is closely tied to uncovering and working through hidden fears, emotional depths, and private struggles. This placement points to a strong inner resilience, with a subconscious need to protect what is emotionally significant to her while navigating the transformative cycles of her inner world.

Lana Del Rey's Aspect Chart:

Here are some key major aspects from Lana Del Rey's birth chart, each showcasing how planetary interactions shape her personality:

- **Sun** (0° Cancer) **Conjunction** Vertex (28° Gemini)
- **Mercury** (16° Cancer) **Sextile** Venus (14° Taurus)
- **Part of Fortune** (25° Sagittarius) **Trine Midheaven (MC)** (25° Leo)
- **North Node** (16° Taurus) **Opposition** Ascendant (15° Scorpio)
- **Saturn** (22° Scorpio) **Square Midheaven (MC)** (25° Leo)

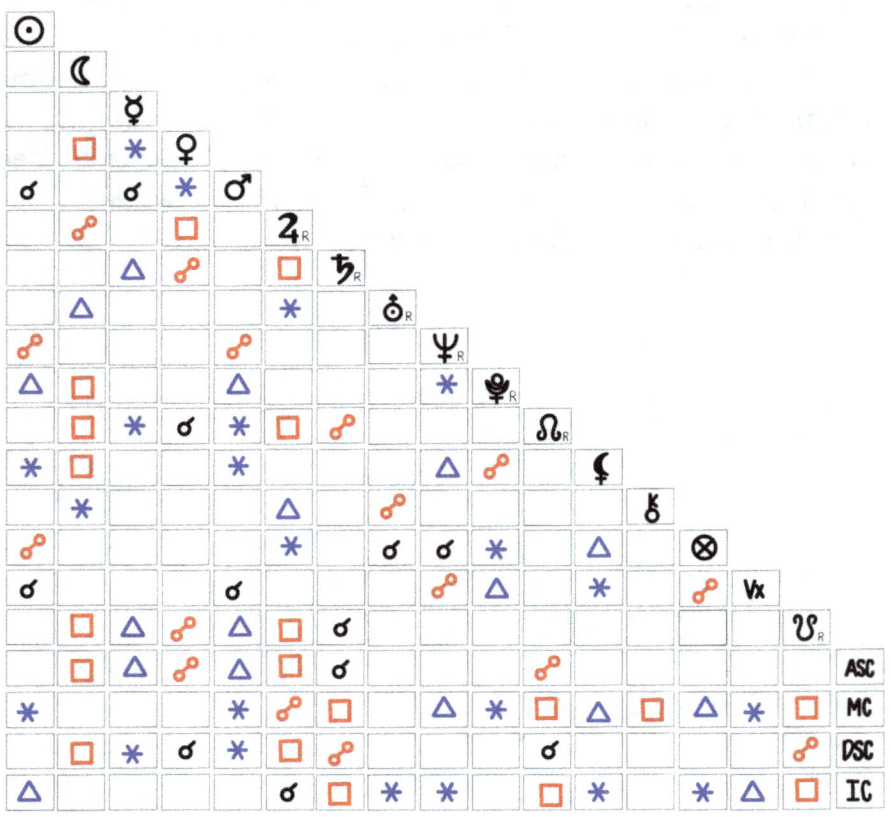

Sun Conjunct Vertex (8th House)

A conjunction between the Sun and the Vertex intensifies themes of identity, destiny, and transformation, linking self-expression to fated encounters and significant turning points. The Vertex represents pivotal experiences and relationships that shape personal growth, and with the Sun in Cancer in the 8th House, these moments are often deeply emotional, centered around intimacy, psychological depth, and personal renewal.

The 8th House connection suggests that self-discovery unfolds through profound emotional exchanges, transformative relationships, and uncovering hidden truths. The Vertex in Gemini adds an intellectual element, indicating that significant turning points often come through communication, learning, or shifting perspectives. This aspect suggests that her identity is continually shaped by deep, fated connections, pushing her toward growth through both emotional and intellectual experiences. Encounters with others play a crucial role in her personal evolution, often acting as catalysts for emotional transformation and expanded understanding.

Mercury Sextile Venus (8th & 6th House)

A sextile between Mercury and Venus suggests that Lana has a natural harmony between communication, creativity, and social interactions. This aspect enhances her ability to express herself in a way that is both charming and emotionally resonant, making it easier for her to connect with others through words, beauty, and refined artistic sensibilities.

With Mercury in Cancer in the 8th House, her thoughts and communication are deeply intuitive, emotional, and reflective, often focused on hidden truths, psychological depth, or transformative experiences. She has an inclination toward expressing her feelings with depth and nuance, often in ways that feel intimate and revealing. This placement suggests a powerful connection between speech and emotional vulnerability, allowing her to engage in profound conversations and articulate complex emotions with sensitivity and insight.

The sextile to Venus in Taurus in the 6th House brings a

grounding and artistic influence to this energy, helping her translate deep, emotional thoughts into tangible, structured, and aesthetically pleasing expressions. Venus in Taurus emphasizes beauty, stability, and sensuality, meaning she may have a strong appreciation for lyrical writing, poetic expression, or artistic communication that feels both meaningful and harmonious. This aspect also gives her a natural ability to bring warmth and grace into her daily interactions, making her communication feel smooth, persuasive, and engaging.

Part of Fortune Trine Midheaven (2nd & 10th House)

A trine between the Part of Fortune and the Midheaven suggests that Lana's sense of fulfillment and success is naturally aligned with her career path and public image. She has an innate ability to attract opportunities that contribute to professional recognition and material stability, as her personal values (2nd House) and ambitions (10th House) work in harmony.

With the Part of Fortune in Sagittarius in the 2nd House, Lana finds fulfillment through freedom, exploration, and expanding her personal resources. She has a strong belief in luck and abundance, thriving when she takes risks or pursues opportunities that align with her ideals. This placement often brings a natural optimism toward financial growth and personal stability, as well as an ability to manifest success through faith in her own abilities.

The trine to the Midheaven in Leo enhances her confidence, ambition, and visibility in the public sphere. She has an effortless ability to step into leadership roles or gain recognition for her talents, as this aspect supports a charismatic and driven approach to career-building. She may be seen as inspiring or visionary in her field, attracting attention and success through her unique perspective and bold self-expression.

This aspect suggests that Lana's career and financial success often feel like a natural extension of her personal fulfillment, allowing her to pursue goals without excessive struggle or resistance. It fosters an ability to trust in her path, with professional achievements often bringing her a deep sense of satisfaction and alignment with her higher purpose.

North Node Opposition Ascendant (7th & 1st House)

This aspect suggests that Lana is meant to move away from self-reliance and intensity (1st House) and toward connection, stability, and cooperation (7th House). She may experience an internal struggle between maintaining personal power and embracing vulnerability in relationships, as her natural inclination is toward independence and self-containment.

With the North Node in the 7th House, Lana's life path is about learning how to trust, build partnerships, and create balance in relationships. However, with her Ascendant in Scorpio, she has an intense, private, and self-sufficient nature, making the process of opening up to others both necessary and challenging. She may naturally gravitate toward self-protection, yet feel a deep pull toward forming meaningful, transformative connections.

This aspect often manifests as a strong desire for deep, committed relationships, but with hesitation or resistance toward depending on others. She may feel torn between maintaining control over her own life and allowing emotional interdependence to develop. The opposition between the North Node and her Ascendant suggests that over time, she is meant to embrace vulnerability, trust, and emotional balance, understanding that partnerships can be a source of stability rather than a loss of control.

Saturn Square Midheaven (1st & 10th House)

A square between Saturn and the Midheaven suggests that Lana's career path, public image, and ambitions are shaped by obstacles, discipline, and a strong sense of duty. She may take a serious or reserved approach to success, often feeling that she must work harder than others to achieve recognition. This aspect can create an internal pressure to prove herself, leading to a long-term, methodical approach to building her career.

With Saturn in Scorpio in the 1st House, Lana carries a strong sense of responsibility, self-discipline, and emotional restraint, which may make her appear mature beyond her years. However, this can also create self-doubt or hesitancy in fully asserting herself, especially in professional pursuits. She may feel a strong need to be in control of her image and ambitions, but this placement can also indicate a fear of failure or a tendency to be overly critical of her own progress.

Since Saturn squares the Midheaven in Leo, a sign associated with visibility and performance, there may be challenges in stepping into the spotlight or fully embracing leadership roles. She may struggle with self-expression in her career, fearing criticism or feeling that her efforts go unnoticed. This tension between Saturn's restrictive energy and Leo's need for recognition may make it difficult for her to fully embrace her public persona, leading to a measured, careful approach to success.

Despite these challenges, this aspect fosters resilience and long-term achievement. Lana's determination and ability to endure hardship allow her to build a career that stands the test of time, often leading to a well-earned reputation and lasting impact. She may take a slow, steady approach to career-building, ensuring that her work aligns with her personal integrity. This placement suggests that, while the road to success may feel demanding, the structure and discipline Saturn imposes ultimately lead to stability, mastery, and professional fulfillment.

"Contradicting" Aspects:

When interpreting aspects in a birth chart, it's essential to consider how they interact with one another. While some aspects create ease and flow, others introduce challenges that require persistence and growth. Rather than working against each other, contrasting aspects often balance the individual's experience, shaping their personal and professional journey in a unique way.

In this case, we see two aspects that influence career and public success in different ways:

While **Part of Fortune trine Midheaven** suggests a natural alignment between career success and personal fulfillment, Saturn square Midheaven introduces challenges, delays, and a strong sense of responsibility toward one's public image and ambitions. These aspects may seem contradictory—one indicating ease and luck in professional pursuits, the other requiring discipline and perseverance—but together, they create a dynamic where success is both fated and hard-earned. Saturn's influence may make early career progress feel slow or demanding, requiring patience and resilience, but the Part of Fortune ensures that once the right path is found, fulfillment and recognition follow naturally. This combination suggests that while external pressures or personal insecurities (Saturn) may initially create obstacles or self-doubt, there is an innate ability to navigate these struggles and ultimately achieve a rewarding and meaningful career (Part of Fortune). Success may not come instantly, but when it does, it is well-earned and deeply aligned with one's greater purpose.

The aspects highlighted in Lana Del Rey's chart offer a glimpse into how planets interact, shaping different areas of life in unique ways. It's important to remember that these are just a few examples among many, as a birth chart is a complex and nuanced map with countless connections between planets, points, and angles. Each aspect adds another layer of influence, contributing to the intricate web of relationships that define an individual's experiences.

This book focuses on the deeper connections between signs, planets, and houses, but aspects provide additional nuance in chart interpretation. Exploring them in detail can offer even greater insight into how different energies manifest and influence personal growth, relationships, and life direction.

Lana Del Rey's Stelliums:

Eighth House Stellium
- **House:** Eighth House
- **Celestial Bodies:** Sun, Mars, Mercury in Cancer and Vertex in Gemini
- **Sign:** Cancer & Gemini

Lana Del Rey's stellium in Cancer in the 8th House, consisting of the Sun, Mars, and Mercury, creates an intense and deeply emotional presence, where themes of emotional security, transformation, and self-protection are central to her identity, drive, and communication. The 8th House governs death and rebirth, transformation, intimacy, shared resources, and psychological depth, making this stellium one of deep personal evolution, where emotions are not just felt but profoundly experienced, processed, and reborn. The presence of the Vertex in Gemini adds another dimension, suggesting that key fated encounters or pivotal life moments will come through communication, learning, or intellectual exploration.

At the core of this stellium is the Sun in Cancer, which defines Lana's self-identity, purpose, and life force. Cancer is ruled by the Moon, making her highly in tune with emotional cycles, nostalgia, and a need for deep emotional security. However, with the Sun positioned in the 8th House, her sense of self is inextricably linked to transformation, intimacy, and hidden power dynamics—she may define herself through personal rebirths, experiences of emotional depth, or profound connections with others. Rather than expressing herself openly, she may have an instinct to guard her emotional world, revealing it only in deeply meaningful or artistic ways. The 8th House's influence on her Cancerian energy suggests that she is naturally drawn to uncovering life's deeper meanings, whether through introspection, relationships, or creative expression.

Mars in Cancer in the 8th House intensifies this energy, adding a strong emotional charge to her ambitions, instincts, and drive. Mars governs action and assertion, and in Cancer, it operates protectively, reactively, and intuitively rather than aggressively. This placement suggests that her motivation is tied to emotional security, deep emotional connections, and themes of transformation. She may have a tendency to act on instinct, defending what is meaningful to her and using emotional depth as a source of personal power. In the 8th House, Mars' drive is linked to themes of intimacy, shared resources, and hidden emotional strength, reinforcing her ability to navigate complex emotional or financial situations with resilience and emotional intelligence.

With Mercury in Cancer also in the 8th House, her thought processes, communication style, and way of processing information are deeply tied to emotion, intuition, and nostalgia. Mercury in Cancer already brings a reflective, emotionally intelligent way of thinking, but in the 8th House, her mind naturally gravitates toward deep, psychological, and hidden matters. She may have a talent for expressing emotions through words, articulating complex emotional experiences with nuance and sensitivity. This placement suggests that she may be drawn to exploring topics related to psychology, healing, or emotional transformation through writing, music, or personal reflection. She likely processes her emotions privately, and when she does express them, it is with deep intention and meaning.

The Vertex in Gemini in the 8th House introduces a fated element to this stellium, indicating that key turning points in her life will be shaped by intellectual connections, communication, or transformative knowledge. The Vertex is often described as the point of destined encounters, meaning that the people or experiences that significantly shape her life may come through conversations, learning, or moments of mental clarity. In the 8th House, these experiences may be intensely emotional, tied to psychological depth, intimacy, or uncovering hidden truths.

This stellium ties together self-identity (Sun), action and motivation (Mars), thought processes and communication (Mercury), and fated experiences (Vertex), under the emotional and transformative influence of Cancer, the communicative influence of Gemini and the 8th House. Lana's Cancer energy manifests in an intensely private, emotionally complex way, where she seeks deep emotional bonds, profound personal evolution, and a sense of security through emotional transformation. She likely experiences emotions with extreme depth, making her relationships, creative work, and internal world rich with meaning.

However, the 8th House requires constant transformation, meaning that this stellium pushes her toward cycles of emotional death and rebirth, where she must confront and release past emotions in order to evolve. The protective, nurturing nature of Cancer contrasts with the 8th House's demand for surrender and transformation, creating a dynamic where she may struggle with letting go of emotional attachments, yet also thrive when she embraces change.

Additionally, the Vertex in Gemini introduces an intellectual component to this deeply emotional placement, suggesting that while her emotions drive her, her fated path may involve learning to detach at times, analyze situations logically, and embrace curiosity. The balance between her deeply intuitive, emotionally protective nature and the intellectual adaptability of the Vertex in Gemini may be a key part of her personal growth.

Lana's Cancer stellium in the 8th House gives her a profound emotional intensity, making her someone who processes life's experiences in a deeply introspective and transformative way. She may be drawn to themes of emotional healing, the subconscious, and personal evolution, constantly navigating the tension between emotional security and the 8th House's demand for profound change. This placement suggests that her greatest strength lies in her ability to channel deep emotional experiences into self-awareness, creative expression, and personal power.

Scorpio Stellium
- **House:** First House & Twelfth House
- **Celestial Bodies:** Ascendant, South Node, Saturn, and Pluto
- **Sign:** Scorpio

Lana Del Rey's Scorpio stellium, consisting of her Ascendant, South Node, Saturn, and Pluto, creates a powerful, enigmatic presence while shaping a deeply private and transformative internal world. This stellium straddles the 1st House (self, identity, physical presence) and the 12th House (subconscious, solitude, hidden matters), meaning that her outward persona and internal experiences are inseparably intertwined, reinforcing themes of control, intensity, and emotional rebirth. Scorpio's influence makes her someone who navigates life with an inherent awareness of power—both personal and external—while operating with a depth that few may truly understand.

At the forefront of this stellium is her Scorpio Ascendant, which dictates how she presents herself to the world. With Scorpio rising, she exudes a quiet but commanding presence, appearing intense, mysterious, and emotionally self-possessed. The 1st House placements—South Node and Saturn—reinforce this sense of control, responsibility, and depth, making her cautious in how she engages with the world. She likely approaches life with a mix of determination, emotional resilience, and secrecy, choosing what to reveal and when. Yet, beneath this structured and composed exterior lies Pluto in the 12th House, suggesting that her most profound transformations happen internally, in solitude, and through deep psychological introspection.

Pluto's placement in the 12th House is significant because it represents hidden power, subconscious regeneration, and themes of endings and rebirth. While her Ascendant gives her a commanding presence, Pluto in the 12th House suggests that much of this power comes from within—often forged through personal crises, deep reflection, and emotional transformation behind closed doors. This placement can create a tendency to withdraw or process difficult emotions privately, making her highly perceptive yet difficult to truly know. The connection between Pluto in the 12th and Saturn in the 1st House further reinforces emotional discipline, self-protection, and a structured approach to life, where past hardships or inner struggles shape her sense of self.

Adding another layer to this stellium is the South Node in the 1st House, which suggests that Lana is naturally accustomed to self-reliance, independence, and navigating life on her own terms. However, with her North Node in the 7th House in Taurus, she is meant to move toward balance, stability, and deeper trust in partnerships. This tension between her South Node and North Node reinforces the Scorpio stellium's underlying challenge: learning when to be in control versus when to surrender, when to embrace vulnerability instead of keeping emotions guarded.

Tying this all together, Saturn in Scorpio in the 1st House acts as the stabilizing force in this stellium, structuring the intense emotional and psychological themes Scorpio brings. Saturn here suggests that self-discipline, maturity, and personal responsibility define her identity, reinforcing a careful and strategic approach to life. This placement, combined with Pluto in the 12th House, can create a highly introspective and private individual, one who processes life's struggles in solitude yet emerges stronger each time.

Ultimately, this Scorpio stellium shapes a person who constantly navigates the duality between control and surrender, intensity and solitude, and external composure and internal transformation. The interplay between her 1st and 12th House placements suggests that her identity is shaped not just by how she presents herself to the world, but by the emotional depths she navigates in private. While she may appear self-assured and composed, much of her personal evolution happens through hidden struggles, spiritual awakenings, and emotional reinvention—making her journey one of quiet power, resilience, and profound self-discovery.

Taurus Stellium
- **Houses:** Sixth and Seventh House
- **Celestial Bodies:** Venus, North Node, Descendant, and Lilith
- **Sign:** Taurus

Lana Del Rey's Taurus stellium, consisting of her North Node, Descendant, Venus, and Lilith, spans the 6th and 7th Houses, creating a strong connection between her daily routines, relationships, and life's greater purpose. Taurus, ruled by Venus, brings themes of stability, beauty, sensuality, and material security, and with multiple placements in this sign, there is an intensified focus on creating balance, comfort, and reliability in both her work and partnerships. The interplay between the 6th House (work, health, daily routines, service) and the 7th House (relationships, partnerships, balance, agreements) suggests that her personal growth, relationships, and daily work are deeply interconnected, and that she is meant to develop security and trust in both her daily life and interpersonal connections.

At the center of this stellium is her North Node in Taurus, which represents her soul's path and karmic growth in this lifetime. With the North Node in the 7th House, she is meant to move away from self-reliance and emotional intensity (indicated by her South Node in Scorpio in the 1st House) and embrace stability, balance, and trust in relationships. This placement suggests that her greatest growth comes from learning how to build partnerships based on harmony, patience, and mutual support, rather than control or intensity. With Taurus energy influencing this path, she is encouraged to develop a steady, grounded approach to relationships, valuing commitment, emotional security, and long-term stability. This placement can also indicate that relationships, both personal and professional, play a key role in helping her build self-worth and establish a sense of peace in her life.

Her Descendant in Taurus reinforces this theme, as it describes the qualities she is drawn to in relationships and how she interacts with others in one-on-one dynamics. The Descendant in Taurus suggests that she is attracted to people who embody loyalty, sensuality, and dependability, valuing partners who bring stability and a sense of grounding into her life. This placement emphasizes her need for peace and emotional security in partnerships, making her likely to seek relationships that feel enduring and comforting. Her Scorpio Ascendant gives her an intense, self-sufficient nature, creating a natural tension with her need to develop trust in others. While she craves emotional depth and passion, she ultimately thrives in relationships that provide consistency, patience, and tangible expressions of love.

With Venus in Taurus in the 6th House, her values, aesthetics, and approach to love are deeply connected to her daily routines, work, and overall well-being. Venus in its domicile sign makes her naturally inclined toward creating beauty and balance in everyday life, suggesting that she finds comfort in routines that allow her to indulge in sensory pleasures and cultivate stability. The connection between Venus in the 6th House and her 7th House placements suggests that she may attract relationships through her work or daily interactions, or that her partnerships directly shape her routines, habits, or professional life. Venus in the 6th House also indicates that she may thrive when her work allows her to express creativity, maintain harmony, or provide service in a way that aligns with her values.

Lilith in Taurus in the 7th House adds a layer of complexity, suggesting that while she seeks stability in relationships, she may also have deep-seated fears, desires, or unconventional experiences related to love, intimacy, and partnerships. Lilith represents the shadow side of femininity, rebellion, and untamed desires, meaning that she may feel a strong need for independence even within relationships, or experience power struggles when it comes to love and commitment. With Lilith in Taurus, there is an underlying tension between wanting long-term security and resisting restrictions that might make her feel trapped. This placement suggests that she may challenge traditional relationship expectations or attract partners who push her to redefine stability on her own terms.

This Taurus stellium across the 6th and 7th Houses creates a powerful connection between her work, daily life, and relationships, suggesting that these areas of her life are deeply intertwined. The North Node and Descendant in Taurus indicate that learning to trust, build stability, and embrace long-term relationships is a major theme in her personal growth. However, Venus and Lilith bring contrasting influences—Venus encouraging harmony and security, while Lilith introduces a rebellious streak, challenging her to find balance between independence and commitment.

Ultimately, this stellium emphasizes the need for her to cultivate patience, emotional stability, and trust in both her relationships and daily life. She is meant to learn how to create tangible, long-lasting connections while balancing her natural intensity (Scorpio Ascendant) with Taurus' need for peace and security. Over time, this stellium encourages her to embrace stability in love, consistency in work, and a steady, grounded approach to life —allowing her to find fulfillment in both her partnerships and personal achievements.

8. Fill In Your Birth Chart:

_____ *was Born on*

____/____/_____ *in* _____,

_____,

_____ *at* ___:___ ____ ____.

"As a well-spent day brings happy sleep, so life well used brings happy death. Astrology is a science that aligns life well."
- Leonardo da Vinci

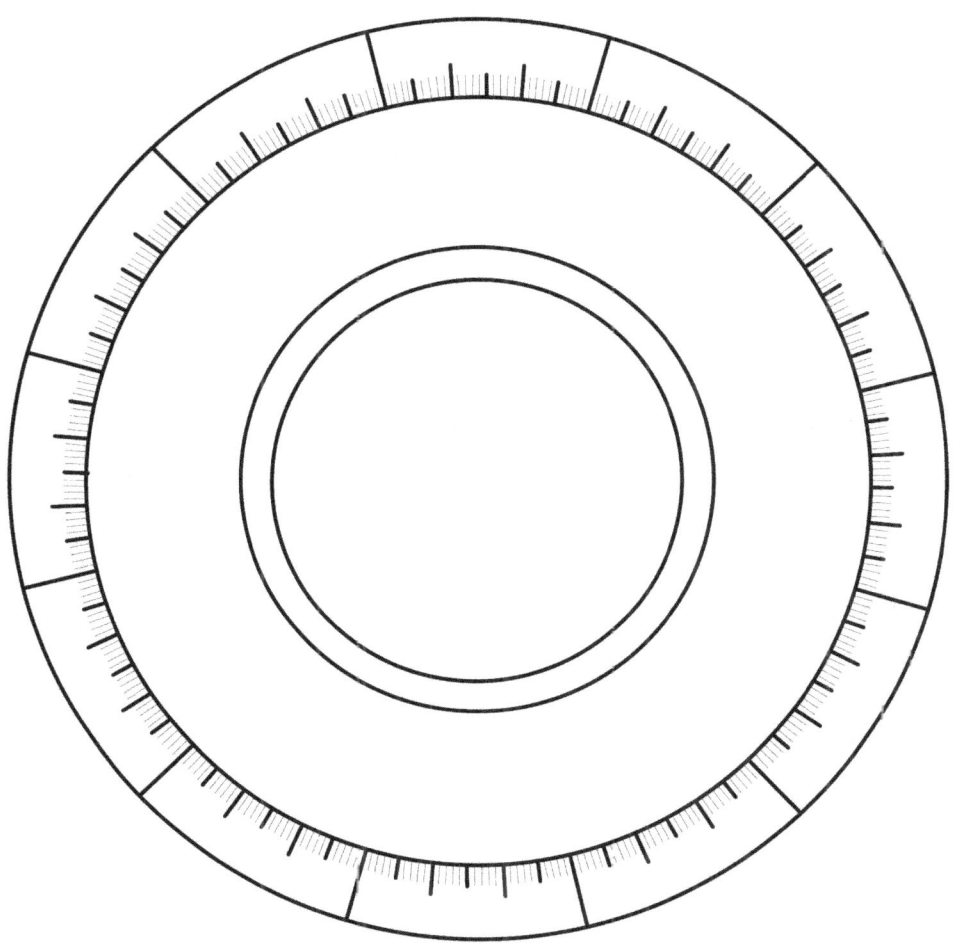

- My favorite website to calculate my birth chart is horoscopes.astro-seek.com
- Since house sizes vary from chart to chart, I've left the house lines out of the sample chart. You can fill them in according to how they appear in your own birth chart.

Fill In Your Birth Chart

_____ _has:_

- Sun ____º in _____ in the _____ House

- Moon ____º in _____ in the _____ House

- Mercury ____º in _____ in the _____ House

- Venus ____º in _____ in the _____ House

- Mars ____º in _____ in the _____ House

- Jupiter ____º in _____ in the _____ House

- Saturn ____º in _____ in the _____ House

- Uranus ____º in _____ in the _____ House

- Neptune ____º in _____ in the _____ House

- Pluto ____º in _____ in the _____ House

- Part of Fortune ____º in _____ in the _____ House

- Vertex ____º in _____ in the _____ House

371

- North Node ____° in _____ in the _____ House

- South Node ____° in _____ in the _____ House

- Chiron ____° in _____ in the _____ House

- Lilith ____° in _____ in the _____ House

- Ascendant ____° in _____ (always on the cusp of the First House)

- Imum Coeli ____° in _____ (always on the cusp of the Fourth House)

- Descendant ____° in _____ (always on the cusp of the Seventh House)

- Midheaven ____° in _____ (always on the cusp of the Tenth House)

Personal Planets:

- Sun ____° in _____ in the _____ House

_____

_____

_____

_____

- Moon ____° in _____ in the _____ House

_____

_____

_____

_____

- Mercury ____° in _____ in the _____

House

_____

_____

_____

_____

- Venus ____° in _____ in the _____ House

_____

_____

_____

_____

- Mars ____° in _____ in the _____ House

_____

_____

_____

_____

Social & Generational Planets:

- Jupiter ____º in _____ in the _____ House

_____

_____

_____

_____

- Saturn ____º in _____ in the _____ House

_____

_____

_____

_____

- Uranus ____º in _____ in the _____ House

_____

_____

_____

_____

- Neptune ____º in _____ in the _____ House

_____

_____

_____

_____

- Pluto ____º in _____ in the _____ House

_____

_____

_____

_____

Points & Objects:

- Part of Fortune ____º in _____ in the _____ House

_____

_____

_____

_____

- Vertex ____º in _____ in the _____ House

_____

_____

_____

_____

- North Node ____º in _____ in the _____ House

_____

_____

_____

- South Node ____º in _____ in the _____
House

- Chiron ____º in _____ in the _____ House

- Lilith ____º in _____ in the _____ House

Angles:

- Ascendant ____º in _____ in the _____
House

_____

_____

- Imum Coeli ____° in _____ in the _____
House

_____

_____

_____

_____

- Descendant ____° in _____ in the _____
House

_____

_____

_____

_____

- Midheaven ____° in _____ in the _____
House

_____

_____

_____

_____

Modalities:

Refer to Modalities section to interpret the modalities within your own chart:

- Cardinal: x____:

_____

_____

_____

- Fixed: x____:

_____

_____

_____

- Mutable: x____:

_____

_____

_____

Elements:

Refer to Elements section to interpret the elements within your own chart:

- Fire: x____:

_____

_____

_____

- Earth: x____:

_____

_____

_____

- Air: x____:

_____

_____

_____

- Water: x____:

_____

_____

_____

Do you have any Critical Degrees?

0°:

_____

_____

15°:

_____

_____

29°:

_____

Critical Degrees of Cardinal Signs:

Critical Degrees of Fixed Signs:

Critical Degrees of Mutable Signs:

Notes:

Ruling Planets

In this section, you'll explore how different areas of your life are linked through the placement of ruling planets in your chart. By discovering where these planets reside, you can gain insight into the connections between your houses and how they influence your life's journey. When using the Placidus system, birth charts can have up to three signs in one house, so I've provided space for this, though you may also have only one sign in some houses.

Signs in the First House:

_____

Ruling Planet of this Sign:_____

Ruling Planet's House Placement:_____

The Connection Between the **First house** and the _____ House:

_____

_____

_____

_____

Ruling Planet of this Sign:_____

Ruling Planet's House Placement:_____

The Connection Between the **First house** and the _____ House:

_____

_____

_____

_____

Ruling Planet of this Sign:_____

Ruling Planet's House Placement:_____

The Connection Between the **First house** and the _____ House:

_____

_____

_____

_____

Signs in the Second House:

_____

Ruling Planet of this Sign:_____

Ruling Planet's House Placement:_____

The Connection Between the **Second house** and the _____ House:

_____

_____

_____

_____

Ruling Planet of this Sign:_____

Ruling Planet's House Placement:_____

The Connection Between the **Second house** and the _____ House:

_____

_____

_____

_____

Ruling Planet of this Sign:_____

Ruling Planet's House Placement:_____

The Connection Between the **Second house** and the _____ House:

_____

_____

_____

_____

Signs in the Third House:

_____

Ruling Planet of this Sign:_____

Ruling Planet's House Placement:_____

The Connection Between the **Third house** and the _____ House:

_____

_____

_____

_____

Ruling Planet of this Sign:_____

Ruling Planet's House Placement:_____

The Connection Between the **Third house** and the _____ House:

_____

_____

_____

_____

Ruling Planet of this Sign:_____

Ruling Planet's House Placement:_____

The Connection Between the **Third house** and the _____ House:

_____

_____

_____

_____

Signs in the Fourth House:

_____

Ruling Planet of this Sign:_____

Ruling Planet's House Placement:_____

The Connection Between the **Fourth house** and the _____ House:

_____

_____

_____

_____

Ruling Planet of this Sign:_____

Ruling Planet's House Placement:_____

The Connection Between the **Fourth house** and the _____ House:

_____

_____

_____

_____

Ruling Planet of this Sign:_____

Ruling Planet's House Placement:_____

The Connection Between the **Fourth house** and the _____ House:

_____

_____

_____

_____

Signs in the Fifth House:

_____

Ruling Planet of this Sign:_____

Ruling Planet's House Placement:_____

The Connection Between the **Fifth house** and the _____ House:

_____

_____

_____

_____

Ruling Planet of this Sign:_____

Ruling Planet's House Placement:_____

The Connection Between the **Fifth house** and the _____ House:

_____

_____

_____

_____

Ruling Planet of this Sign:_____

Ruling Planet's House Placement:_____

The Connection Between the **Fifth house** and the _____ House:

_____

_____

_____

_____

Signs in the Sixth House:

_____

Ruling Planet of this Sign:_____

Ruling Planet's House Placement:_____

The Connection Between the **Sixth house** and the _____ House:

_____

_____

_____

_____

Ruling Planet of this Sign:_____

Ruling Planet's House Placement:_____

The Connection Between the **Sixth house** and the _____ House:

_____

_____

_____

_____

Ruling Planet of this Sign:_____

Ruling Planet's House Placement:_____

The Connection Between the **Sixth house** and the _____ House:

_____

_____

_____

_____

Signs in the Seventh House:

_____

Ruling Planet of this Sign:_____

Ruling Planet's House Placement:_____

The Connection Between the **Seventh house** and the _____ House:

_____

_____

_____

_____

Ruling Planet of this Sign:_____

Ruling Planet's House Placement:_____

The Connection Between the **Seventh house** and the _____ House:

_____

_____

_____

_____

Ruling Planet of this Sign:_____

Ruling Planet's House Placement:_____

The Connection Between the **Seventh house** and the _____ House:

_____

_____

_____

_____

Signs in the Eighth House:

_____

Ruling Planet of this Sign:_____

Ruling Planet's House Placement:_____

The Connection Between the **Eighth house** and the _____ House:

_____

_____

_____

_____

Ruling Planet of this Sign:_____

Ruling Planet's House Placement:_____

The Connection Between the **Eighth house** and the _____ House:

_____

_____

_____

_____

Ruling Planet of this Sign:_____

Ruling Planet's House Placement:_____

The Connection Between the **Eighth house** and the _____ House:

_____

_____

_____

_____

Signs in the Ninth House:

_____

Ruling Planet of this Sign:_____

Ruling Planet's House Placement:_____

The Connection Between the **Ninth house** and the _____ House:

_____

_____

_____

Ruling Planet of this Sign:_____

Ruling Planet's House Placement:_____

The Connection Between the **Ninth house** and the _____ House:

_____

_____

_____

_____

Ruling Planet of this Sign:_____

Ruling Planet's House Placement:_____

The Connection Between the **Ninth house** and the _____ House:

_____

_____

_____

_____

Signs in the Tenth House:

_____

Ruling Planet of this Sign:_____

Ruling Planet's House Placement:_____

The Connection Between the **Tenth house** and the _____ House:

_____

_____

_____

_____

Ruling Planet of this Sign:_____

Ruling Planet's House Placement:_____

The Connection Between the **Tenth house** and the _____ House:

_____

_____

_____

_____

Ruling Planet of this Sign:_____

Ruling Planet's House Placement:_____

The Connection Between the **Tenth house** and the _____ House:

_____

_____

_____

_____

Signs in the Eleventh House:

_____

Ruling Planet of this Sign:_____

Ruling Planet's House Placement:_____

The Connection Between the **Eleventh house** and the _____

House:

_____

_____

_____

_____

Ruling Planet of this Sign:_____

Ruling Planet's House Placement:_____

The Connection Between the **Eleventh house** and the _____

House:

_____

_____

_____

_____

Ruling Planet of this Sign:_____

Ruling Planet's House Placement:_____

The Connection Between the **Eleventh house** and the _____

House:

_____

_____

_____

_____

Signs in the Twelfth House:

_____

Ruling Planet of this Sign:_____

Ruling Planet's House Placement:_____

The Connection Between the **Twelfth house** and the _____ House:

_____

_____

_____

_____

Ruling Planet of this Sign:_____

Ruling Planet's House Placement:_____

The Connection Between the **Twelfth house** and the _____ House:

_____

_____

_____

_____

Ruling Planet of this Sign:_____

Ruling Planet's House Placement:_____

The Connection Between the **Twelfth house** and the _____ House:

_____

_____

_____

_____

Aspects:

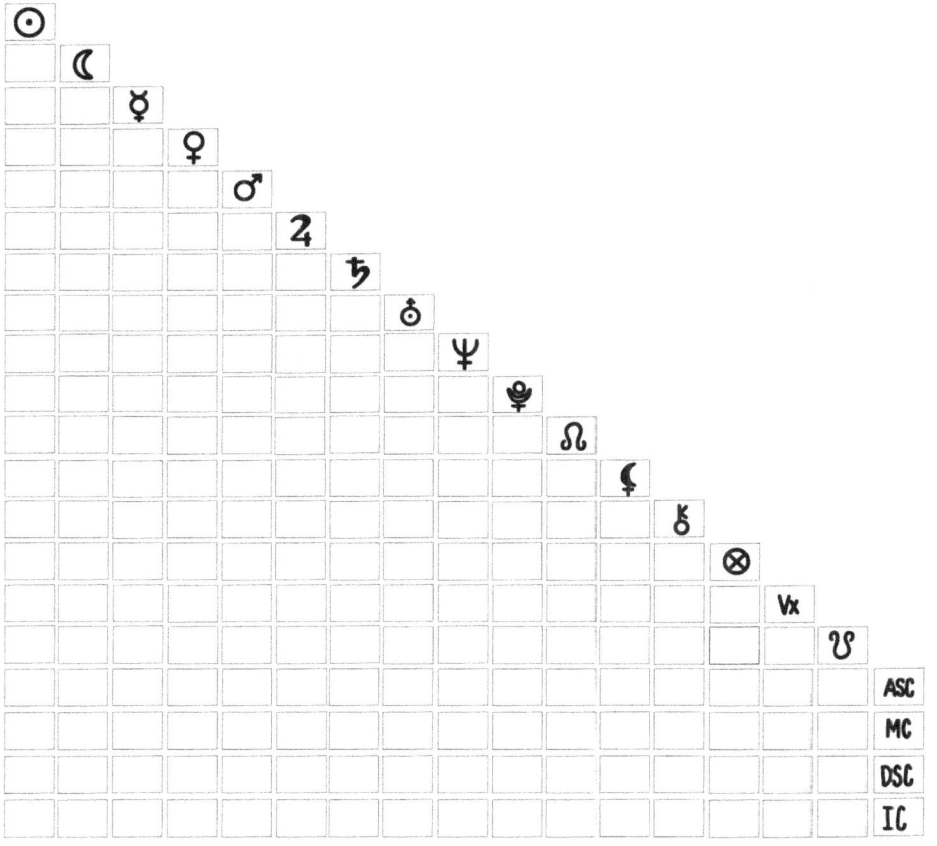

Refer to the chart above to identify your own aspects, then use the spaces on the following pages to write them out in detail.

 Fill In Your Birth Chart

Conjunctions:

1. _____

2. _____

3. _____

4. _____

5. _____

6. _____

7. _____

8. _____

9. _____

10. _____

11. _____

Additional Notes:

_____

_____

_____

_____

_____

_____

_____

_____

_____

Sextiles:

1. _____

2. _____

3. _____

4. _____

5. _____

6. _____

7. _____

8. _____

9. _____

10. _____

11. _____

Additional Notes:

_____

_____

_____

_____

_____

_____

_____

_____

_____

_____

Trines:

1. _____

2. _____

3. _____

4. _____

5. _____

6. _____

7. _____

8. _____

9. _____

10. _____

11. _____

Additional Notes:

_____

_____

_____

_____

_____

_____

_____

_____

_____

_____

Oppositions:

1. _____

2. _____

3. _____

4. _____

5. _____

6. _____

7. _____

8. _____

9. _____

10. _____

11. _____

Additional Notes:

_____

_____

_____

_____

_____

_____

_____

_____

_____

Squares:

1. _____

2. _____

3. _____

4. _____

5. _____

6. _____

7. _____

8. _____

9. _____

10. _____

11. _____

Additional Notes:

_____

_____

_____

_____

_____

_____

_____

_____

_____

Stelliums:

Do you have any Stelliums in your chart?

House(s):_____

Planets:_____

Sign(s):_____

What does the house or houses represent in your life?

_____

_____

_____

_____

What do the planets in your stellium represent

individually?

_____

_____

_____

_____

_____

_____

_____

_____

What is the energy of the sign(s)?

_____

_____

_____

_____

_____

How does all of this tie together, and do you notice any of this energy in your life?

_____

_____

_____

_____

_____

_____

_____

_____

_____

_____

_____

_____

_____

_____

_____

_____

House(s):_____

Planets:_____

Sign(s):_____

What does the house or houses represent in your life?

_____

_____

_____

_____

What do the planets in your stellium represent individually?

_____

_____

_____

_____

_____

_____

_____

What is the energy of the sign(s)?

_____

_____

_____

How does all of this tie together, and do you notice any of this energy in your life?

Any Additional Notes:

Final Words From the Author

Astrology is a tool for understanding yourself and the world around you. By now, you've learned how planets, houses, and signs work together to shape the unique energy of a birth chart. But astrology isn't about memorizing meanings—it's about recognizing patterns and seeing how they apply in real life.

The more you explore your chart, the more connections you'll find. You might notice themes that show up in different areas of your life or gain a new perspective on your strengths and challenges. There's always more to learn, and that's the beauty of astrology—it grows with you.

Whether you use astrology for self-reflection, decision-making, or simply as a way to understand yourself and others better, keep an open mind. Trust your intuition, stay curious, and enjoy the process. Your chart holds endless insights—you just have to keep exploring.

Next Steps & Resources

If you're ready to take your astrology journey further, there are plenty of ways to keep learning and refining your chart interpretations. Here are some next steps you might find helpful:

1. Personalized Birth Chart Readings

Want a deeper, customized breakdown of your chart? I offer in-depth birth chart interpretations where I analyze your placements, aspects, and ruling planets in detail. You'll receive tailored insights and advice on love, career, life path, and more.

- **Book your reading at:** ManifestationMinds.com

2. Get Your Free Workbook PDF

As a special thank you, if you visit my website and sign up for emails, you'll automatically receive the workbook from the back of this book as a free PDF download. This makes it easy to fill in and revisit your insights anytime! This also gives you the opportunity to break down and interpret other people's charts, helping you deepen your understanding and sharpen your interpretation skills!

- Sign up at: ManifestationMinds.com

3. Stay Connected
For more astrology insights, updates, and real-time breakdowns of current transits, you can find me on:
- **TikTok:** Manifestation_minds
- **Instagram:** Manifestationminds_
- **YouTube:** ManifestationMinds
- **Website:** ManifestationMinds.com

4. Upcoming Books & Projects
This book focused on building a strong foundation in astrology, but there's more to explore! My upcoming books will dive deeper into astrology's influence on specific areas of life, helping you apply these insights in practical ways. I'll also be covering how to work with transiting planets for predictive astrology, giving you tools to navigate the future with greater clarity. Stay tuned for updates!

In the meantime, you can also check out my free astrology blog on my website, where I break down current astrological influences and how they may be affecting you.

Thank You
I want to take a moment to thank you for choosing this book and trusting me to guide you through your astrology journey. When I first started learning astrology, I remember how overwhelming it felt —but also how exciting it was to uncover the deeper meanings behind my chart. That's why I wrote this book—to provide a clear, structured way for you to learn and apply astrology to your own life.

Your support means the world to me. If you enjoyed this book, I'd love to hear your thoughts! Reviews help more people discover this resource and allow me to keep creating content that supports your journey.

Thank you again, and happy chart reading!

With all the love,
Jenna

About the Author

Jenna Weston is an astrologer, content creator, and author dedicated to helping others uncover the deeper layers of their birth charts. With years of experience studying astrology and analyzing charts, Jenna specializes in breaking down complex astrological concepts in a way that is both accessible and deeply meaningful. She believes astrology is more than just a system—it's a tool for self-awareness, personal growth, and understanding the intricate connections between the cosmos and human experience.

As the founder of ManifestationMinds, Jenna has built a space for astrology enthusiasts to access insightful birth chart interpretations, astrological resources, and tarot readings. Her approach blends logic with intuition, encouraging others to engage with astrology not just as a belief system, but as a structured, practical method for navigating life's challenges and opportunities.

When she's not immersed in astrology, Jenna enjoys traveling, exploring esoteric philosophies, capturing moments through photography, spending time in nature, painting, and challenging herself in the gym. She is passionate about lifelong learning and continuously seeks new ways to bridge ancient wisdom with modern application.

A Note to Lana Del Rey

Lana (Lizzy),

I want to take a moment to express my deep admiration for you and your work. You have been such an inspiration to me, not only through your music but through the artistry and depth you bring to everything you create. Your ability to capture emotion, nostalgia, and storytelling in a way that resonates so deeply with so many people—including myself—is truly remarkable.

I chose to use your birth chart as an example in this book because I admire you and the unique energy you bring into the world. I hope you take it as the highest form of flattery. My intention was never to overstep but rather to appreciate and explore the astrological influences behind the brilliance that has meant so much to me. It was also incredibly fun to see how the astrological placements in your chart ring so true with what you reveal about yourself on your public platform, how you carry yourself, and the energy you exude. It made reading your chart all the more fascinating and reaffirmed how beautifully astrology reflects the essence of who we are.

I thoroughly enjoyed interpreting your chart, and if you ever wanted a personal reading, I would be honored to do one for you anytime.

Thank you for being a source of inspiration—not just in music, but in life!

With admiration,
Jenna

www.ingramcontent.com/pod-product-compliance
Lightning Source LLC
Chambersburg PA
CBHW071701120626
46550CB00001B/59